JACOB EPSTEIN
SCULPTOR

JACOB EPSTEIN

SCULPTOR

by

RICHARD BUCKLE

THE WORLD PUBLISHING COMPANY

CLEVELAND AND NEW YORK

Published by The World Publishing Company
2231 West 110th Street, Cleveland 2, Ohio

Library of Congress Catalog Card Number: 63-11957

FIRST EDITION

GB

To
GEORGE HAREWOOD and JACK LYONS
friends to Epstein's fame
who rescued the four carvings from Blackpool
then helped Kathleen and me
to mount the Edinburgh Exhibition

CONTENTS

1880–1902: Youth in America   *page* 9

1902–1905: Study in Paris   14

1905–1907: Early years in London   20

1907–1908: Strand Statues   24

1908–1912: Portraits and a tomb   38

1913–1915: The Vortex   65

1916–1920: Maturity   80

1920–1929: Works Sacred and Profane   106

1930–1939: Men and Gods   170

1940–1949: Children, Warriors and Nudes   252

1950–1959: Late Harvest of Commissions   332

1959–1963: Postscript   416

Catalogue raisonné (chronological)   424

List of Illustrations (alphabetical)   431

Index of works, persons, etc. (alphabetical)   436

ACKNOWLEDGEMENTS

To a certain extent the layout of the book had to precede the writing of it, and after making a beginning on this I found the calculating of centimetres so arduous that I called in Michael Jackson to help me. He came for two weeks and stayed two years, bringing not only a superior mathematical ability and a neater pencil but many ideas which made the layout more varied than it would otherwise have been. He was also assiduous in research, in the compiling of the *catalogue raisonné* and the index.

Astrid Zydower, herself a fine sculptor, and one Epstein admired, gave me many suggestions and criticisms and her practical understanding of the sculptor's art has been of great help to me.

I am deeply indebted to Studio Books for allowing me to quote at length from Epstein's 'Autobiography'; to *The Times*, and the *Burlington Magazine* for permission to quote from their pages; to Mr. Henry Moore and the *Sunday Times* for permission to quote from Mr. Moore's posthumous article on Epstein; to Sir Basil Spence and Geoffrey Bles for an extract from 'Phoenix at Coventry'; to the Library of the United States Embassy in London, to Canon Mortlock, to Mr. Louis Osman, to Mr. Paul Vaughan, to Mrs. Anna Bazell, to Mr. Alan Collingridge and to Mr. Leslie Jarman for information; to the late Mr. Tyson-Smith and to Adams, Holden and Pearson for the loan of photographs.

PHOTOGRAPHERS

Hans Wild, who took most of the photographs, has collaborated with me from the start. He has taken photographs in London, Blackpool and Oxford, besides working with his assistant Laurence Brooman throughout two whole nights in Edinburgh. Laurence Brooman took a number of photographs himself.

Paul Laib was commissioned by Epstein to photograph most of his work from 1918 till the second world war. The following photographs are by him: 13, 70, 140, 141, 157, 158, 169, 179, 194, 199, 211, 212, 213, 217, 218, 219, 228, 230, 231, 233, 235, 239, 240, 242, 253, 254, 255, 260, 263, 264, 265, 266, 273, 274, 275, 276, 278–282, 283–285, 295, 300, 301, 302, 304, 306, 310, 311, 312, 314, 318, 321, 322, 324, 325, 326, 329, 331, 332, 333, 337, 342, 343, 346, 349–354, 358–362, 365, 366, 372, 373, 374, 376, 377, 406, 421, 422, 470, 487, 505.

Other photographs are by the following photographers: James Ashworth, Bolton, 404; Associated Press, 308, 662; Stewart Bale, Liverpool, 619, 620; National Gallery of Canada, 113; Carbonara, Liverpool, 622, 623; E. de Cusati, Yale University Art Gallery, 103, 105; Fairmount Park Trustees, Philadelphia, 590, 591; Reproduced by permission of the Syndics of the Fitzwilliam Museum, Cambridge, 551; Helmut-Gernsheim, 446; Hulton Picture Library, 42–45, 47; Geoffrey Ireland, 543, 544, 545, 562, 579, 582–588, 600, 601, 602, 607, 611, 612, 621, 626, 641, 647, 655; Ida Kar, 478, 529, 539, 550; George King, Sevenoaks, 79; Mort Lesser, Toronto, 114; London Art Service (Photographic) Ltd., 536; City Art Gallery, Manchester, 130; Reproduced by permission of the Metropolitan Museum of Art, New York. Rogers Fund 1924, 138; Studio Morgan, Aberdeen, 407, 408, 409; James Mortimer, 315, 338, 387, 388, 434, 435; Sidney Newbery, 229; Mr. Pegg, Leeds, 417–419; Jerome Robbins, 357, 447, 481; Senett & Spears, Jersey, 305; Bertram Sinkinson, 651; Soichi Sunami — Reproduced by permission from the Collection of the Museum of Modern Art, New York, 107, 428, 429; Strickland Studios, 504; Stanley Travers, Cardiff, 627; *The Times*, 29, 31, 48, 49, 63, 106, 648, 663; Van Dieren — Reproduced from his book on Epstein, 37, 74, 99, 108, 109, 112, 118, 133, 135; Victoria and Albert Museum, 23–30, 38, 71, 72; Studio Wesselo, Johannesburg, 57; Raymond Wilson, Beaconsfield, 559, 560; York Museum, 396.

EXPLANATION

This book was undertaken at the invitation of Lady Epstein: and many of the facts in it were supplied by her, though the opinions expressed in it are my own. It is not a biography, though as much of Epstein's life story as is relevant to his sculpture is included; nor is it a critical assessment of Epstein's position in the history of sculpture, though an attempt has been made from time to time to place him in relation to other sculptors: it is something both more modest and, I hope, more useful — a pictorial record of the sculptor's work, with notes on individual pieces and on changes in his style. It is a chronicle.

The story is told chronologically. I have tried to be as accurate in dating the portraits as possible, but, for reasons explained below I may sometimes have been a year or two out. The only conscious exceptions to the chronological sequence of arrangement are as follows.

In the section dealing with the Strand Statues I have followed a description of their creation with an illustrated account of their destruction so as to have the whole tragedy in one chapter. I have put photographs of a statue taken in 1962 alongside a photograph of it as it was half a century ago. When Epstein made several portraits of one woman — as he did of his two wives, his daughters, of Norman, of Dolores, and Oriel Ross — on the occurrence of the final portrait I have in some cases set beside it for the sake of comparison a resumé of earlier heads reproduced on previous pages; so these flashbacks are placed out of chronological order. The rough drawings or studies for a monumental work (and I have included nearly all the few drawings for sculpture Epstein ever made — besides some early drawings he made before he ever became a sculptor) are sometimes reproduced alongside the resulting works and sometimes, as when the sculptor's first idea for a work was certainly separated by a period of years from its final realisation, several pages before.

My publishers allowed me to choose — and in many cases to commission — the photographs I wanted, because from the beginning I determined to plan the lay-out along with the text. My purpose for insisting on this unity — apart from the desire to make a handsome book — was to present the story with the greatest possible clarity. It may not sound a very original idea to have every picture juxtaposed with the text which discusses it, but I believe it is comparatively rare in art books, and such was my aim.

Not every surviving work of Epstein's is illustrated here. (He destroyed nearly all his student work from 1902 to 1907.) Sometimes no cast of a known bronze could be found and the plaster was missing: sometimes it was thought that a surfeit of commissioned heads of business-men in a given year would prove indigestible. When I have not reproduced a work I have tried to mention it in the *catalogue raisonné*. Out of Epstein's 514 known works 446 are illustrated here. All known surviving works of Epstein and a few he is known to have destroyed are listed with an attempt at accuracy in the chronological *catalogue raisonné* on page 424. Anyone wishing to look at pictures of a specific work should look it up in the alphabetical List of Illustrations on page 431. The Index lists people, places and works.

The reader will notice a disparity between the early and later chapters. Whereas the story of the sculptor's youth and apprenticeship, to which there are few illustrations, can be read as a consecutive narrative, the chapters from 1908 onwards tend increasingly to be divided into an introduction and notes on individual works. This was inevitable in view of the nature of the book, text being largely subordinate to illustrations. Likewise, it may seem awkward that while certain works are discussed at length, others are passed over almost without comment. But I thought that in the long run this awkwardness would be less annoying to the reader than a steady stream of repetitive commentary.

My chief sources of information are as follows: Lady Epstein's memory; the catalogues of sixteen exhibitions of the sculptor's work held at the Leicester Galleries, and the recollections of their proprietors; albums of photographs annotated by the first Mrs. Epstein up to 1939; Hutchins Hapgood's *The Spirit of the Ghetto* with illustrations by Epstein; Bernard Van Dieren's *Jacob Epstein*, a truculent and wordy essay published by John Lane in 1920 with 50 illustrations; Hubert Wellington's *Jacob Epstein*, published by Ernest Benn with 35 plates in 1925; Arnold Haskell's *The Sculptor Speaks*, published by Constable in 1930; and above all Epstein's *Let there be Sculpture* published by Michael Joseph in 1940, reissued by the Hulton Press in 1953 as *Autobiography*, and again by Studio Books in 1962. From the last I quote at length.

Occasionally, where the dating of a work by Mrs. Epstein in her albums or in the chronology she helped Haskell to compile for his book disagree with the memories of Lady Epstein it has been necessary either to weigh probabilities or to rely on stylistic evidence.

Some of my notes appeared in the *Catalogue of the Epstein Memorial Exhibition*, which show I arranged for the Edinburgh Festival Society in 1961.

'Going to the Synagogue'

1880–1902

YOUTH IN AMERICA

Jacob Epstein was born in 1880 in lower east-side Manhattan, in the New York ghetto, whose inhabitants were to be the first inspiration of his youthful work. During the eighteen-seventies an increasing number of Jews fled from Russia and Poland to New York, seeking religious freedom and also lured by the agents of the steamship companies. Epstein's parents were among them. He was a third son, one of a large and fairly prosperous family, but from early days, unlike most Jews, he had no family feeling. A long illness in childhood and an aptitude for drawing set him apart from other children; and his father mocked him for his singularity. From the beginning he was himself. Admiring teachers allowed him to neglect his studies for drawing: but he also fed his imagination on books. In his fragmentary autobiography he has recorded, 'When I had got hold of a really thick book like Hugo's *Les Misérables* I was happy.' Lying in bed at night he used to listen to his parents reading aloud to each other. A growing scepticism of Orthodox faith and observances, combined with a tendency to the socialistic and anarchistic ideas which excited many intelligent young Jews at that time, separated him further from his family; and when they moved to 'a more respectable and duller part of the city' he stayed behind in a rented attic to draw and paint. Another young artist, Bernard Gussow, shared this studio and did the cooking.

'New York, New York it's a wonderful town!' sang the sailors in a famous musical show. In the eighteen-eighties and 'nineties, even before its crown of skyscrapers made it a new wonder of the world, Manhattan was a city to enthral and stimulate a growing boy.

'Hester Street and its surrounding streets', wrote Epstein, 'were the most densely populated of any city on earth, and looking back at it, I realise what I owe to its unique and crowded humanity. Its swarms of Russians, Poles, Italians, Greeks and Chinese lived as much in the streets as in the crowded tenements, and the sights, sounds and smells had the vividness and sharp impact of an Oriental city. Hester Street was from one end to the other an open-air market, and the streets were lined with push-carts and pedlars, and the crowd that packed the sidewalk and roadway compelled one to move slowly. . . .

upon the fire-escapes and roofs the tenement dwellers slept for coolness in summer. I knew well the roof life in New York, where all East Side boys flew kites; I knew the dock life on the East and West sides, and I swam in the East River and the Hudson. To reach the river the boys from the Jewish quarter would have to pass through the Irish quarter, and that meant danger and fights with the gangs . . . the children of Irish immigrants.'

A boy may first turn to drawing in imitation of other artists, or from the urge to record some aspect of his surroundings. Epstein was of the latter kind. His earliest stimulus to art came from the life around him. Besides, in New York in the eighteen-nineties there were few works of art readily accessible to him. The public monuments of Manhattan Epstein always remembered as contemptible. The best of them perhaps was Browne's equestrian statue of Washington in Union Square, which the boy must often have passed on his way up-town to Central Park.

The history of sculpture in the United States may be said to have begun in 1785 when Houdon came from France to spend a fortnight at Mount Vernon and make a portrait of the first President. Washington was also sculpted by an enthusiastic Italian, Giuseppe Cerracchi, who travelled to the States — in vain — with the project for a huge monument to Liberty, and, returning to Paris, was executed for conspiracy against Napoleon. Cerracchi's bust served as a model when, on the recommendation of Jefferson, the Governor of North Carolina commissioned Canova to make a marble monument of Washington for their State House at Raleigh: set up in 1821, this became the pride of the State, but was destroyed by fire ten years later. It was not only the sculptors who were imported. No seams of fine marble suitable for carving had yet been quarried in the United States, and the material had to be fetched from Italy. The first marble portrait bust carved in America by an American is believed to be a head by John Frazee, who opened a marble shop in New York in 1818. It was not until 1847 that the first bronze was cast in the United States.

A number of Italian immigrants in the early years of the nineteenth century were stone-cutters who set up

'Friday
Night
Prayer'

business as makers of funeral monuments in New York, Boston and Philadelphia. Mr. Albert Gardner in his *Yankee Stone-cutters* suggests that because Mount Auburn cemetery in Boston and Laurel Hill in Philadelphia became in the sentimental 'twenties and 'thirties the scene of fashionable promenades, their avenues of sculpture, such as it was, could be said to constitute the first museums in America. The mawkish academism of the day was castigated by Emerson, who wrote, 'The art of sculpture has long ago perished to any real effect.' Meanwhile, the infiltration of Italian carvers was counter-balanced by a surge of Americans to Italy. Suddenly, in the 'twenties, a number of young men from all over the eastern states discovered their vocation as sculptors and converged on Rome.

The most celebrated of these Italianate Americans, who imitated Canova and Thorwaldsen, were Greenough, Powers and Crawford. In 1837 Congress commissioned from Greenough a statue of Washington for the Capitol's Rotunda, and this was the first big order given to an American sculptor. Hiram Powers's insipid 'Greek Slave', made in 1843, earned him world-wide fame, and was a hit at London's Great Exhibition in 1851. After the Civil War there was a widespread demand for heroic monuments, which was satisfied by such sculptors as Ward and Saint-Gaudens; and Epstein must have seen a number of boring monumental effigies in and around New York. The equestrian Sherman of Saint-Gaudens, which stands before the Plaza Hotel at the south-east corner of Central Park, was not unveiled till 1903, when the young student was already in Paris, but he saw it on a later visit and thought it better than most.

Until Epstein fulfilled himself on the other side of the Atlantic there were only two American sculptors whose work can hold our attention for other than historical reasons today. The earlier of these, William Rimmer (1816–79), has only recently been studied and acclaimed: Epstein could not have known his work. Rimmer, who believed himself grandson of the Dauphin, was a lonely and tormented character, a doctor, who drew and sculpted in his spare time. His few bronzes, such as the 'Falling Gladiator', the 'Fighting Lions' and the 'Dying Centaur' show an anatomical knowledge which was matched by the power of his imagination and his sense of tragedy. Rimmer died the year before Epstein was born.

The second interesting American sculptor was George Gray Barnard (1863–1938), who met with more acclaim in his day, and carved among a great many other works 'The Two Natures', which Epstein admired, and the Abraham Lincoln at Manchester. Barnard formed the Cloisters Museum in 1925. He was Epstein's first teacher of sculpture.

Naturally the boy drew long before he sculpted, and he could boast casually in his autobiography that he was never reduced, as were so many of his fellow-students, to tinting photographs in order to pay for his classes, because 'I could always sell my drawings'. He spent two terms in his teens drawing and painting from life at the Art Students' League, up-town, where male and female students working from nude models were separated by a curtain. At this time, his brother recalls, he only wanted to be a painter; and it is curious that he never admitted to this first ambition in later years. Mrs. Stuyvesant Fish used to show some of his work to fashionable guests at her weekly *salon*.

His main studies, however, Epstein claimed, were in the quarter where he was born, the crowded 'Ghetto'. Not that his passionate interest in his fellow men was confined to Jews only. From early days he felt a fascination for people of varied race and facial structure which was later to bear fruit in some of his finest works. He tried to sketch Chinamen — 'young men with smooth faces like girls' — but they did not like being drawn, and 'had a curious way of slipping into their houses, suddenly, as

'*He was bewitched by mathematics*'

into holes'. Chinese children too delighted him. He mixed with the vociferous Italians on Mulberry Street and made friends with Negroes. 'Early on', he wrote, 'I saw the plastic quality in coloured people.' He later remembered being criticised for going swimming with Negroes. He 'haunted the docks and watched ships from all over the world being loaded and unloaded', and 'the sailors aloft in the rigging'; saw the new immigrants at the Battery, with their luggage on their shoulders, discomfited to find 'their first steps in the New World greeted with the hoots and jeers of hooligans', and at night through the bright doors of Bowery saloons — one of which, Steve Brodie's, was lined with photographs of boxers and had a floor inlaid with silver dollars — he observed the singers, dancers, sailors and prostitutes moving among lights.

One evening, when he was about nine, exploring on his own, he found himself in the red light district. He had never seen so many pretty women before, and some of them had naked breasts. They called to the boy to enter their houses, but he was too shy to go. The colours, the forms and the joyous climate of welcome seemed like a prospect of paradise. Epstein was never to forget this adventure. In how many of his exuberant busts of women with bare bosoms like fruit — Lydia, Deirdre, Isabel — was he to relive the promise of that Arabian Night!

While he was working at the Art Students' League, Epstein made a habit of dropping in to Durand Ruel's gallery on Fifth Avenue. To a young artist whose experience of original works of art had been limited almost to a few pre-Raphaelites, the Impressionist painters brought over by the French dealer came as a revelation. He saw and loved pictures by Manet, Renoir and Pissarro before he had studied the old masters. The 'sincerity' of some pioneer American painters of the generation before his own also impressed him.

If young Epstein could appreciate the radiant life of a Renoir or one of Winslow Homer's epic landscapes, it may be wondered that he did not paint from nature himself. He loved to be out of doors: would take his book to Central Park, cross Brooklyn Bridge on foot to admire the 'wonderful bay', swim in the surf at Long Island and explore the rocky Palisades overhanging the Hudson. He read Whitman; and glorying in the scale of his untamed continent, would run off with a gang of friends into the Catskill Mountains, to sleep in the woods by night. One winter he hired, with his friend Gussow, a cabin on the shores of Greenwood Lake among the mountains of New Jersey. He tramped 'through snow-clad forests', and cut ice on the lake to earn money. Returning at evening on a sledge from the icefields, he saw 'wonderful snow views of mountain sides ablaze with sunset colours'. 'We enjoyed it very much,' Epstein told Hutchins Hapgood, 'but there were no artistic results. The country, much as

'The Morning Prayer'

I love it, is not stimulating. Clouds and trees are not satisfying. It is only in the Ghetto, where there is human nature, that I have ideas for sketches.'

After this sojourn in the wilderness, in the first spring of the century, Epstein decided to give up painting and be a sculptor. It was Barnard who confirmed him in this decision; and perhaps hewing the ice-blocks had put him in a heroic frame of mind. 'I entered a foundry for bronze casting,' he wrote, 'and attended a modelling class at night.' George Gray Barnard came once a week to give criticisms, and this was the only school of sculpture in New York. Barnard, Epstein recalled, 'would look at a study and give you a penetrating glance (he had a cast in his eye), and then start his talk, in which he would usually lose himself for the rest of the evening. The students would gather round him, and as he was a man of great earnestness, he was very impressive.'

Epstein, however, longed to study in Europe. 'I looked forward to the day when I would be able to see the Ancients and Rodin. I longed to see originals of Michelangelo and Donatello, and Europe meant the Louvre and Florence.' It is sad to think that while Jacob Epstein was growing up, a collection such as Isabella Gardner's was being formed as near as Boston, which circumstances would for ever prevent him from seeing. Philadelphia he visited, but a great social gulf was fixed between him and the celebrated lawyer John G. Johnson, so, even if he had known of the latter's fine collection at 510 South Broad Street, it would have been difficult for him to see it. Thus it was not till 1951 when he went to choose a site for his big group 'Social Consciousness' in Fairmount Park, that he beheld the jewelled Van Eyck of 'St. Francis receiving the stigmata', a picture which the old sculptor loved on sight and sent home postcards of.

Epstein came to Philadelphia with an appointment to see Thomas Eakins at his home in Mount Vernon Street. This celebrated and successful painter was so struck with

'a sweat-shop girl moves his fancy deeply'

the boy's talent, as perhaps with his romantic appearance and decisive personality, that he offered to take him into his home, to adopt and teach him: but the independent young Bohemian felt suffocated by the atmosphere of stuffy respectability — perhaps the stiff chairs in the unused parlour put him off — so he refused.

His chance came when he was asked to illustrate a naïve book by Hutchins Hapgood, a minor Mayhew, called *The Spirit of the Ghetto*; and as Epstein himself is one of the characters described in this work, we have from the author a glimpse of the artist's way of life in 1901, just as the artist's own sketches bring alive for us his youthful surroundings. His first poor studio in Hester Street had been burnt to the ground; he had returned to it one morning to find his 'charred drawings (hundreds of them) floating about in water with dead cats'. He was now in an attic over a sweat shop.

'On the corner of Hester and Forsyth Streets', wrote Hapgood, 'is a tumble-down rickety building . . . a miserable iron bedstead occupies the narrow strip of floor beneath the descending ceiling. There is one window, which commands a good view of the pushcart market in Hester Street. Near the window is a diminutive oil-stove, on which the artist prepares his tea and eggs. On a peg on the door hang an old mackintosh and an extra coat — his only additional wardrobe. About the narrow walls on the three available sides are easels, and sketches and paintings of Ghetto types.'

'Jacob Epstein . . . has a melancholy wistful face. He was born in the Ghetto twenty years ago. . . . He went to the public schools until he was thirteen years old. Since then he has worked at various jobs, until now he was an instructor in a boys' outdoor gymnasium near the corner of Hester and Essex Streets.' (Another job the young artist had failed at was that of farm labourer.) Epstein told Hapgood that twelve dollars a month, which he usually managed to make from selling his sketches, was enough to satisfy all his needs. He appeared 'very happy, altho' serious, like his race in general; and full of idealism and ambition'. 'There is no nature in the sweat-shop,' Epstein told Hapgood, 'and yet it is there that my love and imagination call me. It is only the minds and souls of my people that fill me with a desire to work.' Here we may think that one of the two men, probably Hapgood, was laying on the Jewishness a bit thick.

Hapgood recorded that Epstein had held an exhibition at the Hebrew Institute two years before, and shown, along with his drawings, 'a few paintings . . . very crude as far as the technique of colour is concerned.' The writer evidently preferred 'portraits of old pedlers, roughly successful as Ghetto types, in order to retain whom as models the artist was frequently forced to sing a song, for the pedlers have a Jewish horror of the image . . .'.

It is indeed curious to consider that one born of a race

which forbade graven images, and in a land whose Puritan founders were descended from Cromwell's image-breakers, should become the greatest sculptor of modern times. Yet it is conceivable — and this is a theory Epstein used to discuss with his second wife — that the pre-Mosaic Jews were particularly addicted to sculpture, that it became an unholy passion with them, and that the second Commandment was framed to curb their visual and tactile excesses. One day in the nineteen-fifties the sculptor remarked casually that one of the sins of Sodom and Gomorrah was making love to statues. Perhaps his life's work should be regarded as a sudden outburst of this repressed instinct to fashion images of gods and men after three thousand years.

In some of the young artist's illustrations to *The Spirit of the Ghetto* it is impossible not to read the story of his own early years. Is not he himself the son going with his father to the synagogue? In 'Morning prayer' is he — or had he not been once — the boy in shirtsleeves near the stove? We know he was never 'bewitched by mathematics', yet how often, like the studious boy with the pleading mother, must he have refused to spare his eyes and abandon his book. 'In these cafés they meet after the theatre or an evening lecture'; 'A sweat-shop girl moves his fancy deeply': such titles alone evoke the life of a young Jewish intellectual in New York at the beginning of the century.

If one compares these early drawings of Epstein with those of other artists who contributed as he did at that time to the *Century* magazine, one is struck by their greater virility and simplification. Although the shirted women and bentwood chairs exhale an atmosphere of 1900, these are more than period pieces. Drawn in bold strokes of charcoal or soft pencil, they have, besides their story-telling appeal, a violence and pathos which we associate with the German Expressionists of the next two decades — and this despite the fact that they are printed as conventional 'vignettes', like the illustrations to *Sherlock Holmes*.

The influence which is most evident in these drawings, however, and which chiefly accounts for their merit, is that of the caricatures of Steinlen and Forain, and perhaps the drawings of Toulouse-Lautrec, which he may have seen at Durand-Ruel's gallery on Fifth Avenue. As Epstein in his long, busy and productive life as a sculptor was to span so many movements, was to be classical, primitive, abstract, vorticist and realist, bridging, as it were, the gaps between Rodin, Picasso, Modigliani, Brancusi, Gaudier-Brzeska and Moore, it is interesting in these earliest known works of his to be able to connect him with the great French draughtsmen and satirists of the nineteenth century. Yet even more striking than the stylistic problem these drawings present, is their compassion. Throughout his artistic life, with the exception of a brief period of experiment in abstract forms, Epstein was a humanist. When we look at the face of the old praying Jew, lit by candles from below, and at the gnarled hands of the pleading mother, we think of Rembrandt and Van Gogh.

With the money he received for illustrating Hutchins Hapgood's book Epstein bought a passage to France. His mother had to be torn from him by force when the ship was sailing, and though he returned to America once during her lifetime he never saw her again. Like the American sculptors of the eighteen-twenties he set off to discover the Old World of his ancestors and to claim his artistic inheritance.

1902-05

STUDY IN PARIS

In the last months of his life Camille Pissarro wrote to his son Lucien of the pleasure he got from watching the great transatlantic liners steaming in to Le Havre. On one of these Epstein came to France in the autumn of 1902.

At the time of the young sculptor's arrival in Paris Manet had been dead eighteen years, Van Gogh twelve, Seurat eleven and Lautrec one. Degas, a famous but formidable recluse, hid himself and his pictures from the world in the rue Victor Massé, caring only for his collection of drawings by Ingres and paintings by other masters. Monet had just completed a set of views of the Thames and was about to begin his campaign of water-lilies in the garden of his house at Giverny. Renoir, moving about the Midi and trying to keep his rheumatism at bay, would shortly settle at Le Cannet. Cézanne had just built himself a new house on the Chemin des Lauves on a hill above Aix. Gauguin, poor, sick and proud in the remote Marquesas, had seven months more to live.

There were two famous American artists in Europe. Whistler, settled in his studio in the rue du Bac, was in the last year of his life. Sargent, the most sought after portrait painter of his period — if not of any period — was kept uncomfortably busy in London and earned a hundred thousand pounds a year.

Paris in 1902, two years after the great International Exhibition, was the capital of Art Nouveau, of deliquescent forms inspired by Oriental art, which flourished over the gates of the new Métro stations, in Maxim's, and at Billy's gallery, decorated with paintings on silk by Conder; and which we may connect with Lautrec's posters, with the Nabi movement, headed by Bonnard and Vuillard, with the Blue Period of the young Spaniard Picasso, who had just returned on his second visit to Paris and was sharing an attic, a bed and a top-hat with Max Jacob in the boulevard Voltaire, with Mallarmé's poetry — though the poet was dead —, with the *Pelléas et Mélisande* of Debussy and Maeterlinck, first performed that year, and with the sculpture of Rodin.

Auguste Rodin, though still prone to official discouragements, was reaping fame and fortune after a lifetime of struggle. He worked steadily at Meudon,

surrounded by young sculptors who produced lucrative marble replicas of works he had modelled in clay. During the summer of 1902 he had gone to London to see his 'St. John the Baptist' installed at South Kensington, and after a dinner given him at the Café Royal over a hundred students from the Slade and Kensington had taken the horses from his carriage and begun to drag him home.

Yet, though the movement we call Art Nouveau was in full swing, new movements were beginning, and the twentieth century was launched on its heroic orbit of experiment. A big Van Gogh exhibition in 1901 had given an impetus to the painters later known as 'Les Fauves'. When Epstein arrived in Paris, Matisse was thirty-three, Vlaminck twenty-six, Derain twenty-two and Braque twenty. Fernand Léger, aged twenty-one, had been studying at the Beaux-Arts for a year.

The Paris of 1902 was also that of 'La belle époque', the violet-scented world of Comtesse Greffuhle, of Robert de Montesquiou and Anna de Noailles, the world sketched by Boldini, Helleu and La Gandara, whose splendours were pickled by Proust against oblivion.

Two days before Epstein arrived in Paris Marcel Proust had left the city with Bertrand de Fénelon, the chief original of his Saint-Loup, for a tour of the Low Countries, where the carillon at Bruges reminded him of Mme Greffuhle's silvery laugh, and where he decided Vermeer's 'View of Delft' was 'the most beautiful painting in the world'.

Bernard Gussow had preceded Epstein to Paris and had taken a studio for them both in the rue Belloni behind the Gare Montparnasse. 'On my first walk out in Paris to see Nôtre Dame and the Seine,' wrote Epstein, 'I passed over a bridge, where right in the centre was a small building, the morgue, and I had to regret the morbid curiosity that took me into that tragic building.'

The next day, 5 October 1902, the young American attended the funeral of Emile Zola, whose championship of the wronged Dreyfus had kindled the admiration of Jews in the New World as well as the Old. He joined in the huge procession going to the Cimetière Montparnasse and 'witnessed the clashes between the gendarmes and anti-semites'; but he was not near enough in the crowd to

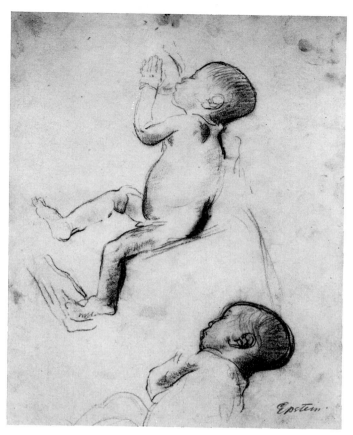

8 SKETCHES OF BABIES

9 SKETCHES OF BABIES

hear Anatole France pronounce over the grave his oration which ended with the famous tribute to Zola, 'Il fut un moment de la conscience humaine.' Towards the end of his life Epstein said that he would never have gone to Zola's funeral if he had known how badly he behaved to Cézanne.

To stout Cortez, 'silent upon a peak in Darien', the Pacific could have been no grander revelation than the Louvre to Epstein. 'Visits to the Louvre opened my eyes', he wrote. 'The great storehouse of painting and sculpture held me for days on end. The thrill of crossing the Pont des Arts to the Louvre.' So the young man set eyes for the first time on the 'Vénus de Milo', on the 'Winged Victory', on Gothic Virgins, on Burgundian tombs, on the two 'Slaves' of Michelangelo. 'On my prowlings . . . I discovered works which were not at all famous then, but have since come into their own — early Greek work, Cyclades sculpture, the bust known as the Lady of Elche, and the limestone bust of Akenaton.'

Three or four days after his arrival, Epstein, who spoke little French, applied for admittance to the École des Beaux-Arts and 'was placed with other students in an amphitheatre to construct a figure from the living model'. He passed this two-hour test and entered one of three modelling ateliers, under an old professor named Thomas. Undeterred by the ragging of the French students who

were ill-disposed to the few foreigners in their class, Epstein set seriously to learn his craft. 'I concentrated with a fanatical zeal entirely at my studies. I worked at the school with a sort of frenzy. I hurled myself at the clay.'

Modelling took place in the mornings. Every Monday a girl model would be produced by the *massier* of the class. '*Massier*' is a word the French use for one who organises the clubbing together of a body of people to pay certain subscriptions, and this man should by rights have been a senior student, but was in fact an *apache* called Cladel from the Butte Montmartre. At the beginning of the week there was always a crowd of students, and as the juniors were relegated to the rear Epstein would dart in and out of the stands to get a close look at the model, then run back to his clay. Cladel, who sat at the back too, and only on Mondays made a pretence of modelling before disappearing for the rest of the week, laughed at the young American's unorthodox behaviour. Epstein answered 'in contempt for a fellow who thought he could do sculpture sitting on a high stool'. By Wednesday most of the students had dropped out of the class and it was easier to study the model.

After a snack, which he brought with him, Epstein went to the carving studio or drew from Michelangelo casts. There was almost no instruction at all in carving.

'One morning', he remembered, 'I decided to attend the anatomy lecture . . . with a corpse as model; when a green arm was handed around for inspection I nearly fainted, and left the class, never to return. I always felt ashamed of this episode, as I knew that Michelangelo and all great Renaissance artists had made intensive research from *cadavres*, until years later I read, in an account of the Ingres atelier, that Ingres himself could never stand dissection, and even objected to a skeleton being in his classroom.'

Epstein remained six months at the Beaux-Arts, working all out and growing in knowledge — although, as he said, he learned more from capable students than from the masters. He described the incident which led to his departure. 'One Monday morning the period of the Prix de Rome Concours commenced, and the new students were supposed to fag for the men who entered concours, and carry clay and stands to the *loges*, and wait upon these immured geniuses. This would have completely cut my morning's work, so I refused point-blank. The French students were astonished, and could hardly believe their ears. I was all the more determined as there were plenty of *gardiens* to fetch and carry. On returning to the atelier next morning, the study I had begun lay in a ruined mass on the ground. I built up a new study, but the following morning it was again on the ground. The Frenchmen stood silently around, watching me. I said nothing, and picking up and shouldering my modelling stand, went over to the Julian Academy.'

It cost money to work *chez Julian*; and the continuance of Epstein's self-education was made possible — as indeed his very existence in Paris must have been — by the payment of a small monthly allowance from his mother. So opposed was his father to the way of life he had chosen, that we can assume there was no question of the parents sending money by mutual consent. The devoted woman must have secretly saved on her budget to keep Jacob alive and learning in Paris.

'This whole student period in Paris', the sculptor wrote, 'I passed in a rage of work; I was aflame with ardour and worked in a frenzied, almost mad manner, achieving study after study, week after week, always destroying it at the end of the week, to begin a new one the following Monday.' He was obsessed with his craft and thought of little outside it. Gussow and he bought their food 'in a near-by cook-shop in the rue de la Gaieté', but sometimes went in the evenings for a change to a Russian students' restaurant near the Jardin des Plantes, where a meal, mostly *kasha*, could be had with free bread for a franc and a half, Russian tea being the only drink, and where the customers waited on themselves. 'In the rue Belloni studios, only the Frenchmen had mistresses, and they naturally laughed at us Americans and English who seemed able to do without. For one thing, the mistress was also the model, and we "foreigners" had to pose for each other and mark up the hours on the walls. Strange proceedings!' Even so, in fine weather the country beckoned: but 'after a Sunday passed in the woods of Chaville, I would return to the modelling class and no one outstripped me in ardour'.

One week at Julian's Epstein decided for a change to draw, instead of sculpting, from life. He went to the class of Jean-Paul Laurens, the historical painter, whose habit was to walk from drawing to drawing, followed by a crowd of students, and give criticisms. When this pundit came to sit on the young American's stool, he looked first at the drawing, then at the model, then at the artist, got up and passed on in silence.

Another day Epstein watched an equally celebrated man giving instruction. Bouguereau, painter of such works as 'Truth', 'Youth and Love' and the sickly 'Vièrge Consolatrice', a hallowed pornographer, was assisted into his chair by two students who seemed 'almost overcome with the honour'.

The independent and irreverent American had nothing but scorn for these academic painters and for academies in general. Of course he was not alone, even in those days, in deriding institutions presided over by a minister who had refused Cézanne the Légion d'honneur. Yet in 1902, as he remarked to Arnold Haskell years later, it was only in France that the Academy was just beginning to be discredited. 'But even when I was a student', he said, 'Rodin was taken as rather a joke by the Academicians, and not recognised as having any merit at all.'

The rebel student gave up taking criticism, and when he saw the master approaching would cover up his figure. Not surprisingly the despised teacher was heard to refer to '*ce sauvage americain*'.

On Sunday afternoons he went to concerts. He heard Paderewski play and saw Richard Strauss conduct. He heard *Pelléas* and was struck by what he remembered as its chaste medieval-Flemish style of production. He greatly admired Isadora Duncan, who shared his Whitmanesque appetite for life, and was present when she first danced surrounded by children, a sight he found beautiful — though he thought Duncan 'looked puny' dancing the Seventh Symphony on the Trocadéro's vast stage. He went to the Comédie Française but did not appreciate the French declamatory style of acting. On the other hand, he was fascinated by Yvette Guilbert, the Bobinet music-hall and the Cirque Medrano.

'During all this period', the sculptor wrote, 'I was sustained by wonderful health and strength.'

After two years of intensive study Epstein left school and tried to work on his own.

One day an English girl he had met called Celia Jerome appeared at his studio and said she had come to live with him. She moved in, together with a hip-bath, a

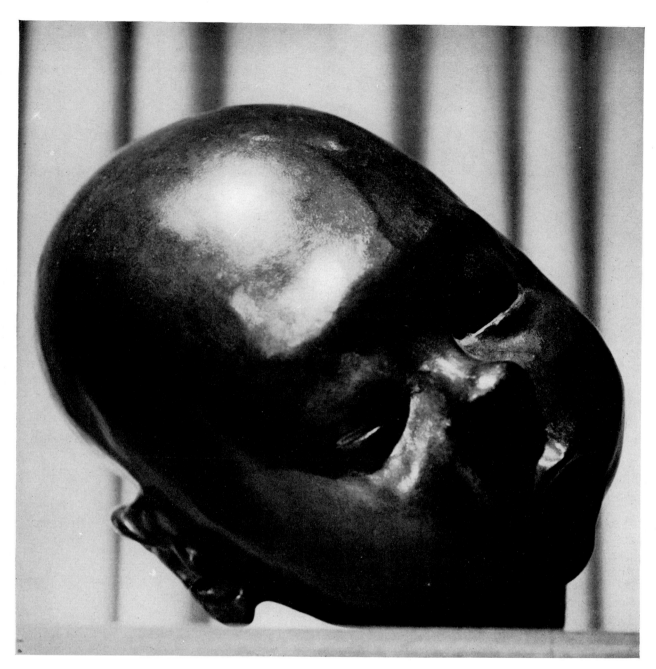

tiger-skin and a 'cello. Epstein made studies of her, none of which has survived. Her attraction to him did not flourish for long in the Spartan conditions of the studio.

At this time Epstein made two short trips out of France. He was given an introduction to an art-loving Italian family who put him up in Florence. The impact on him of Michelangelo and Donatello was overpowering — and yet he only remained two or three days. His hosts were kind to him, but he tended all his life to feel suffo-cated when staying in other people's houses; and he was exasperated by the endless stories of another guest, also a sculptor, and by this man's patronising attitude towards him. But it seems probable that there were more signifi-cant reasons why he fled. The sight of so much greatness — of Michelangelo's Medici Chapel, his David, the un-finished Slaves, the Victory, and the Pietà with Nico-demus; of Donatello's David and St. George; of the golden world of Ghiberti's doors — may have filled him with a divine impatience to get back to work. He was not

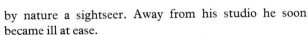

by nature a sightseer. Away from his studio he soon became ill at ease.

'While I was at work at the École des Beaux Arts', wrote Epstein, 'I was asked to dinner by a Belgian, Victor Dave by name, a publisher and anarchist who had suffered imprisonment for two years for activity in anarchist propaganda. He had been associated with Michael Bakunin. I was very cordially received by Victor Dave and his wife in their Passy flat, and there I met the Scottish lady whom I later married.' Epstein was subsequently invited to London and went over for a short visit. He liked the easy and natural manners of the English, and fell in love with the British Museum, whose Elgin marbles were to be one of the chief joys of his life. He went boating on the Thames and even climbed Snowdon. 'I recall this walking trip up the wild Welsh mountains, and how the mountain grandeurs and loneliness impressed me.' England struck him as a place where it would be possible to work.

In 1904 Epstein found himself in a quandary. He had taught himself the basis of his craft: he could observe and analyse form and transfer it *via* clay to bronze, and he could carve it in stone. Technique had made him free to express himself, but, like so many young artists so sure of their vocation, he was suddenly brought up short by the awful question: Have you anything to say? 'I was not at all clear', he wrote, 'how to work out my ideas for sculpture.' He admired so intensely the works of his great predecessors which he had seen in the Louvre, but what was the use of doing something like what they had done before? He was afflicted by the new twentieth-century disease, the fear of being obvious or unoriginal.

The sculptor began to plan two grandiose monuments, a Temple of the Sun and a Temple of Love. The former included a big group of sun-worshippers on which he worked for some time before breaking it up in disgust. He later regretted this and found some early Egyptian figures which bore 'a remarkable resemblance' to his vanished group. It is therefore permissible to assume that the 'Sun-worshippers' were at least partially inspired by Egyptian carvings in the Louvre. (His later relief of 'The Sun God' was certainly Egyptian in style, though not presented in profile). The other 'heroic-sized group' of 'Lovers' was abandoned partly because the male model fell in love with the female, who was Celia Jerome, and the sculptor considered this unforgivably irrelevant of him. He destroyed this group also.

If these Ozymandian projects proved abortive, at least

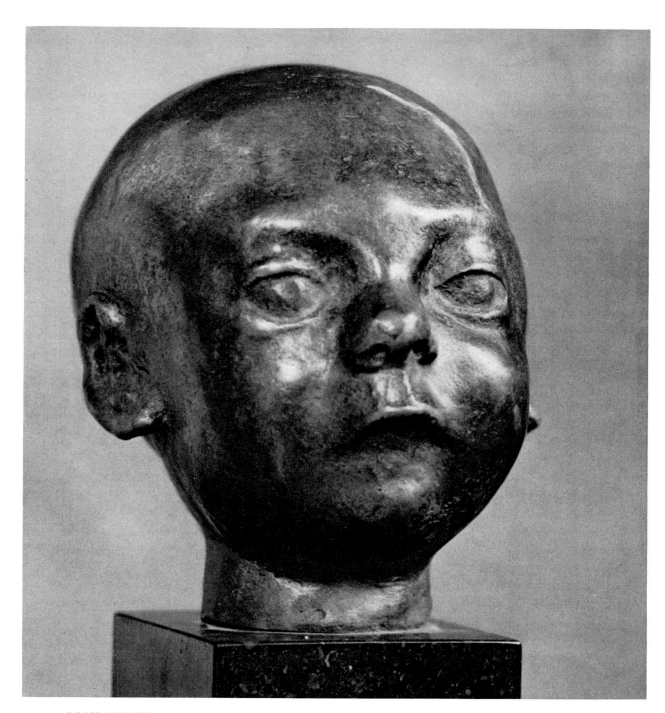

11. 12 BABY AWAKE

two small works survive from the formative period in Paris. There came to his studio door, one day, a girl model with a new born baby. Epstein modelled the baby's head. The tiny portrait SLEEPING BABY with its closed eyes and pursed mouth, so simple and serene, resembles one of those objects the Chinese made to be fondled by an idle hand. It is strange that Epstein's earliest surviving sculpture should be of a baby: this little skull holding the

promise of such great things to come. He went on to model the BABY AWAKE, larger and in a bolder style.

'I was completely at a loss as how to work out my ideas. I had, so it seemed to me, come to a dead end in Paris. I felt that if I went somewhere else and got into new surroundings, I would make a new start. It was in this mood that I debated in my mind whether to return to America or go elsewhere, perhaps to London.'

B 2

[19]

1905-07

EARLY YEARS IN LONDON

So in 1905, the year of the massacre in Red Square and of the Franklin D. Roosevelts' honeymoon in Scotland, the twenty-four year old sculptor, alone and self-sufficient, poor as a stray dog but bursting with ambition and ideas, came to work and to find himself and to seek a living in London. In his head and his hand he carried the new beginning of British sculpture.

His first studio was a room at 219 Stanhope Street, St. Pancras. This was a slum neighbourhood. The lower part of the street, which runs north from the Euston Road, between Albany Street and Hampstead Road, is still much as it was: the northern part, where Epstein lodged, has been torn down and rebuilt with towering apartment blocks in gardens. We can imagine the artist escaping from his cramped quarters in the evening to walk through Cumberland Market into Regent's Park, five minutes away. He slept on newspaper.

What were the earliest sculptures Epstein made in England? The sculptor's first portrait of his first wife was one. MRS. EPSTEIN LEANING ON ONE HAND reminds us of the sort of informal poses given to their sitters by the Impressionist painters or by Sickert. Cézanne certainly painted his 'Jeune Italienne accoudée' (Dr. and Mrs. Harry Bawkins collection) and Degas even modelled the head of a woman leaning on her hand (Sir Kenneth Clark collection). Epstein wrote, 'In the composition itself, I attempted movement which, while very natural, I abandoned in later work, and severely restricted myself to the least possible movement. This I practised as a kind of discipline so that my construction would be more firm. I have always intended returning to the portrait of movement. It is a pity that I have not started on this new departure ere this [he was writing in 1939], but there is time yet for new developments.' In view of the fact that some of his later works in violent movement were his least successful, this reads almost like a threat.

Perhaps the marble RELIEF OF MOTHER AND CHILD, which was certainly carved in the early London period, dates from his stay in Stanhope Street. In the flowing outline of the two figures we can trace the influence of Gauguin and Art Nouveau. The foreshortening of the baby's legs is not rendered successfully, and the mother's hands are weak. Even in the short time he lived in St. Pancras he must have made a number of portraits, for Mr. Robert Jackson remembers his father, a dealer from Manchester, going there to buy from him and returning for more: but (at the time of writing) the whereabouts of none of these is known.

Epstein was not slow in making friends. He probably found his way at once to the Café Royal, since the days of Oscar Wilde the haunt of artists and Bohemians (and where thirty years later, the author of these notes would observe him reverently from a distance, seated with Peggy Jean). It was ten years since Wilde, soon after the triumph of *The Importance of Being Earnest*, had gone to prison, and five since his death in Paris. The 'nineties were dead and the 'Modern Movement' in England had not begun. The plays of Shaw, translations of Ibsen and the novels of Wells already heralded a new spirit of

13 1ST PORTRAIT OF MRS. EPSTEIN

14

14 RELIEF OF
   MOTHER & CHILD

15 DRAWING FOR
   RELIEF OF
   MOTHER & CHILD

15

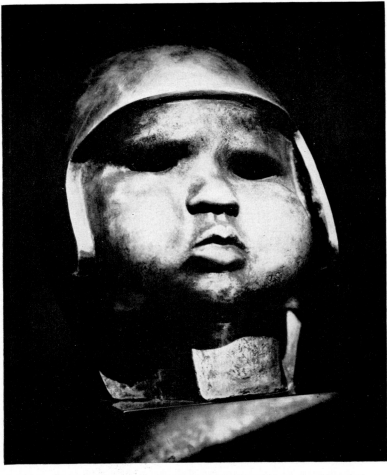

scepticism, social revolution and scientific exploration. Hardy, Conrad, Meredith and James were the other giants of literature. Bridges was Laureate, and Yeats was already well known — had, in fact, lectured in America in the previous year. Bloomsbury was not born. Neither Lytton Strachey, nor E. M. Forster nor Virginia Woolf had, yet been published. The names of Lawrence, of Joyce, of Eliot — even of Hopkins — were still unknown.

Elgar, filling the niche of Sullivan, was the only British composer known to the public. He had already composed his 'Enigma variations' and had been knighted in 1904. Diaghilev had not yet brought Russian music, opera or ballet to Paris, and none would be heard or seen in London for six years. The names of Mussorgsky and Borodine were as unknown there as those of Stravinsky, Schönberg, Bartok and Berg, who were respectively thirty-one, twenty-four and twenty.

In painting Sargent was king; he and such academic painters as Alma-Tadema and Poynter made a lot of money. But Sickert was rampant; Steer and Nicholson had their following; and the Slade, with Tonks, its notable professor, had already produced Orpen, McEvoy and Augustus John. John, whom Will Rothenstein had taken to visit Wilde in Dieppe as early as 1897, had stayed with Lady Gregory at Coole in 1904 and painted Yeats. The first Post-Impressionist Exhibition, which would introduce Gauguin, Van Gogh, Seurat and Matisse to London, was not to happen till 1910.

The only sculptors of repute were academicians, such as Hamo Thornycroft, creator of the Cromwell outside Westminster Hall and Gordon in Trafalgar Square, E. Onslow Ford, Alfred Gilbert, Thomas Brock, who made the tomb of Lord Leighton in St. Paul's, and George Frampton who later carved Edith Cavell. Of these R.A.s Alfred Drury was perhaps the most respectable craftsman.

During his first week in England Epstein met John Fothergill, the literary innkeeper, and drew him. Fothergill introduced him to his friends and made them buy his drawings. Epstein showed some of these, including the 'Calamus' series, to Bernard Shaw, who prophesied a future for him.

One day, feeling extremely discouraged about his work, the sculptor started destroying all that was in the studio. On an impulse he travelled steerage to New York, then, after a fortnight, just as suddenly returned.

Back in London, he took a studio in the Fulham Road by Stamford Bridge, in a building known as the 'Railway Accident'. Here, surprising to relate, his long hair and uncouth appearance aroused the animosity of some of the other residents. 'I heard that the landlady, who lived on the premises, had been requested by the artists to have me removed from the studios, as my clothes were somewhat too Bohemian for the place, not, in fact, respectable enough.' His chief enemies were an Australian sculptor

16. 17 ROMILLY JOHN

and George Belcher, later famous for his well-drawn caricatures of Cockney types in *Punch*. However, the movement to have him expelled was effectively resisted not only by Epstein himself, but, as he relates, by 'the women artists in this beehive'.

Epstein made friends with Augustus John, Ambrose McEvoy, Muirhead Bone and Francis Dodd, all of whom were members of the New English Art Club. From the first he seems to have inspired the admiration and allegiance of these and other British artists, who exerted themselves to get him commissions and advance his career. Both John and Dodd etched portraits of him, while he reciprocated by making, in the course of the next few years, heads of John, of his son Romilly, of Bone and of the wives of McEvoy and Dodd. Mrs. Anna Bazell, daughter of Ambrose and Mary McEvoy, recalls that she was brought up to think of Epstein not just as the best sculptor, but as 'the *only* sculptor'.

Although convinced of his genius and able to inspire conviction in others, Epstein privately still thought of himself as a student. 'My aim was to perfect myself in modelling, drawing and carving, and it was at this period I visited the British Museum and whenever I had done a new piece of work I compared it mentally with what I had seen at the Museum.' There was no one living — in London at least — against whom the young knight-errant of sculpture, who slept in a slum on newspaper, would deign to match himself: when he felt the need to break a lance, as it were, to measure his worth or suffer humiliation in the interests of self-improvement, he had to turn to the giants of the past.

It was while wandering in Bloomsbury, perhaps after one of his visits to the British Museum, that the sculptor met the OLD ITALIAN WOMAN. One of a family of professional models, she used to stand at the corner of Gray's Inn Road and Theobald's Road holding a canary, which for a penny picked your fortune out of a hat. She willingly agreed to pose for Epstein at his Fulham Road studio.

Epstein always said sculpture was entirely a matter of planes. Here we see him exploring the planes of an old face. When he has charted them correctly he knows that character and likeness must follow. Besides this head, which shows the model with hair dragged back into a bun, in typical Italian peasant style, the sculptor tried out another version, OLD ITALIAN WOMAN WITH SHAWL, which is illustrated on page 30 for comparison with a carving based on these portraits. The plaster and bronze of this have disappeared and it is reproduced from Van Dieren's book: but it seems to be the same head with the addition of a shawl pulled tight over her head, its formalised concertina draperies round the neck constituting a kind of decorative base to the bronze.

ROMILLY JOHN, whose portrait is the only other work

18 OLD ITALIAN WOMAN

to survive from this early London period, was a son of Augustus John. His elder brother, now Admiral of the Fleet Sir Caspar John, remembers Epstein visiting their family and playing with the children.

Searching for an extreme simplicity of form, the sculptor made this portrait as 'abstract' as it was possible to make it without sacrificing individual character and expression. The helmet-like bonnet helps to accentuate the stylised nature of the head, which seems almost like a cannon-ball in the process of becoming human. Compare the more particularised and detailed children's portraits of fifty years later.

Although these two portraits from Epstein's early years in London are the only ones — apart from the more Impressionist bust of Margaret Epstein — known to have survived the occasional fits of disgust which led him to destroy the contents of his studio, it seems legitimate to deduce from them that the young sculptor was going through a 'heroic period', and that his aim was to arrive at a grand simplicity by the elimination of detail. This epic mood would carry him through 1908 and 1909 when he made the Strand Statues.

[23]

1907-O8

STRAND STATUES

'One day in the spring of 1907 Mr. Francis Dodd asked me if I could accept a commission from an architect he knew, and decorate a building. This led to my meeting Mr. Charles Holden . . . and to the decorating of the new British Medical Association building in the Strand.'

Holden, shortly before his death in 1960, described to Paul Vaughan, author of *Doctors Commons*, how he gave Epstein the job because he liked the statue of a girl with a dove which was in his studio (this life-size work the sculptor later destroyed, but Plate 19 is a drawing for it), and how 'terribly excited' Epstein was to receive the commission: he was 'almost shaking with excitement'. He undertook to execute the statues for rather less than £100 each, a fee no better-known sculptor would have accepted.

'I set to work and made models of eighteen figures. . . . I moved into a large studio in Cheyne Walk, and began to work. It was a tremendous change for me to move away from the "Railway Accident" to a fine studio, and to receive an advance payment. . . . I thought I was wealthy, and the future looked bright, I could now pay for models, and get to work on large figures. With experience I learned how quickly one's funds could be depleted . . . when you come to reckon up your out-of-pocket expenses against your remuneration, the balance is invariably all on the wrong side. So it was with the Strand Statues. . . .'

However, the twenty-six year old sculptor was exultant at landing the huge and important job. 'I had been like a hound on a leash, and now I was suddenly set free, and I never reckoned the cost. I worked with ardour, feverishly, and within the space of fourteen months the eighteen over-life-sized figures were finished. At first I was some-what held back by the admonitions of the architects, who . . . felt that I might do something rash. I already had a reputation for wildness; why, I don't know. It was quite possible my appearance at this time was that of the traditional anarchist. However, later gathering strength as the architects gathered faith, I managed to impose my own ideas upon the decoration, and had only one bad halt, when they totally rejected one of my figures. . . . I considered it one of the best.' The rejected figure was 'Nature', a young woman holding a leaf, for which Gertrude Williams (see Plate 30) was almost certainly

19 DRAWING OF GIRL WITH DOVE
20 PROJECTS FOR 'STRAND STATUES'
21 PROJECT FOR 'STRAND STATUES'
22 DRAWINGS FOR STRAND 'STATUES'

20

21

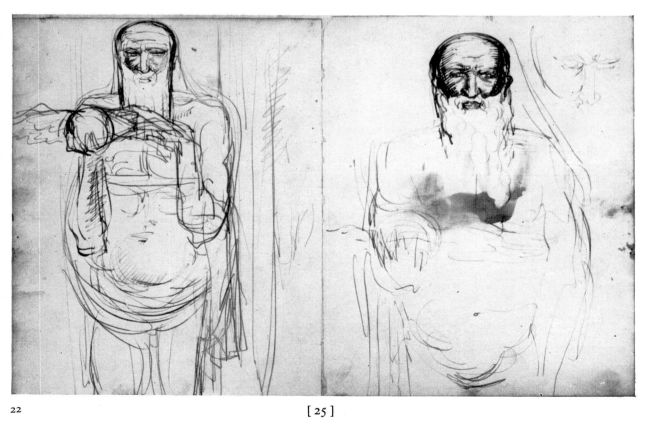

22

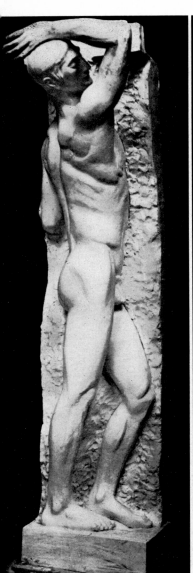
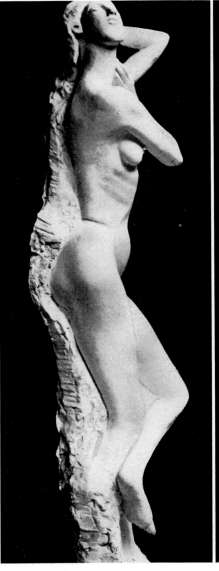
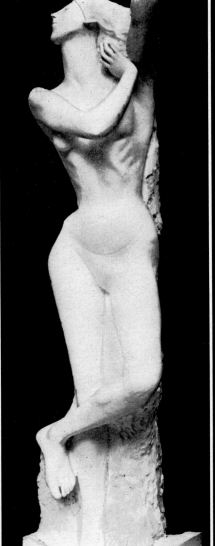
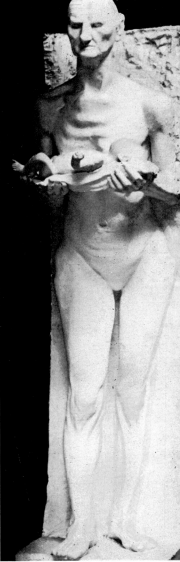

| 23 1st Statue | 24 5th Statue | 25 6th Statue | 26 11th Statue |

PLASTER CASTS OF 'STRAND STATUES'

the model. In the single surviving photograph of the plaster cast her face is far more stylised and decoratively treated than that of the other statues: but it was probably the size of her abundant breasts that the architects objected to.

Epstein's feat in carrying through the STRAND STATUES in so short a time was astounding. He first modelled the eighteen one-and-a-half times life-size statues in clay and cast them in plaster. (He also, of course, modelled the rejected 'Nature' and, according to a photograph, an additional old man — the same old man as the seventeenth statue, but carrying a child instead of a rock.) Having thus made sure exactly what he intended to do, he carved the figures direct from the stone blocks let into the face of the building forty feet above the ground.

Holden's building, at the corner of the Strand and

31 DRAWING OF DANCING GIRL

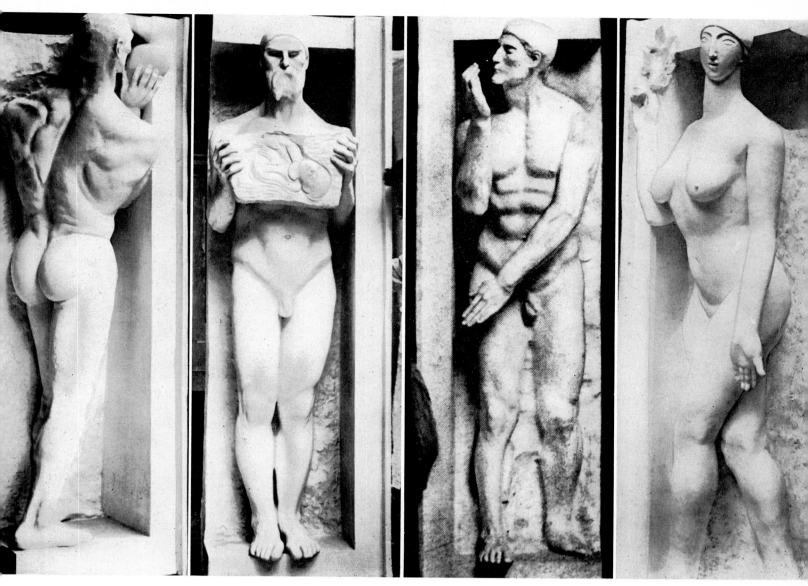

27 16th Statue   28 17th Statue   29 18th Statue   30 Rejected

Agar Street, had elements of grandeur and was devoid of the vulgarity typical of most Edwardian architecture. The lower storeys were in granite, the top two in Portland stone, and the statues carved from the paler material but standing out from the darker, must have been intended, like a sort of fringe, to link the light summit to the sombre base. They were to flank the arched window recesses on the second floor level, fourteen statues framing seven windows up Agar Street, four statues framing two windows on the Strand.

It seems clear, although his single figures were squashed into narrow niches, that Epstein set out to emulate the metopes of the Parthenon. London had no scheme of sculpture so grand, and he would provide it.

In a letter to the *British Medical Journal* Epstein described his statues, but his account is confusing (and he got one wrong) so a new summary is here given, numbering them from left to right, down Agar Street, round the corner and along the Strand.

1 *and* 2. Two men in profile, facing inwards. (1) raises his right hand over his head in a slicing gesture, and his eyes are closed; (2) has his left hand on his chest and he sags at the knees. They are presumably dancing.

3 *and* 4. Two men in profile facing inwards. (3) has head inclined with elbows above it, leans on his left leg, bending the right knee; (4) with knees bent, holds his hands as though clapping or playing cymbals.

5 *and* 6. A man and a woman dancing. (5) is ecstatic, with legs in profile and torso twisted towards the spectator, head thrown back and left arm raised to support it; (6)'s body is turned away from her partner, her left foot is raised to cross her right shin, her left elbow points

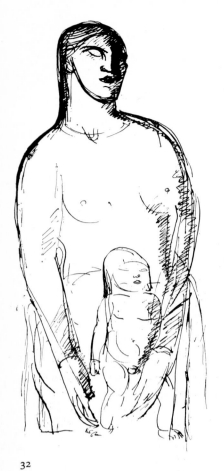

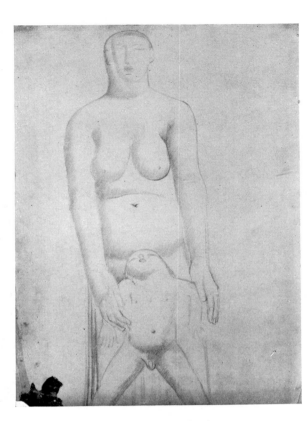

32   1ST DRAWING FOR
     MOTHER & CHILD (INK)

33   2ND DRAWING FOR
     MOTHER & CHILD (PENCIL)

34   DRAWING OF PREGNANT
     MOTHER WITHOUT CHILD

35   CAST OF PREGNANT
     MOTHER (WITH CHILD
     MISSING)

36   9TH STATUE: PREGNANT
     MOTHER WITH CHILD

32

34

35

37

37 OLD WOMAN WITH SHAWL
38 PLASTER CAST OF 11TH STATUE
39 SEVERED HEAD OF 11TH STATUE
40 11TH STATUE
(OLD WOMAN WITH BABY)

upwards, her right arm touches her hair below her left ear, and her head is thrown back.

7 *and* 8. A woman and man. (7) is similar to (6), but faces the spectator. (8) walks to the left but twists his body to show a muscular back. Raising his left elbow forward, he holds his head.

Epstein said these first eight figures represented 'Youth, Joy and Life, youths and maidens reaching out and stretching hands towards each other'; but there are only two girls among them.

9 *and* 10. A woman with a child and a man facing inwards. (9) A young pregnant mother inclines her head tenderly over the child who sits on her hands and embraces her. A draped skirt has slipped below her pelvis. (10) with torso full on to the spectator strides to the left, arms hanging.

11 *and* 12. An old woman carrying a baby, and a man, both full face. (11) with long plaits and a skirt hanging in straight folds, bears the newborn baby before her like an offering. (12) full on, feet together, lifts both arms to cover his eyes, as if stretching after sleep.

13 *and* 14. A man facing and a man back view. (13) feet together, holds a winged skull in both hands. (14) standing in a relaxed attitude, shows his muscular back and reads from a scroll.

41

Turning the corner of the Strand, we come to:

15 and 16. A man's back view and a woman full face. (15) turned to the right, but showing all his highly developed back, holds a retort in both hands (not a scroll as Epstein wrote) and represents 'Chemical Research'. (16) stands full face, a draped koré; she is 'Hygeia', goddess of medicine, and holds (according to the sculptor) a cup and serpent.

17 and 18. An old man full face and a young man facing inwards. Like (16) a forward-facing sentinel, (17) a bearded old man, holds before him a block in which a baby incubates. (18), whose head is turned to his right, though his body faces the spectator, makes with his left hand across his body a gesture as if parting branches, and blows on something which he holds up in his right. Epstein called him 'Primal Energy'; he is meant to be breaking through chaos and breathing life into the atom.

'In symbolism', the sculptor wrote, 'I tried to represent man and woman, in their various stages from birth to old age — a primitive, but in no way a bizarre programme. Perhaps this was the first time in London that a decoration was not purely "decorative"; the figures had some fundamentally human meaning, instead of being merely adjunct to an architect's mouldings and cornices.' Then, in a letter to the *British Medical Association Journal*, he further explained, 'Throughout I have wished to give a presentation of figures joyous, energetic, and mystical.' But he admitted, 'It is very difficult for me to say in

words much that I have wished to put into those figures . . .'; and of course that would always be the trouble. The carvings are classical in the sense that they diverge hardly at all from the Greek and Renaissance tradition, ranging from the realistic to the idealised, and show none of the influence of Egyptian, Mexican or African sculpture which was evident in much of Epstein's later work. 'Hygeia' is an archaic Greek Koré; the realism of the old woman's head is reminiscent of Donatello: the dancing figures can be compared to Michelangelo; and the man with upraised arms, awaking from sleep, recalls Rodin's 'Age of Bronze'. Yet, being intended to be seen from a distance of forty feet, they are bolder and more simplified than, for example, Michelangelo's 'Victory' or his 'Slaves'. There was no question of rendering the veins on the hands.

Taken as a series, a continuous decoration, they are (or were) enormously effective: but the speed with which they had to be planned and carried out may account for certain anomalies. One can understand the artist's idea of framing (16) and (17), the two forward-facing sentinels on the Strand front with two inward-facing figures in movement: but there are in the series of eighteen no less than four full-face sentinel figures who stand to attention bearing something — a baby, a skull, cup and serpent, a rock — before them. (And the serious man with the winged skull holds it, not from beneath, but by the temples, as if it were a ball he was bouncing.) (6) and (7), apart from the direction they face, are strangely similar, and in fact must have been carved after the same plaster model. The anatomy of (14)'s raised arm is peculiar. (Throughout his career as a sculptor Epstein was to take lordly liberties with anatomy.)

The figures are a mixture of prose and poetry. The mysterious choreography of (1), (2), (3) and (4), the ecstasy of (5), and the fantastic treatment of (6) and (7), the dancing nymphs, contrast with the down-to-earth rendering of (11), the old woman carrying the baby, and the detailed musculature of (14)'s and (15)'s backs, which seem almost like technical diagrams provided for the satisfaction of the British Medical Association.

Yet though his eighteen carvings showed no break with tradition, they were entirely devoid of the sentimental academism with which that tradition had come to be associated. The young mother, for instance, was a novel conception, both bold and tender, and was unlike anything that had been done in previous centuries: indeed, perhaps only in the paintings of Renoir — and Renoir only began to 'dictate' his few sculptures to Guino five years later — could one look for so golden a blend of lyricism and monumentality.

[32]

42

43

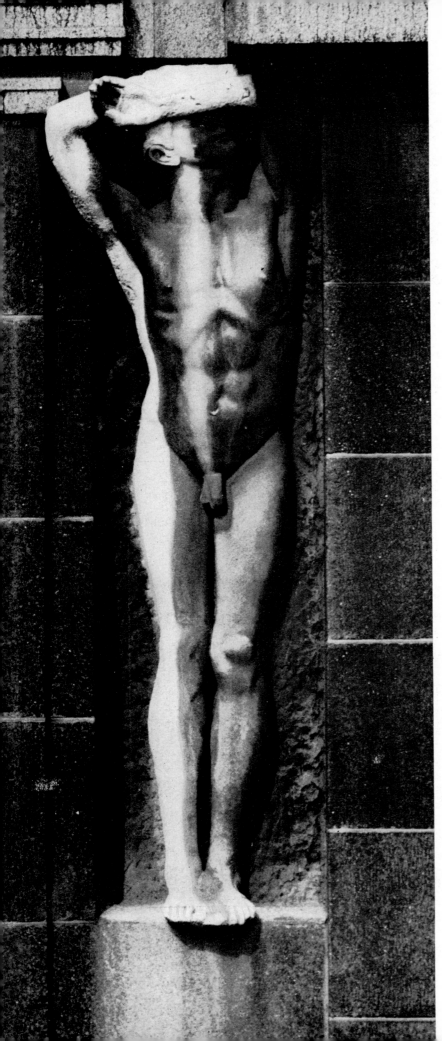

The great scheme of sculpture, Shakespearean in scope, was a tremendous success, and there was nothing to compare with it in London. The young artist, who eight years before had never touched a chisel, could now congratulate himself not only on his technical mastery, but on having something new to say — and having said it in record time.

There were 'disturbances' while the artist was working with his two assistants on the scaffolding, but he 'concentrated on the work and went straight ahead'. However, he was destined to make Londoners conscious of sculpture, and to suffer for it. The plaster cast of the young mother was delivered to the site without her baby: she seemed to be contemplating her own pregnancy. This caught the evil eye of the National Vigilantes Society, who happened to have an office across Agar Street.

In view of the traditional nature of the statues it is hard to understand the violent attacks they were to undergo. 'All was quiet', wrote Epstein, 'until after the scaffolding was removed from the first four figures, then a storm of vituperation burst out [on 19 June 1908] in the *Evening Standard and St. James's Gazette* that was totally unexpected and unprecedented in its fury.' 'They represent a development in art', wrote the anonymous critic, 'to which the British public are not accustomed . . . they are a form of statuary which no careful father would wish his daughter or no discriminating young man his fiancée, to see. . . . The question arises how they were permitted to be erected . . . and inquiries go to show that no authorization is needed to put figures in sculpture on a building.' Thus did a sensation-mongering hack, desperate for copy, set in motion a campaign of denigration which was to reopen with the appearance of nearly every monumental work carved by Epstein until his old age: a campaign which would embitter the vulnerable and childlike artist, endanger his livelihood, deprive London of noble adornment, and indirectly hasten the sculptor's end. A policeman was sent to report on the figures: Dr. Lang, Bishop of Stepney (later Archbishop of Canterbury), declared them to be decent; passengers stood up on the top of open buses to get a better view — the Strand was narrower in those days — and the sculptor was called (on 24 June) to give evidence before the Premises Committee of the B.M.A. (not the Council, as he wrote in his autobiography). The question arose whether Epstein should be permitted to complete his work, and whether the figures should be removed from the building. However, they were defended by a leading article in *The Times*, and by letters from Sir Charles Holmes, Slade Professor, from Charles Ricketts, Charles Shannon and Laurence Binyon: they were allowed to remain.

We must interrupt the chronological continuity of this book to conclude in this chapter the tragic history of the Strand Statues.

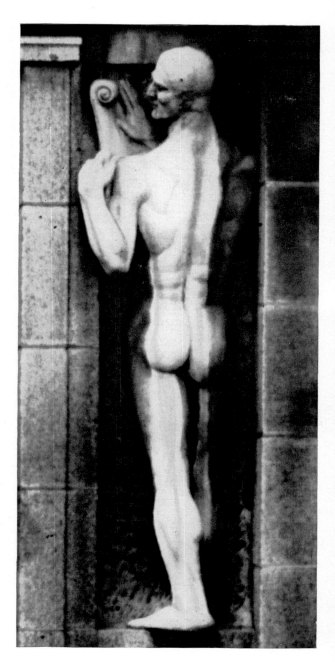

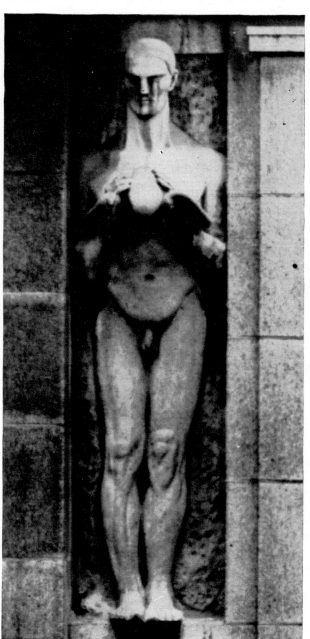

45 14TH STATUE
46 SEVERED HEAD OF 13TH STATUE
47 13TH STATUE

In 1924 the British Medical Association moved to new premises in Bloomsbury and 429 Strand was up for sale. The ground floor had always been let as a shop: now it became a News Theatre. The upper part became offices.

In 1935 the government of Southern Rhodesia bought the building, and the High Commissioner announced in the Press that the statues were to be removed. Sickert protested amusingly in the *Daily Telegraph*. A letter in *The Times* signed by Kenneth Clark, W. G. Constable,

48 1937 PLASTER MOULDERS TAKING
   CASTS BEFORE THE STATUES'
   DESTRUCTION

49 16TH, 17TH, 18TH STATUES
   AFTER MUTILATION

50 RHODESIA HOUSE, 455 STRAND
   IN 1961

Lord Crawford, William Reid Dick, H. A. Goodhart-Rendel, G. F. Hill, Eric Maclagan and J. D. Manson proclaimed that 'If the statues are removed, and still more if they are irreparably damaged in the course of the removal, we find it difficult to believe that this generation will be acquitted by our successors of a charge of grave vandalism'. Sir William Llewellyn, President of the Royal Academy, was asked to sign the letter, but refused; whereupon Sickert resigned from the Royal Academy. The statues were reprieved.

In 1937 decorations were attached to the statues at the time of King George VI's coronation, and when they were being taken down a portion of one of the figures fell. A few of them had indeed weathered badly, considering that they were only twenty-nine years old. This was either due to corrosion by the dripping of rain which had run off metal plates on a superior cornice or because the blocks had been set up contrary to their bed positions, or both. Holden, the architect, is said to have intended the eventual discoloration of the statues. Despite protests from T. W. Earp and Muirhead Bone, the Rhodesian

government began the destruction of the statues. Some inadequate casts were hastily taken: these, together with a few indifferent old photographs, are all that remain to bear witness to the grandest scheme of sculptural adornment ever realised on a London building. Epstein wrote, 'Anyone passing along the Strand can now see, as on some antique building the mutilated fragments of my decoration.'

Holden, who defended Epstein throughout the controversy, employed him again on the Underground Headquarters Building: but he was only given the commission to design the new towered edifice of London University on condition that there were no Epstein statues on it.

After Epstein's death, his widow mentioned to the present writer, who was also directing the Epstein Memorial Exhibition at the 1961 Edinburgh Festival, that she remembered her husband remarking in recent years that he had seen a photograph in some magazine of a function in Southern Rhodesia and had recognised one or more fragments of his Strand Statues in the back-ground. The writer, who had been having trouble finding even photographs of the statues in their original condition — there seemed to be a curse on these too, for the inadequate ones reproduced here are the only ones to have survived — and he asked for help in the Press. (A letter to Government House, Salisbury, had drawn a blank.) From Devonshire came a letter from Miss Reed, a schoolteacher, who remembered an Epstein head which had been the pride of the Coghlan School for Girls in Bulawayo. The Headmistress of this school, Miss Armstrong, confirmed this information, sent a photograph and kindly agreed to lend the head of No. 11, the Old Woman holding a baby, to Edinburgh. So the head of the woman Epstein met in Bloomsbury (herself an exile from her native Italy), and which for thirty years looked down on the rowdy life of the Strand, made a brief excursion to Scotland, then returned to far-off Bulawayo.

Other fragments which came to light are listed in the *catalogue raisonné*.

C

[37]

1908-12

PORTRAITS AND A TOMB

In an interview given to a press reporter, Epstein revealed that after paying his plaster moulders he was £500 out of pocket over the Strand Statues. The result of this was that a chemist called Fels appeared one day and handed him the money.

Epstein wrote: 'It was at the time immediately after my decoration of the Strand building, that I again took in hand my development as a Sculptor. After so much that was large and elemental, I had the desire to train myself in a more intensive method of working; and with that in view, I began a series of studies from the model, which were as exact as I could make them. I worked with great care, and followed the forms of the model by quarter-inches, I should say, not letting up on any detail of construction of plane; but always keeping the final composition in view. . . . I look upon this period as formative.'

Yet during this period of approximately four years the sculptor would also be working on big imaginative carvings, the chief of these being the Tomb of Oscar Wilde. 'I heard of the commission to do the tomb of Oscar Wilde the day after it had been announced at a dinner given to Robert Ross by his friends at the Ritz. In the morning when friends rang me up to congratulate me I imagined a hoax was being played. . . . I had only just finished the British Medical Association figures, and this important commission, following immediately after, was a matter of some excitement. It took me some time to get started on the work. I made sketches and carried them out, but I was dissatisfied and scrapped quite completed work. Finally I determined on the present design, and I went to Derbyshire to the Hopton Wood stone quarries where I saw an immense block which had just been quarried preparatory to cutting it into thin slats for wall-facings. I bought this monolith, weighing twenty tons, on the spot, and had it transported to my London studio. . . .'

By the words 'I made sketches and carried them out' Epstein meant that he made drawings and from them small models in clay. By the time he made the drawing reproduced here he must have decided on the nature of the monument — that it should be the relief of a winged angel in flight: but the folded arms, the extended legs, the poked-forward position of the head and the nature of the crown would all be changed and improved upon. Epstein had already determined — somewhat oddly, it may be thought — that the angel's head-dress should be decorated by personifications of the Seven Deadly Sins. At the foot of this drawing he improvises a list of ten, namely: covetousness, envy, jealousy, anger, sloth, wandering thoughts, fornication, slander, sodomy, evil.

Exactly when, and for exactly how long he worked on the Wilde tomb it is impossible to calculate. The Strand Statues were finished in summer 1908, and if, as Epstein

51 SKETCH FOR TOMB OF OSCAR WILDE

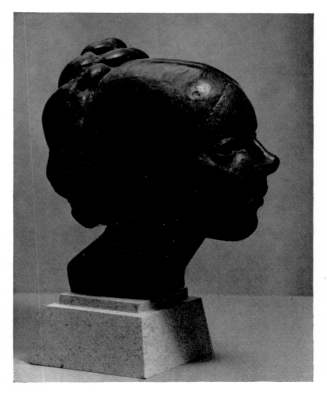

52

53

52 HILDA HAMBLAY
53 ENGLISH GIRL

writes, he had 'only just' finished them when he received the commission and if, as he also wrote, he 'began work immediately and without hesitation continued to labour at it for nine months' he could have finished the tomb as early as 1909. How long elapsed before he bought the stone in Derbyshire? Was he accurate in saying he worked on it for just 'nine months'? What we do know is that he threw open his Cheyne Walk studio to the public and the Press, and that reviews of the sculpture appeared in June 1912, shortly before it was transported to France. If Epstein finished the carving in 1909, 1910 or 1911, even allowing for the polishing of the stone, would he have waited so long to show it and to dispatch it to its permanent site?

Epstein had become a British citizen in 1907. Among the heads he was to model in 1909 and 1910 there were several of women whose features seem peculiarly English. This would not be worth commenting on if he had not shown in later years a preference for exotic beauty, and even come to be predominantly associated in the mind of the public with 'colourful' Negro, Jewish and Oriental types. Of course, a young and poor artist must take what models and commissions he can get: but it does seem, when one looks at such heads as the one he called, perhaps pointedly, 'English Girl', at 'Hilda Hamblay', at

'Mrs. Chadburn' and 'Mrs. McEvoy' (the last two of which will be found on the following page) that the Paris-trained, American-born Polish Jew was studiously regarding the women of his newly adopted country, eager to probe the secrets of a land which had borne George Eliot and Victoria, Becky Sharp, Kathy, Tess and Alice. In later years he would say that English women had always looked to him very 'Greek'.

The eyes of the ENGLISH GIRL — who, by the way, seems identical with Gertrude Williams (Plate 76) — are rather perfunctorily rendered. Epstein had not yet solved the problem of how to model eyes — a perennially difficult one for sculptors — and that may be why many of his sitters at this period are portrayed looking down. Soon (1916) he would marvellously indicate the inspired eyes of W. H. Davies; and in later years he would find a number of ways to bestow on his artifacts the boon of sight.

HILDA HAMBLAY, though another English type, is not such a 'good sort' as the English Girl, nor so sweet and noble as Mrs. Chadburn, but she is evidently short, pert, pretty and flirtatious. A pointed face set off by a halo of plaited hair; eyes wide with surmise; a snub nose; parted, provocative lips; a dimpled chin.

[39]

54

The MARBLE BUST OF MRS. CHADBURN is one of Epstein's only two carved portraits. He decided early on that the subtleties of surface which reveal character were rendered better in clay, and that marble should be kept for ideal and monumental works. It is curious to recall that Rodin believed women's portraits should be in marble, men's in bronze. As Rodin never carved with a chisel himself, his marble heads of women, like his imaginative groups, were all copies by assistants from his own clay models. No work of Epstein's, however, was ever touched by an assistant's hand, although at the end of his life he had stonemasons cut away the rough of his T.U.C. carving. (He never took his plaster casts himself, though, deeming this to be waste of time.) With her hair swept back into a bun, her fine brow, her slightly pursed lips and strong jaw, Mrs. Chadburn seems the sort of woman Millais might have painted. Her eyes look down, but they are not closed; and her expression is one of sweetness.

MRS. MCEVOY, born Mary Spenser-Edwards, is another quiet English gentlewoman, whose windows clearly open on a mown lawn and an apple tree. She left her home in Somerset to study painting at the Slade, and was introduced to McEvoy, also a Slade student, by Augustus John in front of Titian's 'Noli me tangere', which John was then copying, in the National Gallery. The sensitive bust was modelled by candlelight as the electricity had been cut off. Of the four portraits on this and the previous page, Mrs. McEvoy's is the most individual: and not only because of the subtlety of modelling. It is as if Epstein has not only made the portrait of a woman in thought, looking down, but also the portrait of a *moment* — the fraction of a second when, say, a vague sensation of love for her husband turned into the anxious question

54 MRS. CHADBURN (MARBLE)
55 MRS. MCEVOY (BRONZE)
56 MRS. MCEVOY (BRONZE)
57 MRS. MCEVOY (MARBLE)

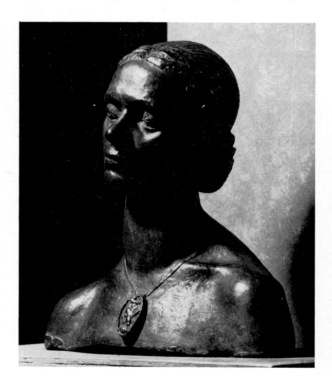

55

56

of whether she could afford to give him cream with his gooseberry tart for lunch.

For the only time in his life Epstein then went on to copy his cast in marble. The MARBLE BUST OF MRS. MCEVOY, a rare and remarkable work, is a faithful version of the bronze and retains its living quality. The hair is simplified and the suggestion of a plain dress replaces the pendant medallion. This precious carving, whose exis-

tence has long been forgotten in this country, found its way to the Johannesburg Art Gallery in South Africa as early as 1910.

Nan Condron was a gypsy and a professional model, a big angular woman with a stately carriage, who wore her long hair hanging straight down her back. When she strode down the street boys called 'Gippo!' after her, and she resented it. She also posed for Orpen and Rothenstein,

58

58   DRAWING OF NAN
59   FIRST PORTRAIT OF NAN   59
60   FIRST PORTRAIT OF NAN

but becoming devoted to Epstein, she gave up working for other artists for several years. She seldom spoke and asked for nothing except to be taken to the music-hall once a week. Epstein did a number of studies of her; this FIRST PORTRAIT OF NAN, made in 1909, being one of the earliest.

The heavy brow, large nose, full lips and strong chin are meticulously modelled, with no thought of improving or refining them; and the sculptor seems to have exaggerated the irregularities of the face. For instance, when looking at the bust full on, one observes that the nose slants in one direction and the chin in the other. The resulting portrait is grandiose. Nan knows she is a princess of wild places, and seems content that Epstein at least should so acknowledge her. As if in tribute, the sculptor cast in bronze a pair of barbaric earrings like inverted fans and had them fixed to the ears of the bust. In the casting which belongs to the Tate Gallery and which is illustrated here, they have been broken off. Nan's is the first of several portraits which Epstein decked out with fantastic jewellery. A version of the bust with bare shoulders also exists.

Besides his nude studies of Nan (Plates 82–6) Epstein made a 'Second Portrait of Nan', reproduced in Van Dieren but not here.

From his earliest days in Paris Epstein had been impressed by the sculpture of India and China, then little regarded, and he had studied it further in the British Museum. African masks too had excited his admiration at the Trocadéro as early as 1902, before they were generally considered to have anything but anthropological interest. In 1906, shortly after Epstein had left Paris, Picasso, whom he was not to meet till 1912, in turn made the discovery of African art: the introduction of two African faces with long concave noses into his picture called 'Les Demoiselles d'Avignon' initiated his short 'Negro Period', which led to Cubism.

In 1910, influenced by visits to the British Museum and perhaps by the forty-one paintings of Gauguin in the first Post-Impressionist Exhibition at the Grafton Galleries during the autumn of that year, Epstein began what was to be the first 'primitive' sculpture made in England in modern times. He started work on 'maternity' in his Cheyne Walk studio, and exhibited it unfinished at the Allied Artists Exhibition in the Albert Hall in 1911. When he moved to Guildford Street in 1916 the heavy figure was stored in a shed where he sometimes worked in Emerald Street nearby. In the early 'twenties he made a start at continuing work on it, but evidently gave up at once, for the figure remained unchanged except for some vertical grooves representing the folds of the skirt (as the photographs on page 46 show) between its only two

[42]

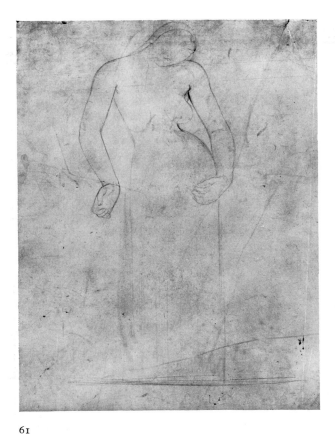

61

exhibitions, at the Albert Hall in 1911 and in the Waverley Market, Edinburgh, exactly half a century later.

Epstein was continually inspired by the process of generation and the idea of motherhood. He had already carved in the Strand 'Mother and Child' one pregnant woman, and he would make others. This drowsy MATER-NITY with closed eyes has the calm of a Buddha in meditation (compare the face of 'Night', Plate 255, carved in 1928–9), though her assertive breasts recall the voluptuous dancing goddesses of Hindu sculpture. It is these breasts, however, which spoil the statue: their formalised, knob-like nature belong to a different convention from the rest of the figure — an African one — and the fact that they are placed dead level throws the whole thing out. 'Maternity' is nevertheless the first unsentimental treatment of motherhood in sculpture (except for the Strand 'Mother and Child') since the Renaissance. It is a tentative work which only partly resolves the conflict between form and expression: but, seen from the front its outline has an exciting flow. It is as if this pregnant goddess is rehearsing in her mind the movements of the sacred sexual dance which, incidentally, brought her to her present predicament, and which countless millions of her unborn descendants will perform after her in order to populate the earth. The hands are sensitively carved, and seem to be conscious of the miraculous new life within the belly they are grasping. Perhaps the back, with its heavy plait of hair, like a loaf of Jewish bread, is more successful than the front. The braided hair reminds us of the Chosen Virgin in Stravinsky's *Sacre du printemps*, and we remember that this revolutionary work, the first

61 DRAWING FOR 'MATERNITY'
62 DRAWING OF HANDS
63 EPSTEIN WITH 'MATERNITY'

62

64. 65. 66
'MATERNITY' (in 1911)

67. 68
'MATERNITY' (in 1961)

64

65

66

67

68

69 SUNFLOWER

70 SUN GOD (detail of the unfinished relief)

'primitive' ballet, with its angular choreography by Nijinsky and designs by the archaistic Roerich, was first performed in Paris in 1913. 'Genesis' was also to have a braided plait.

During the same year, 1910, the sculptor began to carve a big relief, somewhat Egyptian in style — though the figure was not in profile — of a SUN GOD with flaming hair: this was soon put aside, like 'Maternity', though unlike that statue, it was resumed and finished twenty years later (see Plates 274 and 311).

SUNFLOWER, an interesting experiment in semi-abstraction, also carved (in San Stefano stone) at this time, was another smaller variation of the Sun theme. Observing it, we note that even before his meeting with

Picasso, Modigliani and Brancusi in 1912, Epstein was drawn towards the rectilinear and the abstract. Raised on its stalk or neck or obelisk, the round disc with its double halo of dog-tooth rays, petals or curls, is at once a face, a flower and a sun.

We have seen that Epstein regarded the period of his life following the completion of the Strand Statues as 'formative': he was still learning. Indeed he was at a cross-roads, experimenting in a variety of styles. Besides the careful and exploratory studies of models such as Nan, he began to execute portrait commissions very much in Rodin's style; then, he was tackling big carvings such as the Wilde tomb and 'Maternity' in a primitive or Oriental manner — and at least one of his portrait

[49]

71

recently discovered in the Victoria and Albert Museum, to assume that he made and destroyed several naturalistic nudes at this time, and that these might have been either modelled or carved or both. GARDEN FIGURE is the only one of these to survive: like the Strand Statues it was first modelled, then carved.

Lady Ottoline Morrell describes in her memoirs how in 1909 or 1910 Augustus John wrote asking her to help Epstein, who was very hard up. The Morrells went to his studio in Cheyne Walk and found him almost starving. 'We gave him an order for a garden statue, and I took likely clients to see him, amongst others W. B. Yeats and Lady Gregory.' Later Lady Ottoline sold the carving to Arthur Clifton of the Carfax Galleries for the price she had paid for it, namely £25. It passed to Clifton's second wife, and has stood for many years in a garden in Kent.

71 NARCISSUS (clay)
72 PLASTER SKETCH FOR GARDEN FIGURE (1910)
73 GARDEN FIGURE

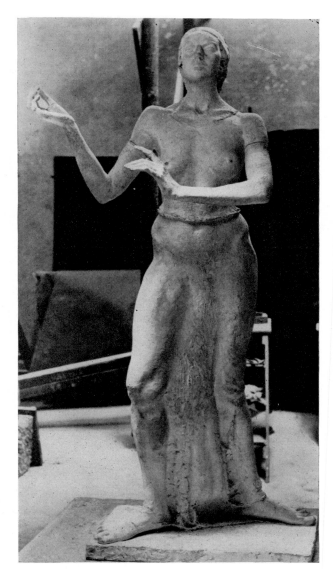

bronzes, as we shall see, showed the influence of Buddhist art as well; finally he was making smaller, more delicate statues which can only be described as modern Renaissance or modern Greek.

He had destroyed along with much else the statue of a 'Girl with a Dove' (the drawing for which is Plate 19), the work that aroused the enthusiasm of Holden the architect. It seems reasonable on the evidence of the surviving photograph of a standing NARCISSUS in clay

72

20

74

74 1ST BUST OF EUPHEMIA
75 2ND BUST OF EUPHEMIA

'Garden Figure', for which Euphemia Lamb was the model, is unique among Epstein's surviving carvings, the rest of which were all conceived in far more monumental terms. Even the dancing nymphs in Agar Street were not given such delicate, capricious and, as it were, conversational gestures of the hands. The formalised archaic treatment of rippling drapery in contrast to the little modern sleeves of Euphemia's clinging dress is strange too.

Euphemia posed for a number of artists, including John and her husband; and there is a McEvoy of her in the Tate Gallery.

Epstein made two portraits of Euphemia. Her very English looks must have appealed to him. In the FIRST BUST OF EUPHEMIA, which has part of the arms and breast, he modelled her looking upwards: in the SECOND BUST OF EUPHEMIA, which is just a head and shoulders, she looks down, her head slightly leaning to the left. The two busts

[52]

76

in marble: and this is the only period of his work of which such a thing can be said. With her closed eyes, her unlined face, her sloping shoulders and smooth formalised hair falling behind her, Marie Rankin projects a convent calm which may be the result of Epstein's admiration for certain Buddhist sculpture. Only a flicker of the lips suggests the possibility of laughter or tears.

In an awkward but appealing life-size statue of a STANDING MOTHER AND CHILD (only cast in bronze after his death) Epstein combined the portraits of Marie Rankin and Romilly John.

76 GERTRUDE
77 STANDING MOTHER AND CHILD
78 MARIE RANKIN

contrast strangely. The first could only be a modern portrait of a modern woman. The second, not only because of the way it is cut off traditionally below the shoulders, but also from the delicacy of its modelling, its reticence and the life it breathes, might almost be a work of the Florentine *Quattrocento*.

Gertrude Williams was a model of whom Epstein made several nude studies, only one of which has survived. She may have posed for the rejected Strand Statue; and she seems to be the same person as 'English Girl' (Plate 53). The HALF-LENGTH FIGURE OF GERTRUDE is curious in that the wrists sink handless in the base.

According to Haskell's chronology, compiled with the aid of the first Mrs. Epstein, there were two versions of the head of MARIE RANKIN, the first made in 1907, the second — once known as 'Irish Girl' — in 1911. The latter has survived and is one of Epstein's most successful early portraits. Although in this 'formative period' the sculptor was occupied on 'research' and the analysis of physiognomy, he could still occasionally produce portraits of a simplicity so monumental that they might be mistaken — in a photograph particularly — for carvings

77

78

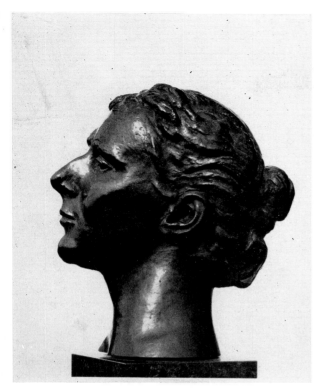

so the head may have been a delayed wedding present.

'I began at this time', the sculptor wrote, 'to do commissioned portraits of people. The artist who imagines that he puts his best into a portrait in order to produce something good, that will be a pleasure to the sitter and to himself, will have some bitter experiences.'

The portrait of Augusta Gregory, friend of Yeats, author, and founder of the Abbey Theatre, was commissioned by her nephew Sir Hugh Lane, the collector. It was Ottoline Morrell who first took LADY GREGORY, with Yeats, to the Cheyne Walk studio.

Epstein wrote: 'The bust progressed to my own satisfaction, and was about completed, when one morning Lady Gregory turned up with the most astonishing head of curls: she had been to her hairdresser and wished me to alter the head. I was not inclined to do this, as the bust had up to then been planned to give Lady Gregory the air of the intellectual, somewhat "school-marmish" person that she was, and her usual appearance was all of a piece and quite dignified. I told Lady Gregory that I could not imagine the bust any better if I altered it . . . and in my headstrong way kept to my guns: this practically terminated the sittings. When Sir Hugh Lane saw my bust . . . he threw up his hands in horror and exclaimed, "Poor Aunt Augusta. She looks as if she could eat her own

79 MRS. ARTHUR CLIFTON
80 MRS. FRANCIS DODD
81 LADY GREGORY

If certain heads of this period were in the manner of Rodin (Lady Gregory's, for example), the head of MRS. CLIFTON commissioned by her husband, Arthur Clifton of the Carfax Galleries, has the grace, charm and sentiment of Carpeaux or Dalou. The elegant disorder of the rippling hair, the sophisticated naturalness of the smiling eyes and parted lips are in the French rococo tradition. Only the curious prolongation of the eyelids to form solid rims of eyelash is an innovation — and an unsuccessful one (see also the 'Head of Lillian Shelley', Plate 123). Throughout his career as a sculptor Epstein showed a fascination for the various ways hair grew and could be dressed; and he explored innumerable possibilities of methods to render it in clay. Arthur Clifton had been a friend of Oscar Wilde, had visited him in prison and sent a wreath to his funeral. Wilde had thought his wife 'so like Rossetti's wife — the same lovely hair — but of course a sweeter nature. . . .'

Also in a somewhat French manner is the head of MRS. FRANCIS DODD, with her fine profile. To make this portrait of the wife of his painter friend (who etched him), Epstein travelled daily to Greenwich possibly because the model was pregnant or could not leave her baby. The Dodds had recently been married,

82

83

82 DRAWING FOR NAN (THE DREAMER)
83 NAN (THE DREAMER)
84 NAN SEATED
85 NAN SEATED

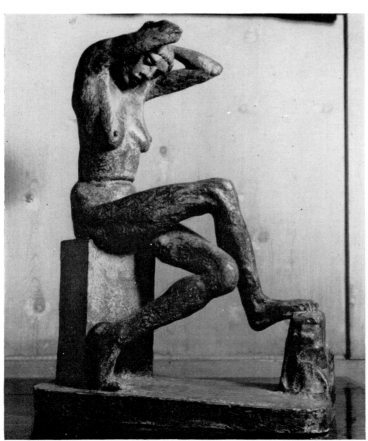

84

85

86 NAN (THE DREAMER)

children." Later I was to get used to this sort of reception of a work, but at the time it nonplussed me, for I had put many days of work with long sittings, and much labour into it. Nevertheless Sir Hugh Lane hurried the bust over to Dublin in time for Horse Show week.'

Epstein made a number of drawings of Nan, the Gypsy model (see Plates 58–60), and one of these at least he translated faithfully in clay. THE DREAMER is very like the artist's drawing of Nan in a semi-recumbent pose, but she leans on her left hand, not her elbow. Her eyes are closed (in the earlier bust they were only lowered) and the fingers of her right hand are raised as if she were drumming on the ground the rhythm of a song which had come into her head. This curious piece of naturalism reminds us of the sublime 'Zeus with a Thunderbolt' in Athens, the toes of whose extended foot curl upwards off the ground.

'The Dreamer' is a very careful anatomical study: it also has a lyrical quality. NAN SEATED is less refined, more stylised, perhaps grander. While the model's arms, raised to adjust her back hair, are in a pose beloved of Degas, her angular attenuated limbs anticipate the kind of work Lehmbruck would be doing in Paris a year or two later. Gaudier described this study in a letter to Sophie Brzeska as 'a little bronze, very beautiful, quite the nicest work of his I have seen — alive and sincere . . .'.

Between the group of studies from Nan, of which only these two have survived, and the numerous reclining nudes he made from Betty Peters and Marie Tracy about the beginning of the Second World War, Epstein appears to have modelled only two small nudes from life, those of Dolores (Plate 182) and Sunita (Plate 275).

Two events of this period may be recorded as touching Epstein's career as a sculptor: his proposal for membership of, and rejection by, The Royal Society of British Sculptors, and his meeting with Gaudier-Brzeska. He had already experienced the antagonism of the Press; he now ran into the Philistinism of official art circles; and he would soon find the genuine 'intellectuals' of Bloomsbury were also against him. The defiance and suspicion he now began to feel towards a large percentage of his fellow men certainly affected the nature of his work. One might have thought that this bitterness would be mitigated by the sympathy of other artists like John, Dodd and Bone, who were good friends to him, or by the admiration of younger sculptors like Gaudier, whom he encouraged as he was later to encourage the youthful Henry Moore: yet he was entering on a period of misanthropy which would last till old age.

Ezra Pound, another new friend of this period recorded the story of Epstein's first meeting with Henri Gaudier-Brzeska, as told by Frank Harris to Brodzky. 'G, *aetatis suae* XVIII or thereabouts, met Epstein, who said, mustering the thunders of god and the scowlings of Assyrian sculpture into his tone and eyebrows, "UMMHH! Do . . . you cut . . . direct . . . in the stone?" "Most certainly!" said Gaudier, who had never yet done anything of the sort. "That's right," said Epstein; "I will come around to your place on Sunday". So Gaudier at once went out, got three small stone blocks, and by working more or less night and day had something ready by Sunday.'

By the spring of 1912 Epstein had completed the carving of the TOMB OF OSCAR WILDE, and he invited the Press and the public to see it in Cheyne Walk before it was shipped to Paris. The reaction this time was favourable.

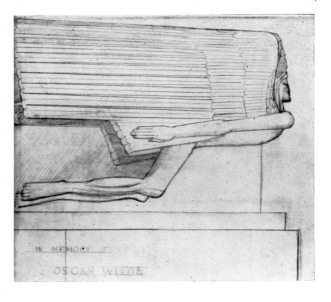

87 DRAWING FOR THE TOMB OF OSCAR WILDE
88 THE TOMB OF OSCAR WILDE
89 THE TOMB OF OSCAR WILDE (detail)

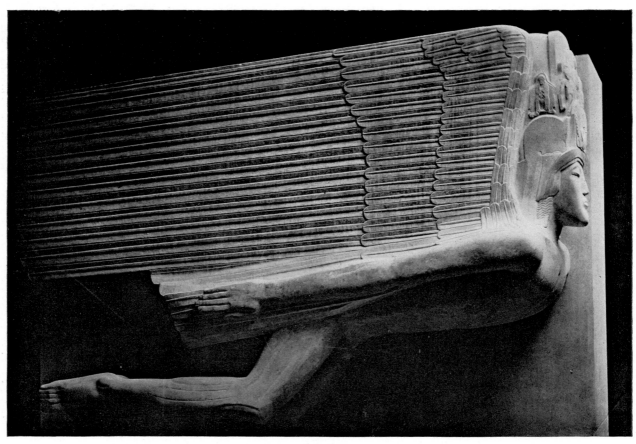

London society flocked to see the monument. In later years the sculptor recalled the visit of Ellen Terry.

In a foreword to Herbert Read's edition of T. E. Hulme's *Speculations* (Kegan Paul, 1936) Epstein recalled his first meeting with Hulme at this time and the latter's interpretation of the Wilde monument as 'Some theory of projectiles'. Hulme was to become a close friend of the sculptor and a buyer of his work, and it may be that his theories influenced Epstein during the 'Vortex' period.

Epstein had to pay customs duty of £120 to take his tomb into France and Lytton Strachey organised a petition to the French authorities to remit the duty. This appeal, signed by Shaw, Wells, Lavery, Robert Ross and Bakst was unsuccessful: but it is interesting that Strachey, one of the stars of the Bloomsbury *pléiade*, should at this time have come to Epstein's aid, for Bloomsbury was soon to turn against him.

It was the French authorities who reacted against the tomb. Arriving one morning in October at the cemetery of Père Lachaise to put finishing touches to the head, Epstein found his work covered with a tarpaulin and guarded by a gendarme. He was told the tomb was banned.

Despite the protests of French journalists and men of letters a bronze plaque was fixed over the sexual organs of the angel. This was removed during a night raid of poets and artists. The statue was again covered with a tarpaulin, which remained there until the outbreak of war.

A less independent artist, an academician, say, when faced with the problem of commemorating the great but scandalous Oscar, might have thought it more tactful or even more Christian to avoid allusions to his purple sins, to concentrate on his 'nicer side'. Not so Epstein. He carved a fallen angel, an angel of debauch, with bags under his eyes, and wearing the Seven Deadly Sins in a diadem worthy of Heliogabalus. The angel's face with its closed, slanting eyes, high cheek-bones and protruding lower lip seems Mongolian; the rigid rendering of the limbs is Egyptian, while the highly formalised but meticulously detailed wing, whose rectangular shape respects and emphasises the original cubic form of the stone block, recalls the great Assyrian winged bulls from Khorsabad in the British Museum. The total effect is curious. Never before had the idea of flight been conveyed in terms of such ponderous bulk.

The sculpture seems not to relate to the verse from 'The Ballad of Reading Gaol' which is carved on the back of the tomb:

> And alien tears shall fill for him
> Pity's long-broken urn
> For his mourners will be outcast men,
> And outcasts always mourn.

Epstein describes how, when distinguished French men-of-letters were getting up a petition in defence of his monument, the aid of Rodin was sought. 'A beautiful Russian-English girl, who knew Rodin, volunteered to go as an emissary to enlist his support with photographs of the tomb. Without looking at the photographs, Rodin started to upbraid her for bringing to his notice the work of a young sculptor who, he imagined, was her lover, and declared he would do nothing to help her. A plain girl would have been a better emissary to Rodin.' Such, at least, is Epstein's account of the matter, based no doubt on what the girl told him. But perhaps Rodin did not like Epstein's tomb.

The two sculptors never met. Epstein was taken to a gathering at Rodin's, but was too shy to push himself forward.

À propos of Rodin, Oscar Wilde and fallen angels, it is perhaps amusing to recall what Wilde wrote about Rodin's (of course posthumous) statue of Balzac. His opinion crops up in a letter to Robert Ross (who, of course, commissioned Epstein to make the tomb), written from Paris on May 1, 1898.

'Rodin's statue of Balzac is superb — just what a *romancier* is, or should be — the leonine head of a fallen angel, with a dressing-gown. The head is gorgeous, the dressing-gown an entirely unshaped cone of white plaster. People howl with rage over it. A lady who had gazed in horror on it had her attention directed to Rodin himself who was passing by. She was greatly surprised at his appearance. "Et pourtant il n'a pas l'air méchant," was her remark.'

So Balzac was modelled by Rodin, and Rodin's work criticised by Wilde, and Wilde's tomb carved by Epstein — to be described by me.

In a letter to Georges Bazile thanking him for his support in the French Press, Epstein mentioned that he was about to sail at once for South Africa to carve some lions in granite at Pretoria. 'I have signed a contract and promised to go. . . .' But nothing came of this interesting project, whatever it was.

Gertrude Stein remembered Epstein during his earlier stay in Paris as 'a thin rather beautiful rather melancholy ghost who used to slip in and out among the Rodin statues in the Luxembourg Museum'. Now she found him 'a large rather stout man, not unimpressive but not beautiful'.

In 1955 Epstein revisited the Oscar Wilde monument with his second wife and laid some sunflowers before it.

One more work survives from 1912, the over-lifesize SELF-PORTRAIT IN A CAP (reproduced over the page). Modelling himself in his working cap, the sculptor turned it into a Roman helmet and himself into an emperor who scans the landscape for his enemy's approach.

[63]

91 SELF-PORTRAIT IN A CAP

1913-15

THE VORTEX

During the summer and autumn of 1912, when he was in Paris for the erection of the Wilde tomb, Epstein met Picasso, Modigliani and Brancusi. Picasso had just moved from the Butte Montmartre to Montparnasse: his *papiers collés* were leading him to synthetic cubism. Modigliani went round the cafés in the evening selling for next to nothing drawings he had made in the morning. Brancusi did not frequent cafés and Epstein remembered that 'no matter when one called . . . he was always at work'.

This was a crucial six months (June-November) in the sculptor's career, and for more reasons than one. It was his first direct contact with some of the most revolutionary spirits in the modern movement. Influenced by Picasso he might have sought an equivalent to cubism in sculpture. Influenced by Brancusi's pursuit of pure forms, he might have fallen for the heady release of abstraction. Enthusiastic, like both these artists and Modigliani too, about African carvings, which he was now collecting, he might have 'gone African': and, as it was, he felt the pull of the primitive more strongly than ever. Seduced by the fever of creation in Paris, by the *'douceur de vivre'* between café and studio, he might have decided to settle there permanently. In fact, he and Modigliani spent a day looking for a vacant plot with a hut on the Butte Montmartre where they could work in the open air.

Epstein took a studio and began carving, but 'no sooner had I got started than my neighbour, who lived below, complained of my hammering. He was a baker who only slept during the day. The landlord explained that it was a painter's studio and not a sculptor's. These rows and continual interruptions finally decided me to leave Paris for good'. Yet though he left Paris, Paris did not yet let him go. The semi-abstract carvings he was to make in the next few years bear witness to the strength of the impressions he had received there in 1912.

'Coming to England I rented a bungalow on the Sussex coast at a solitary place called Pett Level near Hastings, where I could look out to sea and carve away to my heart's content. . . . It was here I carved the "Venus", the three groups of doves, the two flenite carvings and the marble "Mother and Child". . . . This was a period of intense activity and were it not for the

war and the impossibility of living in the country and making a living, I would have stayed there forever.'

From his earliest days in England Epstein had been friends with John, McEvoy and artists of the New English Art Club. Now he joined a more radical set.

In 1913 the painters who called themselves the Camden Town Group joined up with the Vorticist Group to form the London Group. Of this Epstein and the young Gaudier-Brzeska were founder members. In 1914 appeared the first number of *Blast*, edited by Wyndham Lewis, Vorticist painter and writer, the violence of whose effusions should not make one overlook his talent as a draughtsman, or the genuine merit of Gilman and Ginner, whom he reproduced. Epstein contributed two drawings in the Vorticist manner to *Blast*.

What was 'The Vortex'? With Picasso and Braque inventing Cubism in France, with Kandinsky painting the first abstract pictures in Munich, and Marinetti setting off the alarum of Futurism in Italy, Vorticism in London seems a desperate provincial attempt not to be left out. Wyndham Lewis's manifestoes can hardly have represented the opinions of Gilman and Ginner, whose admirations were for Gauguin, Van Gogh and the Fauves; but the similarity of Vorticist drawings by Wyndham Lewis, Etchells, Wadsworth, Nevinson, Gaudier-Brzeska and Epstein argue that — for a short time anyway — these artists shared what was not only an artistic credo but an attitude to life.

They were against respectability, the Greek tradition, the nineteenth century, Bloomsbury, Brangwyn and Galsworthy. They thought they had gone further than Picasso. 'By Vorticism', wrote Lewis, 'we mean (*a*) ACTIVITY as opposed to the tasteful PASSIVITY of Picasso; (*b*) SIGNIFICANCE as opposed to the dull or anecdotal character to which the Naturalist is condemned; (*c*) ESSENTIAL MOVEMENT and ACTIVITY (such as the energy of a mind) as opposed to the imitative cinematography, the fuss and hysterics of the futurists.'

Gaudier's manifesto in the first number of *Blast* suggests that the Vortex saw themselves as the reincarnations of such artists as had painted the Dordogne caves in the Palaeolithic era, had flourished in ancient Egypt, in

[65]

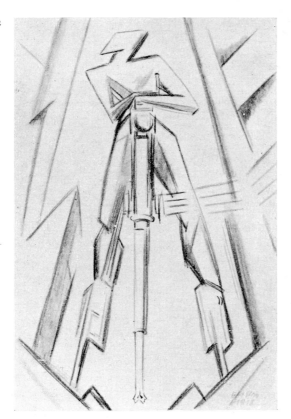

94

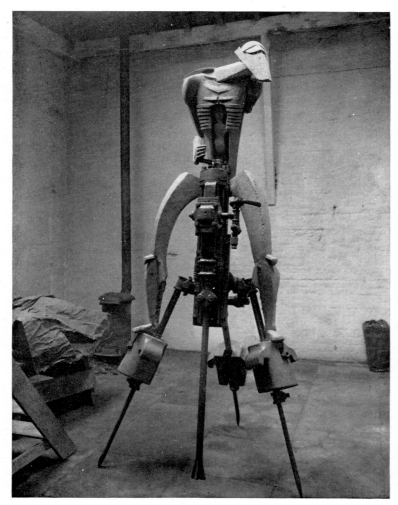

92. 93 DRAWINGS FOR ROCK DRILL
94 ROCK DRILL ON MACHINE BASE
95 ROCK DRILL
96 ROCK DRILL

the 'Shang and Chow' dynasties of China, and among the Aztecs of Yucatan. They were in favour of the sea, of ports, of hairdressers who made 'clean, arched shapes' and 'angular plots', of various music-hall

95

as Caravaggio painted Medusa's head on a shield? And if so, where did Epstein's 'ardour for machinery' come in? Was the driller of rock portrayed as an angular robot because he was a monster or because straight lines and African simplifications were the latest fashion in art?

I believe that Epstein subscribed temporarily to the Futurist admiration for speed, noise and machinery; that a masked man drilling rock, held for him the fascination of a heroic, demonic, even sexual image; that he was happy to borrow some of the angularity of Cubism, to glorify the Vorticist ideal of energy, and to have hit on what all his colleagues must have welcomed as a highly 'contemporary' subject.

'I exhibited this work complete in plaster [the full-length figure was mounted on a genuine rock-drill, a sort of tripod] at the London Group, and I remember Gaudier-Brzeska was very enthusiastic about it when he visited my studio in 1913 with Ezra Pound to view it. Pound started expatiating on the work. Gaudier-Brzeska turned on him and snapped, "Shut up, you understand nothing!"'

'Later I lost my interest in machinery and discarded the drill. I cast in metal, only the upper part of the figure.'

The visor-face, with its long terrible beak, the thrust of the neck, the flat planes of the piston arm contrasting with the curved box of cutlet ribs which surprisingly enclose the foetus of a little unborn monster — these have the beauty of a streamlined machine.

97

artists including Gaby Deslys, of Swift and Shakespeare.

The Vorticists wanted to make artifacts which were essential, clear-cut, significant and dynamic. Their ideals were perhaps best embodied in some of Gaudier's carvings, in Epstein's ROCK DRILL and his drawings for it. Before starting work on modelling his 'Rock Drill' Epstein made a number of drawings in charcoal and pencil, of the robot figure drilling into the rock, one of which was reproduced in *Blast*. 'It was in the experimental pre-war days of 1913 that I was fired to do the rock drill, and my ardour for machinery (short-lived) expended itself upon the purchase of an actual drill, second-hand, and upon this I made and mounted a machine-like robot, visored, menacing, and carrying within itself its progeny, protectively ensconced. Here is the armed, sinister figure of today and tomorrow. No humanity, only the terrible Frankenstein's monster, we have made ourselves into.'

This statement shows some confused thinking. Epstein was a man of strong feelings, but his concepts were often mixed up. Why had 'we' made ourselves into a 'terrible Frankenstein's monster'? By inventing cars, guns, machinery and rock-drills? Was it wrong to drill rock, and was a man who did it a monster to be depicted in horror,

97 FLENITE RELIEF (obverse)
98 FLENITE RELIEF (reverse)
99 FIGURE IN FLENITE
100 FEMALE FIGURE IN FLENITE

98

99

Having acquired a few pieces of flenite, a substance as hard as it is rare, Epstein resolved to put them to good use. It seems likely that the FLENITE RELIEF was carved first as an experiment.

FEMALE FIGURE IN FLENITE, the formal rendering of a pregnant woman, shaped like a question mark, grand despite its small scale, may be inspired by the fertility charms carried by the women of Baluba (Congo), but its design was more probably suggested by the odd shape of the flenite block. Epstein would want to waste as little as possible of the precious and almost unworkable material.

Regarded simply as an object, the carving gives pleasure because of the colour, markings, hardness and smoothness of the flenite. As a shape to be seen in profile

against the sky it is daring and wonderful. But the figure is also a pregnant mother, like 'Maternity', like the ninth Strand Statue and like the 'Genesis' to be carved in the late 'twenties. Everything focuses on the projecting belly which contains the miracle: the strong legs slope up to it, the back curves away from it, the arms and hands enclose it, the head hangs over like a heavy flower to contemplate it. The sculptor made of this intractable substance a curve charged with meaning and came close to the solemnity of certain Egyptian statuary.

This was one of several carvings bought by T. E. Hulme in monthly instalments.

A similar but less successful FIGURE IN FLENITE, with a more pointed head and with a skirt concealing the legs

E

[69]

and feet, was in the John Quinn collection, but its whereabouts are unknown to the present writer. These flenite
carvings were among works shown at Epstein's first
exhibition which took place at the 21 Gallery in 1913.

The sculptor carved two marble Venuses at Pett Level.
He must have been dissatisfied with the first or he would
not have undertaken another work so similar. In the
FIRST VENUS the flat planes of her featureless face and
slab-like legs contrast with the rounded forms of the
pendant African breasts and the swelling belly. An im-
placable figurehead, the goddess of procreation rides on
the backs of two birds, her knees sagging like those of a
surf-rider who has to keep his balance when travelling at
speed.

The SECOND VENUS, eight foot tall, is more attenuated
and seductive — if such a word can be used of a creature
so elemental. Her flattened brow and held-in chin increase the S-shape of her outline; her small breasts are
protuberant instead of pendant; her coupling doves form
a higher prow, and the uppermost of the two has a crest.
The flat and rounded planes are more subtly alternated.

This remarkable carving was one of many Epstein
works bought by the American lawyer John Quinn, a
voracious buyer and propagandist of new trends in art.
His huge collection was dispersed in several sales after
his death in 1924, and the big 'Venus' is now at Yale.

101 FEMALE FIGURE IN FLENITE

102 1ST VENUS

103 2ND VENUS

104 1ST VENUS

105 2ND VENUS

106 EPSTEIN WITH THE UNFINISHED GRANITE MOTHER & CHILD

A mystery surrounds the fate of a big GRANITE MOTHER AND CHILD of which Plate 106, showing it incomplete, is the only trace this writer has been able to find. John Quinn in an article for *Vanity Fair* dated October 1917 mentioned it as one of the works in his collection: but the tradition in the sculptor's family was that it had been sent to Quinn in America, that Quinn had said 'No, a mistake has been made, I wanted the

107

107 MARBLE MOTHER
    AND CHILD

108 CURSED BE THE DAY
    WHEREON I WAS BORN

108

"Marble Mother and Child" [mentioned below], and that Epstein had impatiently told his brother, who acted for him in New York, to dump it in the East River. It seems unlikely, however, that this operation — almost as difficult, one would think, as selling the heavy statue — actually took place. The child beginning to emerge from the block of granite in our photograph resembles the squatting (or kicking or dancing in the air) child in the Flenite Relief. Perhaps the mother was based on the Female Figure in Flenite; but this seems improbable as she would have to be holding this child out in front of her.

The MARBLE MOTHER AND CHILD, a curious experiment in the style of Brancusi, an essay in the juxtaposition of ovoid and spheroid forms, the most 'abstract' sculpture Epstein ever made, is in the Museum of Modern Art.

'CURSED BE THE DAY WHEREON I WAS BORN', the stylised representation of a screaming negro, made in an African convention in scarlet-painted plaster, was also bought by Quinn. This seems to have disappeared.

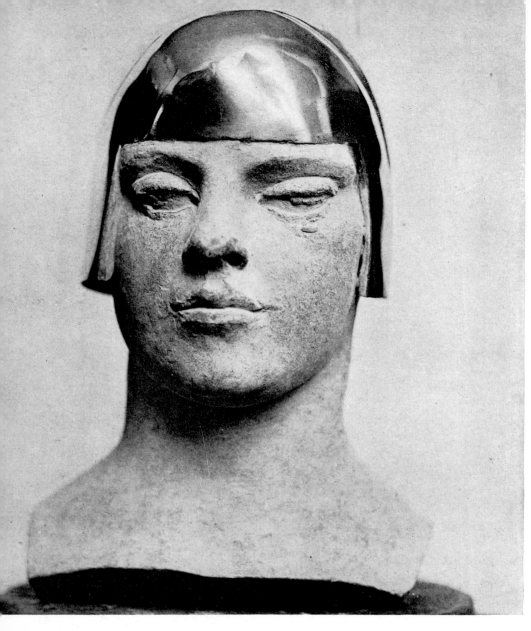

109   IRIS TREE
110   BILLIE GORDON
111   MARIE BEERBOHM
112   COUNTESS OF DROGHEDA

In 1916 Epstein portrayed IRIS TREE, the intellectual daughter of Sir Herbert Beerbohm Tree, the actor-manager, as well as her cousin MARIE BEERBOHM. The 'Iris Tree' is one of the sculptor's most striking heads of the Vorticist period. In the casting bought by John Quinn the hair was burnished a bright and brassy gold.

The monumental bust of the COUNTESS OF DROGHEDA with her striking looks, harks back to Epstein's early days in England, to a time when it seems he was indifferent as to whether a work should be realised in clay or in marble, when he could model his Strand Statues before carving them, and when his head of 'Marie Rankin' in bronze had the simplicity and impassivity of a stone Buddha. The 'Countess of Drogheda' is one of those original and yet eclectic portraits which posterity will be able to date — within twenty years — at a glance. The stylised shoulders are Florentine; the locks of hair are the tendrils of Art

113 MASK FROM
BILLIE GORDON
114 MARCELLE
115 T. E. HULME

Nouveau waterlilies; and yet there is something about the way the eyes are framed in exaggerated ridges which is Chinese. Lady Drogheda's husband made her sell what is believed to be the only bronze casting of the bust to John Quinn and it is probably now somewhere in America.

BILLIE GORDON, of whom Epstein made a portrait in a mob cap which remained uncast, was a red-head who frequented the Café Royal. The present writer saw for the first time what is presumably the only bronze casting of 'a mask' cut out of this portrait-head on a visit to the National Gallery of Canada.

MARCELLE, oddly described by Quinn as 'a French girl of great beauty', was a waitress. Hers is another very simple head, which, however, the sculptor has somehow charged with the atmosphere of Lautrec's brothels. Marcelle looks 'so very French', as our grandparents might have said, implying the worst.

Looking at the alarming profile of T. E. HULME, one feels relieved not to have known him: but Epstein

thought highly of his intelligence and character. 'He had the reputation of being a bully and arrogant', the sculptor wrote, 'because of his abruptness. He was really a candid and original nature like that of Samuel Johnson, and only his intolerance of sham made him feared . . . with artists he was humble and always ready to learn. . . . Someone once asked him how long he would tolerate Ezra Pound, and Hulme thought for a moment and then said that he knew already exactly when he would have to kick him downstairs.'

Hulme was the first of an intellectual group which included Ford Madox (Hueffer) Ford, Ashley Dukes, Wyndham Lewis and G. R. Orage, editor of the *New Age*, and he held Tuesday evenings at his house in Frith Street. When he was killed in Flanders in 1917 a book he was writing on Epstein's sculpture disappeared and was presumably destroyed.

Epstein wrote 'Early during the [First] War, Francis Dodd, R.A., asked me to do a bust of Lord Fisher for the Duchess of Hamilton. It was to be begun that very morning and "would I get my clay and other things together and start?" I packed everything into a cab and was taken to the Duchess of Hamilton's flat in the St. James's district.

'Fisher had an extraordinary appearance. . . . In posing he was tireless. He began at ten every morning . . . and went on until six o'clock in the evening.'

In the first state of the portrait, of which the cast exists, the admiral had his epaulettes and part of his arms. Epstein then took a wax impression and from this made a second plaster (as was his usual practice when he wanted to try a variation), from which he cut the shoulders and arms. This was because he felt the epaulettes on top of all the decorations made the work too heavy and ornate. The bronze illustrated here, which is in the Imperial War Museum, was cast from this second state.

In 1916 Epstein was still under the influence of the Vortex, and the portrait of ADMIRAL LORD FISHER shows evidence of a struggle between 'likeness' and stylisation. The railway-tunnel effect resultant from cutting off the shoulders (which also occurs in 'Lady Gregory') heightens — perhaps fortuitously — one's feeling that at this time the sculptor felt a good portrait was not enough — it had to be an interesting object as well. 'Admiral Lord Fisher', whatever conflict of ideas went into the making of him, turned out to be one of Epstein's most striking studies.

Epstein's DUCHESS OF HAMILTON was a grandiose but subtly characterised work in the sculptor's 'Rodin style'. The sitter's fine bare shoulders emerge from an impressionistically suggested evening dress rather as so many of the older master's demon lovers, with their pearly passionate limbs, spring like fountains from formless rock.

116 ADMIRAL LORD FISHER
117 ADMIRAL LORD FISHER
118 DUCHESS OF HAMILTON

The sculptor made at least four carvings of doves at Pett Level of which the FIRST MARBLE DOVES have only recently come to light after many years. Another, less successful, which we might call the 'Second Marble Doves', was in the Quinn collection, and was illustrated in the catalogue of his fifth and last sale, 12 February 1927. Pound mentioned yet another, 'A Bird pluming itself' in a review published in *The Egoist* on 16 March 1914.

It is hard not to believe that the THIRD MARBLE DOVES, belonging to Mr. Billy Rose, were the finest of the several carvings: indeed they are the masterpiece of Epstein's Vorticist period. Marvellously serene — although in fact the doves are copulating — this group achieves perfection in a style Epstein would now abandon forever.

'Clean', 'clear-cut', 'hard', 'durable', 'geometrical': these were words of praise among Hulme and the Vorticists. The 'Marble Doves', like Gaudier's 'Sleeping Doe' or the 'Laughing Torso' of Nina Hamnett would seem to fulfil all the qualifications.

Gaudier had been killed in June 1915, and Vorticism would not long survive him.

119, 120   FIRST MARBLE DOVES
121, 122   THIRD MARBLE DOVES

121

122

1916-20

MATURITY

If 1916 to 1920 seems an arbitrary division it can be accounted for in the following way: it was a period of transition for Epstein. In 1916 he finished with Vorticism and abstraction: he also left the country retreat where he had been carving for three years, and settled again in London. In 1917 he was called up, in 1918 he was demobilised. By 1920 he would be forty, half way through his life, a mature artist. He would not only have made the 'Risen Christ' his first monumental bronze but modelled the bust of 'Mrs. Epstein in a mantilla' which could be called the first of his great masterpieces of portraiture. Then, in 1921 a new phase of life would open for him after his meeting with Kathleen Garman.

123 1ST PORTRAIT OF LILLIAN SHELLEY
124 W. H. DAVIES

'Had I an income', wrote Epstein, 'I would like to live in the country and work, but I have found it impossible to work in the country and keep in touch with galleries and others who might want my work. My three years, 1913–16 at Pett Level, near Hastings, were productive of many carvings, but I had constantly to run up to London to see if I could dispose of something or get a portrait to do.' This reason, and the interest taken by the local police in an 'alleged sculptor' with a foreign name who lived on the coast in war time and kept pigeons — though these were too fat to fly — drove him back to London.

The sculptor and his wife, still very poor, had a room for a time over Harold Monro's Poetry Bookshop in Devonshire Street, W.C.1, where he met the 'Georgian' poets, and another attic in Great James Street. Then he took a house, 23 Guildford Street, opposite the old Foundlings' Hospital, the first floor of which was to be his studio for twelve years.

Lord Derby, the War Minister, refused to employ Epstein as a 'war artist' despite the urging of Lord Beaverbrook: and in 1917 he was called up in the Artists' Rifles and posted to Plymouth. He was offered a commission, but refused it; fell ill and spent some time in hospital. After a short while he was discharged.

The FIRST PORTRAIT OF LILLIAN SHELLEY was made in the Great James Street attic: it was commissioned by a Sassoon. Shortly before the war Mme Frida Strindberg had opened a night-club in a cellar called the Cave of the Golden Calf. Epstein had made two elaborate pillars in painted plaster for it; and Lillian Shelley, like Dolores, another of the sculptor's models, had sung and danced there. She was a dark, romantic beauty from Bristol, who acquired lovers and a legend, but died in poverty (see also Plate 148).

W. H. DAVIES, the Welsh poet, was introduced to the sculptor by Harold Monro, over whose Poetry Bookshop the Epsteins lodged for a short time, and his head was modelled at 23 Guildford Street during the same year.

The fine head might be that of a heroic Welsh footballer, were it not for the light of genius which the sculptor has so miraculously captured in the eyes. They seem to be observing clouds moving, and the change of

seasons on the landscape over which their owner tramped. In this portrait we can see Epstein already beginning to give to his clay the rough surface for which, in his middle period, he became known.

Epstein made three heads of Van Dieren, whom he had met in 1915. The FIRST HEAD OF BERNARD VAN DIEREN illustrated here, gives him the air of a Regency dandy — or, as Epstein wrote 'one of Napoleon's generals'. Epstein and Van Dieren admired each other's work and the composer was to write an essay on the sculptor — a pretentious and provocative apologia. It seems that Van Dieren's arrogance appealed to Epstein, who had always been a rebel and was entering on a misanthropic period. He introduced, about this time, Cecil Gray and Peter Warlock (Philip Heseltine) to the composer, and they became his close friends and supporters.

Van Dieren, as Epstein wrote, 'was strikingly hand-some': the sculptor saw in him a quality of force allied to something mystical, and made a powerful portrait.

Two other friends whom Epstein modelled in 1916 were Muirhead Bone and Augustus John. McEvoy, Dodd and other painters of the New English Art Club, had continually put themselves out to get him commissions and defend him from persecution. In fact, one has the impression, looking back to Epstein's arrival in London in 1905, that he had been acclaimed in enlightened artistic circles as a kind of Messiah. There had been and were good painters in England, but there was no sculptor of imagination. Of all these friends none was a stouter champion of Epstein than Muirhead Bone. In 1908 he had written to the *British Medical Journal* in defence of the Strand Statues; in 1924 he arranged for the sculptor to model Conrad, then offered the bust to the National Portrait Gallery, who refused it (they now have one); he helped, through support at a meeting of the Royal Society, to get Epstein the commission for the Hudson Memorial, then, later, wrote to *The Times* in defence of it, and sent a memorandum to the First Commissioner of Works, which saved it from being removed from Hyde Park; in 1929 he invited the critics to inspect 'Night' and 'Day' on the Underground Headquarters Building; in 1937, having protested in vain at the destruction of the Strand Statues, he had plaster casts of the carvings made at his own expense. (Three of these survive and are very crude.)

The head of MUIRHEAD BONE is in Epstein's smooth style, and seems like the work of an earlier period. The bald head and contemplative expression increase the effect of simplicity, but the portrait is not really as stylised as it first appears. Compare, for instance, 'Romilly John' (Plates 16, 17) or 'Marie Rankin' (Plate 78).

The head of AUGUSTUS JOHN is rougher again, but the

125   BERNARD VAN DIEREN
126   MUIRHEAD BONE
127   AUGUSTUS JOHN

128
MASK OF MRS. EPSTEIN
129
TIN HAT

sittings were interrupted and it remained a sketch. Epstein wrote, 'John sat to me in my Guilford Street studio. I had wanted to do a head of him for some time, and as he had made two etchings of myself and several drawings, I was eager to do him justice. . . . John's head had plenty of dignity, but there was much more to it than that, and I wanted to capture a certain wildness, an untamed quality that is the essence of the man. . . .'

At Epstein's first one-man show at the Leicester Galleries in 1917 two castings of Augustus John's head were to be sold for a hundred guineas each, one to Lady Tredegar, the other to the painter.

In 1916 the sculptor made a mask of his first wife. Of the SECOND PORTRAIT OF MRS. EPSTEIN (WITH EARRINGS) he wrote, 'In this mask, I immediately made what I think is one of my subtlest and most beautiful works. The serenity and inward calm is there, and . . . the simplicity

is that achieved by antique sculpture. I can recall that I worked at this mask without effort, achieving it happily, and was pleased with the result.'

Gertrude Stein wrote of Mrs. Epstein, in her *Autobiography of Alice B. Toklas* that she 'had a very remarkable pair of brown eyes, of a shade of brown I had never before seen in eyes'.

The strangeness of Mrs. Epstein's heart-shaped face, from which projects a very definite and determined nose, is accentuated by the smooth fringe enclosing her forehead and the plait which crowns her head.

Apart from his bust of Admiral Fisher, Epstein marked the passing of the First World War by three portraits of soldiers, the Tommy in 'The Tin Hat', an 'American Soldier' and 'Sergeant Hunter V.C.'.

THE TIN HAT is a vigorous sketch of a proletarian type: it is also an experiment, perhaps unsuccessful, in incor-

F

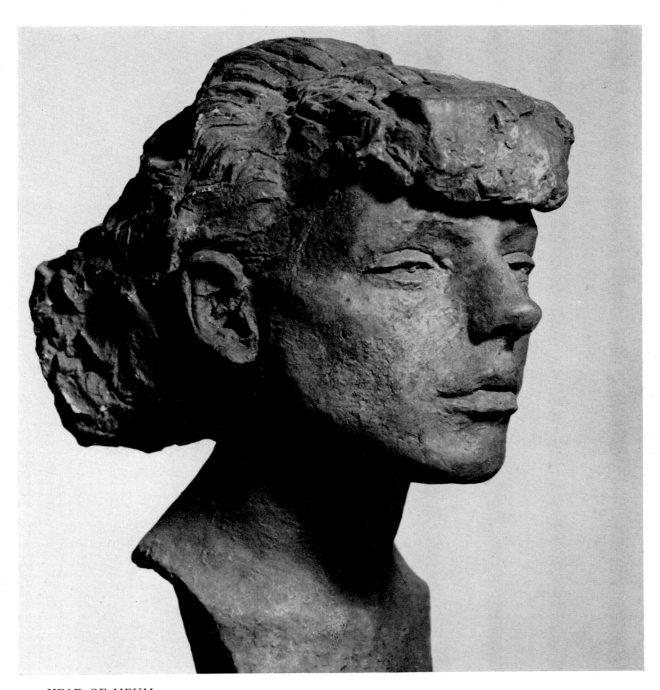

131 HEAD OF MEUM

porating a real object, namely a helmet, with a work of art. Could the head have been done with the idea of showing that the sculptor might prove more useful as a war artist than as a mere serving soldier? If so, the attempt was unsuccessful, for Epstein was called up in 1917.

'Meum' Lindsell-Stewart was an extraordinarily pretty blonde typist. She married an officer during the First World War, then became one of Mr. Cochran's Young Ladies. She was later the friend of Clifford Bax, the playwright. In his FIRST PORTRAIT OF MEUM, a bust, Epstein modelled her with a mischievous Mona-Lisaish half smile and bare shoulders emerging from impressionistic drapery.

Another study, this time a small bust — that is to say without shoulders — the SECOND PORTRAIT OF MEUM, was made in the same year. A mask and a half-length figure with a fan would follow within two years.

[87]

130 BUST OF MEUM

132 DORIS KEANE

133 MARGUERITE NIELKE

In February 1917 Epstein, although in the army, had his first exhibition at the Leicester Galleries, and to judge by the sales it was a considerable success. Three copies of the early 'New-born Baby' were sold at 40 guineas each, busts of Nan and Euphemia, heads of W. H. Davies, Augustus John, Meum and 'The Tin Hat' at prices varying from 100 guineas to 200 guineas. The head of W. H. Davies was bought by the Hon. Evan Morgan (later Viscount Tredegar), himself a minor poet: he left it years later to the Art Gallery, Newport. Sales totalled £1,661, from which, naturally, the gallery deducted a commission. But Epstein wrote to John Quinn complaining that he found 'almost without exception every influential critic bitterly hostile', while Sargent could sell a portrait for £10,000. This did not prevent Quinn claiming, in the article in *Vanity Fair* mentioned above, that Epstein, who 'has been the storm centre of English art for the last ten years . . . has now arrived'. Quinn, who, after the exhibition, bought the 'Venus', the 'Granite Mother and Child', 'The Rock Drill', one of the flenite carvings, 'Cursed be the day I was born', the 'Marble Mother and Child', 'Romilly John', the 'Mask of Mrs. Epstein with ear-rings', the second 'Bust of Euphemia Lamb', 'T. E. Hulme', the first 'Bust of Meum', 'Lady Drogheda', 'Augustus John', 'Bernard Van Dieren' and the 'Old Italian Woman', lists favourable articles on Epstein's work in the *Fortnightly Review*

by John Cournos, in the *New Statesman* by Laurence Binyon and by Bernard Van Dieren in the *New Age*.

The account books of the Leicester Galleries record the sale of a 'Marble Clock' for £500 to Miss Deacon, then staying at the Coburg Hotel. Gladys Deacon, an intelligent American, had been brought up in artistic circles in Venice and Paris. She knew Rodin, and on meeting Epstein was relieved to find '*un génie qui est jeune*'. They became friends, presumably as a result of the Leicester Galleries exhibition, and as the marble clock was never made it can be guessed that her commissioning of this unlikely object was a way of helping the sculptor financially. He also made her portrait, and it is one of his strangest works.

The striking looks of GLADYS DEACON are rendered with a grand archaic simplicity which recalls nothing so much as the Delphic charioteer and seem the more fantastic because of her chic modern fringe, permanent wave and necklace of graded pearls. Gladys Deacon married the ninth Duke of Marlborough in 1921.

DORIS KEANE was a feature of wartime London. She was the star of a play called *Romance* which ran for years. It was the thing to do to see this play regularly, and officers on leave from France would boast of the number of their visits.

MARGUERITE NIELKA was a Swedish singer.

During his service in the Artists' Rifles, Epstein was

[88]

134 GLADYS DEACON
(LATER DUCHESS OF MARLBOROUGH)

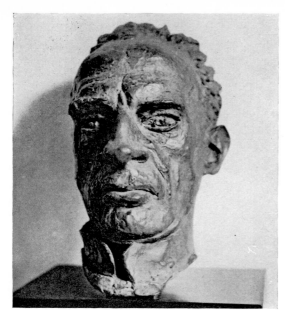

135

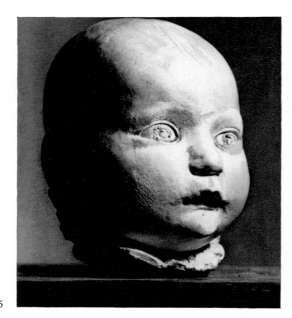

136

137

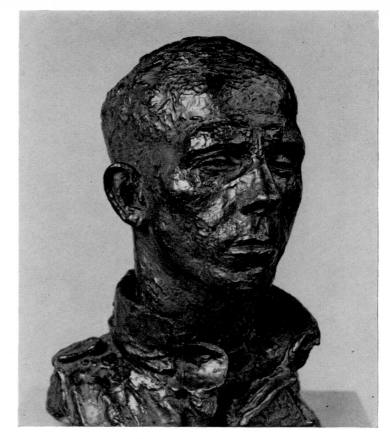

138

135 JOSEF HOLBROOKE
136 ELIZABETH SCOTT-ELLIS
137 CLARE SHERIDAN
138 AMERICAN SOLDIER
139 SGT DAVID FERGUSON HUNTER V.C.

stationed at Plymouth. He fell ill and was for a time in the military hospital at Mount Tovy, where he made some drawings of nurses and fellow patients. The authorities must have been liberal with leave or sick-leave — that is, if the chronology compiled by Mrs. Epstein and Haskell is correct — for the sculptor made twelve portraits in 1917. But as only five works are listed under 1918, the year Epstein was demobilised, it seems probable that some may be a year later than the compilers thought.

Lord Howard de Walden, who had been splendidly modelled by Rodin, and who was a generous patron of artists, notably Wilson Steer, commissioned a head of his infant daughter, ELIZABETH SCOTT-ELLIS. To make the study of this wide-eyed and wondering baby Epstein travelled to Chirk Castle in Wales.

The portrait of JOSEF HOLBROOKE must also have been modelled as a result of the sculptor's association with Howard de Walden, for the latter, under the name of T. E. Ellis, was Holbrooke's librettist. Their principal collaboration was an opera trilogy, *The Cauldron of Anwyn*.

Besides staying at country houses we also find Epstein at this time attending smart lunch parties, such as that of CLARE SHERIDAN, the sculptress and first cousin of

139

Winston Churchill, which he described in his autobiography. 'When I arrived, Clare Sheridan was engaged
on a statuette of H. G. Wells. Wells was sitting on a stand
rolling a pellet of clay in his hand, a procedure which
would have maddened me. . . . I pointed out that one
of the essentials of Wells's facial makeup was his overhanging eyebrows, which she had not put in.'

It was in the Café Royal during September, 1917, that
Epstein met August Franklin Kopf, whose portrait was
called AMERICAN SOLDIER. Kopf was 'battle-weary' and
on leave in London. The story as he told it later was that
he was sitting with two Anzacs at the Café Royal when

Epstein spoke to him from the next table; the sculptor
said he had been commissioned to make busts of soldiers
of the Allied Armies for the British Museum — an unlikely tale (either Epstein was trying something on, or
Kopf remembered it wrong) and the unfortunate
American was persuaded to give up a large part of the
rest of his leave for five sittings 'in a studio in Russell
Square' — obviously Guilford Street.

Another soldier modelled in 1917 or 1918 was
SERGEANT DAVID FERGUSON HUNTER, V.C. With his
folded arms and rolled-up shirt sleeves he confronts the
spectator fearlessly and is obviously Scottish.

[91]

140 3RD PORTRAIT OF MRS. EPSTEIN
141 4TH PORTRAIT OF MRS. EPSTEIN
142 5TH PORTRAIT OF MRS. EPSTEIN
143 5TH PORTRAIT OF MRS. EPSTEIN
144 5TH PORTRAIT OF MRS. EPSTEIN

142

140

In 1918 Epstein made two more studies of his first wife Margaret Dunlop, before embarking on the final and finest portrait of her. (He does not mention these two intermediary studies, the THIRD PORTRAIT OF MRS. EPSTEIN (WITH A RIBBON) and the FOURTH PORTRAIT OF MRS. EPSTEIN (WITH A SCARF) in his autobiography.) 'This bust', wrote Epstein, '. . . is the most profound of the three works, and it has that quiet thoughtfulness that

141

143

144

I had unconsciously striven for in the other two; or most likely as I matured in my work, I naturally brought into full play all my powers of observation and expression, and so made this one of my gravest, and I think one of my most beautiful busts. This work was unhurried and brooded over, and the drapery was worked with great care, the lines, all running downwards like the rills of a fountain, are essential to the effect of the bust, and help to express its innermost meaning.'

Three photographs of FIFTH PORTRAIT OF MRS. EPSTEIN (IN A MANTILLA), taken from the same angle, but with different lighting, reveal more clearly than words the subtleties of this portrait, which might well be considered Epstein's finest work to date.

[93]

145

The MASK OF MEUM was one of three 'masks' Epstein modelled between 1916 and 1918. The idea of making masks, that is, faces with no backs to them, was probably inspired by African sculpture: it was to catch on in the 'twenties, when there would be a fashion for hanging polychrome or silvered faces of high-cheekboned ladies on 'studio' or mews-flat walls.

Looking at the half-length figure of MEUM WITH A FAN, one wishes that Epstein had stopped at the shoulders. His arms are too often either serpentine or formless: Meum's are weird. Though they make an interesting pattern, with the ostrich feather sticking out at a right angle to the body, the conception was superior to its final realisation. Her face and hair, though, are delightful.

[94]

146

The MARCHESA CASATI, celebrated for her striking looks, her wealth, extravagance and eccentricity, for her costume balls at the Palais Rose in the Avenue du Bois, at Villa San Michele in Capri, and at the Palazzo Venier in Venice, died in London in straightened circumstances in 1957: Epstein had met her at the luncheon of Clare Sheridan's, and asked her to sit. 'The Marchesa arrived in a taxi-cab at two o'clock and left it waiting for her. We began the sittings and her Medusa-like head kept me busy until nightfall. It was snowing outside, and a report came in that the taxi-man had at length made a declaration. He did not care if it were Epstein and if it were a countess, he would not wait any longer. On hearing this Casati shouted: "He is a Bolshevik! Ask him to wait a little longer." He was given tea and a place by the fire and shown the bookshelf. The winter light had failed, and I had many candles brought in. They formed a circle round my weird sitter with the fire in the grate piled high to give more light. The tireless Marchesa, with her over-large blood-veined eyes, sat with a basilisk stare. . . . The Medusa-like mask was finished the next day.'

In the BUST OF LILLIAN SHELLEY, of whom Epstein had already made a head in 1916, the model's rippling hair and flowing draperies, her delicate hands and her conversational expression all contribute to the romantic nature of the portrait. (In its original state, according to a photograph in Van Dieren, she wore a bangle.)

Like Lillian Shelley and Dolores, Betty May was a model known for her beauty and Bohemian behaviour. Born in Tidal Basin near the Victoria Docks to a half-French mother and an absentee father, she was reared in conditions of extreme poverty. As a teen-age vagabond, five feet high, she arrived at the Café Royal. Here, according to her autobiography, *Tiger Woman*, Epstein

147 MARCHESA CASATI
148 2ND PORTRAIT OF LILLIAN SHELLEY

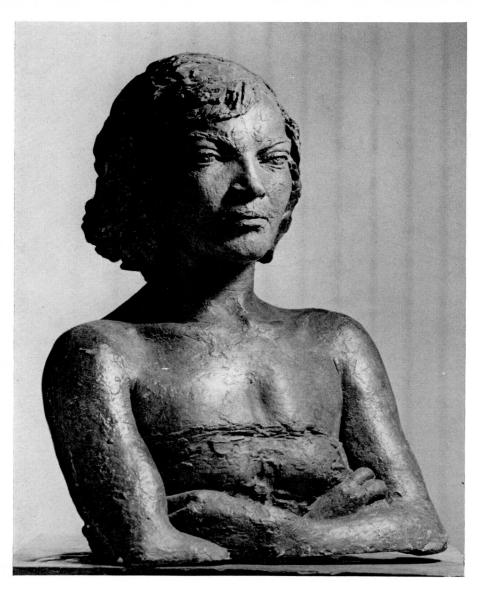

149 BUST OF BETTY MAY
150 HEAD OF BETTY MAY

150

saw her and said 'You're very young to be here, little
girl, aren't you? ' He asked her to his table and they made
friends. A year or two later, at tea in Guilford Street, the
sculptor said 'Betty, I think the time has come for you to
sit for me.' She would arrive at the studio every morning
at nine, and often stay till seven or eight in the evening.
Sometimes Epstein said 'Sing something, Betty', and she
would oblige with 'Sigh no more, ladies', 'The Raggle-
taggle Gipsies' or 'Bonnie Earl o' Murray' — a curious
repertoire. She was taken to dine at the Isola Bella in
Soho, where, apparently, could be had a 'famous egg-flip'
which Epstein was very fond of. At a farewell dinner
given at the Harlequin before she left with her third
husband Raoul to join Alastair Crowley's lodge of sorcery
in Sicily, Epstein is alleged by her to have said 'Don't go,
Betty. If you do, one of you will never come back again.'
Raoul in fact did not return, but corroborative evidence
of Epstein's prophetic powers is lacking. If she was not

151 DRAWING FOR 'RISEN CHRIST'
152 2ND HEAD OF BERNARD
VAN DIEREN

the most 'statuesque' of the sculptor's colourful models, she was certainly the fieriest, and made up in temperament what she lacked in inches. Epstein once gave evidence as to her character in Marlborough Street after she had been had up for throwing a glass at Horace Cole in a restaurant. She died mysteriously. In his FIRST POR-TRAIT OF BETTY MAY with folded arms the sculptor has oddly sliced through the forearms to form a base for the work. His SECOND PORTRAIT OF BETTY MAY, done about the same time, Epstein thought resembled the young Beethoven.

Epstein's monumental figure of the 'Risen Christ', referred to in his book as his 'First Christ', began as a portrait, the SECOND HEAD OF VAN DIEREN whom the sculptor had modelled a year before, and whom he now visited on his sick-bed in 1917.

'Watching his head, so spiritual and worn with suffering, I thought I would like to make a marble of him. I hurried home and returned with clay and made a mask

which I immediately recognized as the Christ head, with its short beard, its pitying accusing eyes and the lofty and broad brow, denoting great intellectual strength.'

Next Epstein decided to make a full-length figure, and to embody in it all his feeling for the pity, horror and tragedy of war. Until 1914 he had looked upon the human body as an object of beauty and character, a source of pleasure and inspiration: now he recognised it as an instrument which could not only inflict but suffer pain. He saw his RISEN CHRIST in the attitude of 'Noli me tangere', pointing at the wound the world had given him.

'With haste I began to add the torso and the arms and hand with the accusing finger. This I then cast and had, as a certainty, the beginning of my statue. . . . I then set up this bust with an armature for the body. I established the length of the whole figure down to the feet. The statue rose swathed in clothes. . . . I was interrupted on this work for . . . a whole year . . . and it stood in the centre of my studio in Guilford Street unfinished.

[99]

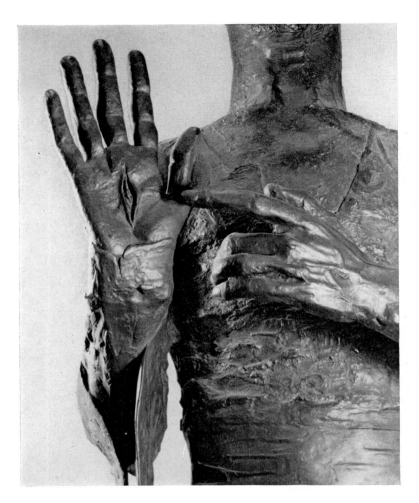

153 RISEN CHRIST (detail)
154 RISEN CHRIST (detail)
155 RISEN CHRIST

153

When I resumed work on it, it was only to finish the feet.'

Christ, seven foot two inches high, stands upright, feet slightly apart, wearing curious clinging grave-clothes with a ground-length skirt and long close-fitting sleeves. His right hand is raised, wounded palm towards the spectator, and his left hand points at it. Were it not for the treatment of the drapery, which suggests a crepe garment dipped in plaster, for the slightly over life-size hands, and the deeply-accented and stylised eyes, the statue could be described as realistic — even startling in its realism. This is a man of our century, with short parted hair in the modern style, an intellectual's brow, fastidious nose and scornful mouth.

Epstein described him as 'the modern living Christ, compassionate and accusing at the same time', but the modernity and the accusation are more evident than the compassion.

This is the first of the sculptor's works with a 'message'. His didactic side would become more pronounced in later years. 'I should like to re-model this Christ,' he wrote. 'I should like to make it hundreds of feet high, and set it up on some high place where all could see it, and where it would give out its warning . . . to all lands.

The Jew — the Galilean — condemns our wars, and warns us that "Shalom, shalom" must still be the watchword between man and man.'

When, in February 1920, the 'Christ' was exhibited at the Leicester Galleries, the attacks began in the Press. Of these one by Father Vaughan, an exhibitionistic Jesuit, must be quoted as it contains probably the most ignorant, racialistic — i.e. Fascist — observations ever made by an educated person on a work of art in this country. 'I felt ready to cry out with indignation that in this Christian England there should be exhibited the figure of a Christ which suggested to me some degraded Chaldean or African, which wore the appearance of an Asiatic-American or Hun-Jew, which reminded me of some emaciated Hindu, or a badly grown Egyptian swathed in the cerements of the grave. . . . As I came out of the gallery I noticed that Mr. Epstein's statue stands near a certain type of shop round Leicester Square.'

Bernard Shaw replied: 'Now that Father Vaughan is going in for art, many terrible shocks await him. Imagine him at Bruges, looking at the Christs of the Netherlands school. . . .'

[100]

I

156

157

156 GABRIELLE SOENE
157 HELENE
158 EVE DERVICH
159 HEAD OF A GIRL

GABRIELLE SOENE, a Belgian who had posed for Modigliani, liked to wear a crimson dress which Poiret had made her in exchange for a Modigliani painting. HELENE was a half-caste married to a musician named W. Yellin. EVE DERVICH was a professional model, who died shortly after Epstein made her portrait. HEAD OF A

158

159

GIRL, with fringe and bunches of hair, is of a sitter whose identity has been forgotten.

Epstein had always been fond of children. In October 1918 Peggy Jean was born and he had one of his own. He was fascinated by the baby's changing expressions and began to try to catch them in clay. Within the first three years of her life Epstein made at least ten studies of Peggy Jean: before she married and left home he would have made at least fourteen. I say 'at least', because in trying to put the portraits in order I may have overlooked some of which plaster casts no longer survive in the studio or of which photographs have never been taken.

From the earliest heads the FOURTH PORTRAIT OF PEGGY JEAN (AT EIGHTEEN MONTHS), the FIFTH AND SIXTH PORTRAITS OF PEGGY JEAN (AT TWO), which together form 'The Putti', and the THE SEVENTH PORTRAIT OF PEGGY JEAN (AT TWO) are reproduced.

160

161

162

163

160 4TH PORTRAIT OF PEGGY JEAN
161 5TH & 6TH PORTRAITS OF PEGGY JEAN
162. 163 7TH PORTRAIT OF PEGGY JEAN

164

166

164. 165. 166. 167 SELF PORTRAIT WITH BEARD

Epstein's second and last head of himself, SELF PORTRAIT WITH A BEARD, was made in this year. Modelled during a period of doubt and depression for the artist, this work projects something of his misanthropic state of mind. It has the haunted look of Van Gogh's self-portraits and the rough surface seems in keeping with the violent mood of the subject.

Cecil Gray, who had posed for Epstein in 1918 and also stood for the hands of Christ, tells a story of the sculptor at this time — possibly the following year — which illustrates his disillusioned mood. Gray, Van Dieren and Epstein went to see Busoni after hearing him play at the Wigmore Hall, and Gray compared the pianist and the sculptor. 'It would be difficult to find two men more completely contrasted in most essential respects, but one thing they certainly possess in common — a highly developed persecution-mania. For Busoni, as for Epstein, everyone is a potential enemy. . . . Epstein said, after the concert, in his usual direct and abrupt manner: "What struck me most, Busoni, when I heard you play for the first time, was the way in which you looked at the audience, with such hatred and contempt," and Busoni positively beamed with pleasure.'

In 1919 Epstein had visited Italy with Cecil Gray, seeing the Sistine Chapel for the first time, returning by Carrara, Spezia and Livorno. The reason his head of Gray is not reproduced here is that it was one of the only plasters, after the mass destructions of his youth, which he allowed to be broken up.

GIRL, with fringe and bunches of hair, is of a sitter whose identity has been forgotten.

Epstein had always been fond of children. In October 1918 Peggy Jean was born and he had one of his own. He was fascinated by the baby's changing expressions and began to try to catch them in clay. Within the first three years of her life Epstein made at least ten studies of Peggy Jean: before she married and left home he would have made at least fourteen. I say 'at least', because in trying to put the portraits in order I may have overlooked some of which plaster casts no longer survive in the studio or of which photographs have never been taken.

From the earliest heads the FOURTH PORTRAIT OF PEGGY JEAN (AT EIGHTEEN MONTHS), the FIFTH AND SIXTH PORTRAITS OF PEGGY JEAN (AT TWO), which together form 'The Putti', and the THE SEVENTH PORTRAIT OF PEGGY JEAN (AT TWO) are reproduced.

160

161

163

162

160   4TH PORTRAIT OF PEGGY JEAN
161   5TH & 6TH PORTRAITS OF PEGGY JEAN
162. 163   7TH PORTRAIT OF PEGGY JEAN

164

164. 165. 166. 167 SELF PORTRAIT WITH BEARD

Epstein's second and last head of himself, SELF PORTRAIT WITH A BEARD, was made in this year. Modelled during a period of doubt and depression for the artist, this work projects something of his misanthropic state of mind. It has the haunted look of Van Gogh's self-portraits and the rough surface seems in keeping with the violent mood of the subject.

Cecil Gray, who had posed for Epstein in 1918 and also stood for the hands of Christ, tells a story of the sculptor at this time — possibly the following year — which illustrates his disillusioned mood. Gray, Van Dieren and Epstein went to see Busoni after hearing him play at the Wigmore Hall, and Gray compared the pianist and the sculptor. 'It would be difficult to find two men more completely contrasted in most essential respects, but one thing they certainly possess in common — a highly developed persecution-mania. For Busoni, as for Epstein, everyone is a potential enemy. . . . Epstein said, after the concert, in his usual direct and abrupt manner: "What struck me most, Busoni, when I heard you play for the first time, was the way in which you looked at the audience, with such hatred and contempt," and Busoni positively beamed with pleasure.'

In 1919 Epstein had visited Italy with Cecil Gray, seeing the Sistine Chapel for the first time, returning by Carrara, Spezia and Livorno. The reason his head of Gray is not reproduced here is that it was one of the only plasters, after the mass destructions of his youth, which he allowed to be broken up.

166

1920–29

WORKS SACRED AND PROFANE

Epstein had always had a rage for work: during the 'twenties his productivity increased. If obliged to generalise one might say that there was a growing tendency to exaggeration and dramatisation in his heads: they became more 'expressionist'. But he seems to have forced his effects least when a sitter inspired him, as was evidently the case with Dolores and Sunita; and a study such as that of his daughter Peggy Jean which he called 'The Sick Child' could only be described as classical in its simplicity and restraint. As ever, he was capable of working in a number of styles during a given period. It must be remembered that never before in history had an artist been exposed to influence from the art of so many countries and periods: archaeology, easier travel, photographic reproduction and an increase in the commerce of art having made available whole civilisations which were hitherto unknown. Epstein's mind was a meeting-place for many cultures.

During this decade following the 'Risen Christ' he modelled two more monumental bronzes; and religious compositions were much in his mind at the time. He only received two commissions from public bodies during this period. Both were carvings and both were triumphantly successful. Both, however, were greeted with derision by sections of the Press and public: the tarring and feathering of 'Rima' made him more notorious than ever.

*   *   *

Nineteen twenty-one began with the sculptor making two busts of a Russian girl, the FIRST PORTRAIT OF MIRIAM PLICHTE, and a SECOND PORTRAIT OF MIRIAM PLICHTE (WITH ARMS).

The NINTH PORTRAIT OF PEGGY JEAN (LAUGHING) is one of Epstein's most remarkable studies of children. Lying in wait to pounce and fix an expression, he has amazingly caught the moment when a child's look of incomprehending wonder turns into laughter. The harvest of curls helps to make this head a delightful object.

168   1ST BUST OF MIRIAM PLICHTE
169   2ND BUST OF MIRIAM PLICHTE
170   9TH PORTRAIT OF PEGGY JEAN (LAUGHING)

168

169

[108]

171 1ST PORTRAIT
     OF KATHLEEN
172
SENEGALESE GIRL

172

In August 1921 the sculptor met Kathleen Garman, who, after thirty years, was to become his second wife. The following day he began a study of the twenty-year-old girl, the FIRST PORTRAIT OF KATHLEEN, a head. Even in this passionately observed portrait of someone whose beauty and personality captivated him at once and for ever, Epstein deliberately exaggerates the irregularities of the face. He makes one eye higher than the other, scoops out a hollow over the right eyebrow, leaves the forehead and cheeks rough but smooths the nose and chin. The sculptor told Haskell, 'It is the rough surface that gives both character and likeness to the face, not just the rough surface as such, but the particular individual treatment. No face is entirely round and smooth. The face is made up of numberless small planes and it is a study of where those planes begin and end, their direc-

tion, that makes the individual head. . . . It would be an easy matter to polish and sandpaper until the material was entirely smooth, but to do that would be really to produce a grave distortion. The reflection of light would play havoc with all the sculptor's effects, while the rough surface breaks up the light, and accentuates the characteristics, giving life to the work. . . . The texture is a definite and inseparable part of the whole; it comes from inside so to speak; it grows with the work.'

Epstein met Madeleine Béchet, walking proudly and beautifully down Southampton Row. When he asked her to pose she agreed readily. On hearing she came from Senegal Epstein told her he was reading a book by a French doctor about that country whose author described buying a girl slave and later marrying her. Madeleine revealed that these had been her parents.

[109]

173. 174
JACOB KRAMER

175
WEEPING WOMAN

'The Leeds painter, Kramer,' wrote Epstein, 'was a model who seemed to be on fire. He was extraordinarily nervous. Energy seemed to leap into his hair as he sat, and sometimes he would be shaken by queer tremblings like ague.' JACOB KRAMER's striking idealistic features and his mane of hair were rendered with tremendous vigour by the sculptor. He is wearing an ordinary woollen undervest buttoned up the front.

A few months after Epstein had made the portrait of Kramer, in 1922, a model he knew who had once posed for Whistler came to the studio weeping and complaining that her son had been carried off to America by a musician. The sculptor suddenly saw her as a mourning Magdalen, and began her portrait. He then had the idea of including it, with Kramer's as St. John, in a group of the Deposition, but this idea came to nothing. Apart from some of the dancing figures in the Strand THE WEEPING WOMAN was the first work in which the sculptor attempted

174

176   2ND PORTRAIT OF KATHLEEN

to convey violent movement. It was bold to try to suggest this weeping, wailing and wringing of hands, but he brought it off. He would not always be so fortunate with later experiments.

The SECOND PORTRAIT OF KATHLEEN was made six months after the first. Although modelled in the winter — in January 1922 — it has a sultry summer afternoon quality very different from the radiant visionary first portrait. Lips parted, eyes half closed, Kathleen basks sensuously, full of honey.

In 1922 Epstein made portraits of FEDORA ROSELLI, a singer who had appeared in *Chu Chin Chow* with Oscar Ashe, and who was reported to have been dismissed because her voice was bigger than that of Mrs. Oscar Ashe; of SELINA, his long-faced, bedraggled-looking Cockney cleaner of Italian descent, whose gaunt appearance may have put him in mind of Donatello's 'Repentant Magdalen'; and of OLD SMITH, a humble Isaiah, who used to call upon passers-by to turn from their sinful ways and prepare themselves for the final judgement, in Piccadilly. Smith's is a noble head, which one can understand the sculptor being interested in.

177 FEDORA ROSELLI
178 SELINA
179 OLD SMITH

177

Because Epstein made five studies of the model Dolores within a year we are able to compare these varied works and follow the progress of his search for her character without interrupting our chronological sequence.

'My first work from Dolores', wrote the sculptor, 'I abandoned and thought a failure, and yet years afterwards, when I came across the plaster again, I realised that it was a very vivid and spontaneous sketch of her, and I cast it in bronze. It became instantly popular.' This was the bust called LA BOHEMIENNE in which the model is shown hanging slightly forward, but with head raised to flatter the line of the neck, eyes lowered and lips parted in a half smile. One senses that Dolores had not a good figure. In each of her portraits her hair is done differently. In this first it is cut short and hangs in thick untidy streaks, with a heavy straggling fringe combed slightly to the left over a forehead which it conceals entirely. The all-over broken surface is typical of Epstein's 'twenties manner.

In the SECOND PORTRAIT OF DOLORES the fringe has been pushed aside to reveal her forehead. 'The second study', wrote Epstein, 'was again a failure.' We can understand that there was some quality about the woman's beauty he despaired of catching.

Next he modelled a small RECLINING STUDY OF DOLORES in the nude. Left arm behind her head, right

181

180 1ST PORTRAIT OF DOLORES
(LA BOHEMIENNE)

181 2ND PORTRAIT OF DOLORES

182 RECLINING STUDY
OF DOLORES

182

hand on her chest, she lies back against invisible cushions and surveys the spectator with mocking indifference.

The THIRD PORTRAIT OF DOLORES, a bust with folded arms — 'was', wrote its creator, 'tragic and magnificent; Dolores was a model who was extremely suggestionable, and after I had made this bust, she always strutted about keeping her arms folded in the pose of the bust, and with the same tragic and aloof expression fixed upon her face, and she took great care that she never relaxed into those careless smiles of the first head. In the studio she was the devoted model, never allowing anything to interfere with posing, taking it seriously; a religious rite.'

In this bust Dolores has her hair parted in the middle, and it falls in waves to the nape of her neck, but revealing

[116]

76

183. 184 3RD PORTRAIT OF DOLORES

H

185

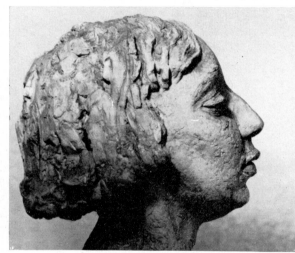

186

187

her ears. In an early version of the bronze she had large star-shaped ear-rings. The head is held up as in the first two portraits, though the expression is different. Draperies conceal the lower half of her breast; her left hand touches without grasping her right arm. The upper arms are rather short. The surface is like beaten copper.

Who was Dolores, of whom Epstein made these several studies? She had black hair and a white skin, and no one knew if she came from the East End of London or the slums of Marseilles. She liked taking off her clothes, lived on anyone who would support her, told cynical stories of her own misdeeds and was an extreme exhibitionist. Of all the girl models, noted for their looks or their lovers and notorious for their Bohemian behaviour, the height of whose glory was to pose for Epstein, and the reward for whose adulation was to form part of the circus which toured from Guildford Street to the Eiffel Tower Restaurant and on to the Café Royal, none was more flamboyant than Dolores. 'She became the High Priestess of Beauty,' wrote the sculptor, 'and this role she carried to ridiculous lengths. She even gave as an excuse to a magistrate, before whom she appeared for some indiscreet conduct in Piccadilly, that my being in America had disorientated her, and this was taken as sufficient excuse, together with a small fine, by a magistrate indulgent to a Phryne of modern times.'

'In 1923', the sculptor wrote, 'I made one more head of her, which I think is the best work I did from the beautiful and fantastic Dolores.' Indeed this FOURTH PORTRAIT OF DOLORES is one of Epstein's most masterly heads of any period. This time the hair is drawn back to fall in waves at the back and to reveal the line of the cheekbones; a straight fringe is combed down to the brows; there is no neck. The surface, though irregular, is in the main smoother. Epstein had seized the secret of Dolores at last.

With her glorious bone structure, smouldering eyes and lips parted like a greedy orchid, Dolores is so alive and modern in this final portrait; yet the sculptor has given her a classic, eternal quality, and there is a Greek breeze blowing in her hair.

'Her endless amours were a boon to Fleet Street journalists, and when she died of cancer, suddenly, they must have regretted the passing of a character so colourful and so accessible.'

185 1ST PORTRAIT OF DOLORES
186 2ND PORTRAIT OF DOLORES
187 3RD PORTRAIT OF DOLORES
188 4TH PORTRAIT OF DOLORES

189. 190 4TH PORTRAIT OF DOLORES

In 1923 Epstein made his first carving since he had finished with Vorticism in 1916. MARBLE ARMS is said to be inspired by the sight of Kathleen Garman's arm resting on a table, which prompted the sculptor to dash off a pencil sketch. Then, having a block of marble just over three foot long, he decided to make on a heroic scale a carving of two arms, hers and his own, with her left hand resting on his right. But the resulting work is too grandiose and generalised in treatment to be considered a study from life.

Since the Romantic eighteen-thirties minor sculptors had liked to model or carve detached hands or feet to stand as decorative objects on tables, or to act as paper weights. It was Rodin who, around 1890, began to model, in a more serious spirit, limbless torsos and disembodied limbs — such as his over-life-size 'Hands' — intending them as sculptures complete in themselves. Perhaps Epstein was trying to emulate him. He had not Rodin's anatomical knowledge, though he had an eye trained to observe. Then, of course, Rodin never carved marble himself, but had his assistants copy his clay model.

Epstein's old friend, the American Gladys Deacon, of whom he had made the archaic-looking bust in 1917,

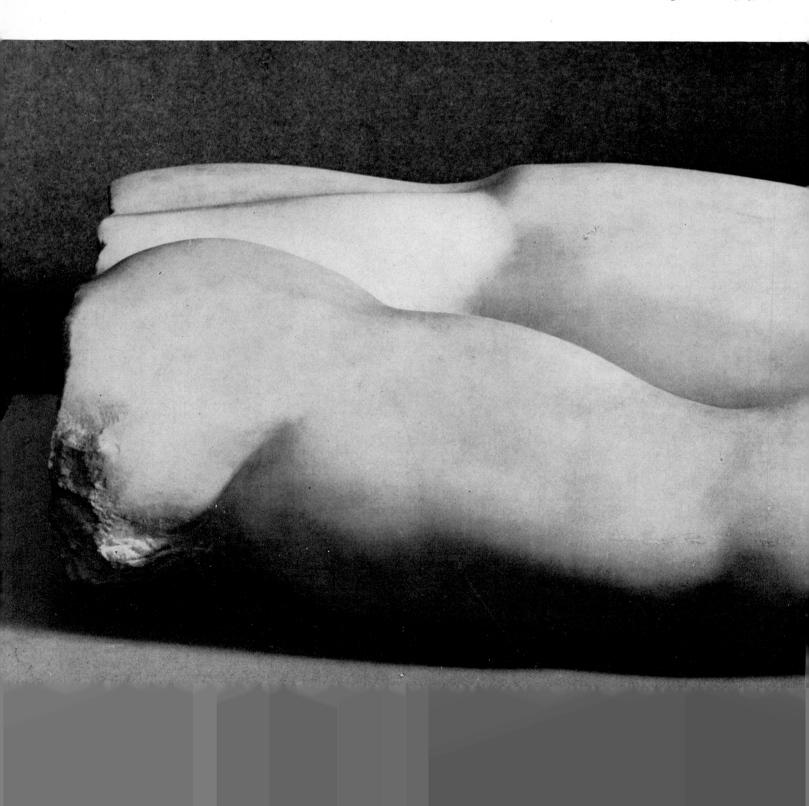

was now married to the Duke of Marlborough, and she determined that Epstein should make a portrait of her husband to take its place with his ancestors in the entrance hall at Blenheim. 'It was thought', wrote the sculptor, 'that sittings given in the Palace itself would materially help to solve the problems involved. I made fairly good progress with the head, which I wanted to get first go off, before beginning the bust. I completed the head and started on the bust, and that was where the trouble began.

'The Duke thought he would look best as a Roman bust with nude shoulders, but to my mind it was best as a

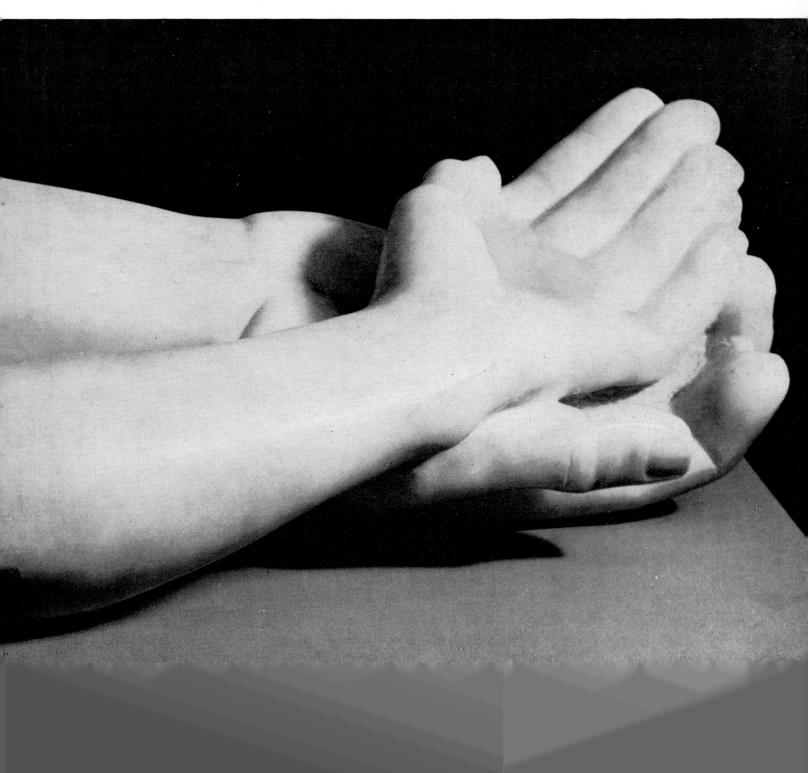

192

193

194

192. 193 SKETCH HEAD OF
DUCHESS OF MARLBOROUGH

194 HEAD OF
DUKE OF MARLBOROUGH

man of his period and I was not particular as to what the costume should be as long as it was something that he wore. The Duchess agreed with me, but we came to no understanding, and I gave up working on the bust, after an acrimonious debate which ended in ill-temper on both sides. [The bust was completed two years later.]

'My stay in Blenheim Palace in 1923 was quite pleasant because of the beautiful parkland, mostly wild. . . . In my careless working costume . . . I was more than once called upon by the gamekeepers to explain my presence. . . . Also the Duchess of Marlborough had an organist to come and play the organ for me . . . and the day began with an hour of Bach. The Duke disliked Bach.'

No doubt a good likeness, the HEAD OF THE DUKE OF MARLBOROUGH seems also to be the portrait of a type of English gentleman of its period. Much can be read from it: the years in the Household Cavalry, the vistas of gilded rooms, the eternal parkland, the big shoots, the Turkish cigarettes — even the dislike of Bach.

While at Blenheim Epstein began another study of the Duchess's interesting face but this SKETCH HEAD OF THE DUCHESS OF MARLBOROUGH remained unfinished. Photographs of the plaster are included, though, for the sake of illustrating one of the sculptor's works in an intermediary stage. Such portraits as 'Haile Selassie' and 'Einstein' were unfinished too, but they were carried further than this one.

In R. B. CUNNINGHAME GRAHAM, the Scottish writer and explorer, Epstein found a model after his heart, and he made of him one of his most effective and characteristic portraits.

'Imagine Don Quixote walking about your studio and sitting for his portrait!' wrote Epstein. 'This was R. B. Cunninghame Graham, and you could see him on horse-back any day in Hyde Park on his small American mustang, seated in a high saddle, riding along Rotten Row in a bowler hat. . . . No man with easier manners, more debonair and courteous. . . . I should have gone on with his head and made it into a bust and full figure and mounted it on a horse, and had it set up in Hyde Park, where his ghost now rides.'

Cunninghame Graham helped to get Epstein the commission for the Hudson Memorial in the following year, and the sculptor recorded how he came to see him working on it in Epping Forest, and how when they walked afterwards through the woods the seventy-three-year-old 'Don Roberto' jumped the brooks with astonishing agility. The author was also to bring the Polish Ambassador to see Epstein's bust of Conrad, offering to start a fund for its purchase for Poland with a contribution of his own, but nothing came of this generous scheme.

'In the head I modelled he seems to sniff the air, blowing from the Sierras, and his hair is swept by a breeze from afar.'

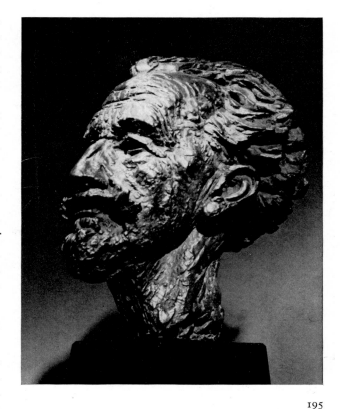

195

195. 196
R. B. CUNNINGHAME
GRAHAM

196

[125]

[126]

197 OLD PINAGER
198 EILEEN
        PROUDFOOT
199 DR. OKO

198

Of OLD PINAGER Epstein wrote: 'He sits with his matches every evening on the doorstep of a shop labelled "Old Masters". His head is bowed. He is the image of abject patience. He is quite pleased to sit in the same position in my studio where it is warm. . . . He accepts himself as a natural failure.' The life-story is told again in clay, and Pinager is perpetuated by the sculptor's pity, his life not wasted after all.

EILEEN PROUDFOOT was a South African art student, who died shortly after her portrait was made.

DR. ADOLPH S. OKO met Epstein in New York about 1898, and they remained friends until Oko's death after the Second World War. Dr. Oko created the Hebrew Union College Library, Cincinnati, Ohio. On retirement in 1932 he came to England to pursue his studies of Spinoza. It was at this time that the sculptor and the scholar saw most of each other, but Oko's portrait was made on an earlier visit to London in 1923. Epstein was

199

200
FEROSA
RASTOUMJI

201
ANGEL OF THE
ANNUNCIATION

later to make portraits of Oko's second wife and of his daughter Pearl and a drawing of his son Benjamin. His friendship with Oko was one of the most enduring he ever enjoyed. That with Matthew Smith was another.

The distinctive features of the Parsee pianist FEROSA RASTOUMJI, with their aloof, spiritual expression, gave him the idea of using her for an ANGEL OF THE ANNUNCIATION, but this work remained unfinished.

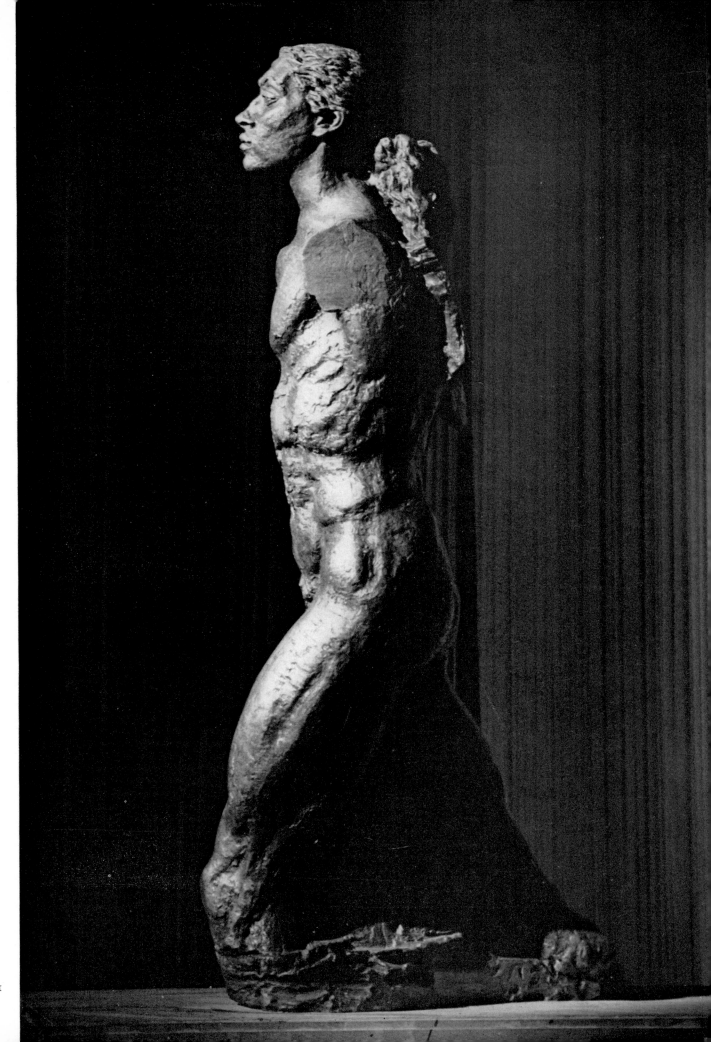

202

'Muirhead Bone had arranged that I should do a bust of Conrad for him.' Epstein drove down to Kent and put up at the village inn of Bridge, near Canterbury, as he preferred being independent to staying with people. He stayed three weeks working on his portrait of JOSEPH CONRAD.

'Conrad was an absorbing study. He took posing seriously and gave me good long sittings until one o'clock, when we lunched and talked. . . . A sculptor had previously made a bust of him which represented him as an open-necked, romantic, out-of-door type of person. In appearance Conrad was the very opposite. . . . He was worried if his hair and beard were not trim and neat as became a sea Captain. . . . He was crippled with rheumatism, crotchety, nervous, and ill. He said to me "I am finished." . . . I had no hesitations while at work

owing to his very sympathetic attitude . . . he would beam at me with a pleased expression and forget his rheumatism. . . . Conrad had a demon expression in the left eye, while the right eye was smothered by a drooping lid, but the eyes glowed with a great intensity of feeling. . . . The whole head revealed the man who had suffered much. . . .'

Conrad wrote to Richard Curle, his biographer, 'The bust of Ep has grown truly monumental. . . . It is wonderful to go down to posterity like that.' He died five months later. Sir Muirhead Bone offered the noble bust to the National Portrait Gallery, but it was refused. They later acquired a casting, however.

It is believed that only the original casting of Conrad's bust, still in the possession of the Bone family, has the correct upswept moustache which gives the writer's face much of its gallant character. The plaster must have been

[130]

202. 203 JOSEPH CONRAD

204 ELSA LANCHESTER
205 SHEILA
206 THE SERAPH

damaged and repaired perfunctorily by the plaster-moulder, for in subsequent castings, such as that in the National Portrait Gallery, the moustache is represented as being waxed into points.

ELSA LANCHESTER, later to become the wife of Charles Laughton, was an actress who, with Harold Scott, ran a nightclub called the Cave of Harmony.

SHEILA — surname forgotten — was a girl who, with her mother, used to frequent a club called the Harlequin, where Epstein possibly met her. Her head, instinct with life, is in Los Angeles.

THE SERAPH is a perhaps somewhat idealised portrait of Marie Collins, younger sister of José Collins, the actress and singer, star of *The Maid of the Mountains*, *Catherine* and *The Last Waltz*. At a time when Epstein's mind was turning to religious groups he met this girl whose striking head he thought could be used for an angel figure. He modelled her, but the cast was set aside for thirty years, till elements of it were incorporated in the bright visage of the Llandaff 'Christ in Majesty'.

[133]

207

207 RELIEF OF W. H. HUDSON
208 SKETCH FOR RIMA
209 RIMA (HUDSON MEMORIAL)

208

In 1924 the Royal Society for the Protection of Birds commissioned Epstein to make a memorial to W. H. Hudson, the writer and naturalist, to be erected in Hyde Park. A RELIEF OF W. H. HUDSON himself was rejected by the Office of Works. The artist was asked for something more symbolic. At a meeting of the Society, during which he was attacked by Galsworthy, he agreed to make a model incorporating Rima, the heroine of *Green Mansions*. His sketch was accepted by the Office of Works.

The sculptor found a shed in Epping Forest overlooking Monks Wood, a rustic and isolated spot, though only thirteen miles from Charing Cross. He worked on the panel of Portland stone throughout the winter from October to April, 'solitary, surrounded by silent and often fog-laden forest'.

The decorative panel of RIMA is cut in high relief and gives an archaic impression, though it is hard to say whether this is Minoan or Aztec. The composition seems to be inspired by the fifth century B.C. Greek Sarcophagus in the Museo delle Terme in Rome, which represents the Birth of Venus and is known as the 'Ludovisi Throne'. Epstein admitted later in his life that he had probably had this work in mind. One phrase in Hudson's book had particularly struck and inspired Epstein, namely that

which describes Rima's fall to death from a treetop into the fire beneath 'like a great white bird'. But, I must admit that until told this I had not thought the relief represented her death fall. Rima, shown from the thighs upwards, extends her arms in an ecstatic butterfly W, as though dancing in her virgin forest. Her head is thrown back and her hair flows free. The rest of the rectangle is filled out with four birds, native to South America, who fly triumphantly around her. Rima is conceived as an elemental being, a primitive wood nymph — but not a Greek one. Her pronounced frontal bone, strong straight arms, big hands, clearly circumscribed and pointed breasts, her nipped-in waist, heroic pelvis and belly like an inverted pear — even the unclassical hunching of her shoulders — these must have appeared startling to a public of park-promenaders who had grown to accept Achilles, Prince Albert and Peter Pan. The boldly conceived birds, particularly the two in the 'foreground', are remarkable for the way they combine the monumental with a feeling of life. But in the relief, of course, it was not her death fall he chose to represent.

'On a fine May morning,' wrote the sculptor, 'the memorial was unveiled in Hyde Park.' A crowd, music, speeches from Stanley Baldwin and Cunninghame Graham. Then the Prime Minister pulled the string and uncovered the monument. 'Cunninghame Graham would relate, with some humour, how he saw a shiver run down the spine of Mr. Stanley Baldwin. . . . The small and inoffensive panel produced a sensation wholly unexpected on my part. . . .' 'Take this horror out of the park,' the *Daily Mail* demanded. A Member asked in the Commons that 'the terrible female with paralysis of the hands called "Rima" be instantly removed from the park'. In October the *Morning Post* commented that 'were not the English a tolerant people, it would have long ago been broken in pieces'; and a month later was able to report, 'The inevitable has happened to Mr. Epstein's "Rima". She has been ingloriously daubed with green paint.' A letter demanding the removal of the memorial was signed, among others, by Hilaire Belloc, Conan Doyle, Frank Dicksee (President of the Royal Academy), Alfred Munnings and Bernard Partridge. However, Muirhead Bone defended 'Rima' in *The Times* and his letter was endorsed by, among others, Arnold Bennett, Samuel Courtauld, G. Eumorfopoulos, Lord Howard de Walden, John Lavery, Ramsay MacDonald, Ambrose McEvoy, Michael Sadler, Bernard Shaw, Sybil Thorndike, Hugh Walpole, Cunninghame Graham, Holbrook Jackson, Augustus John, George Moore, Henry Nevinson, William Orpen and Francis Dodd; 170 students of the Royal College of Art and 85 of the Slade also protested against the monument's removal. It was saved by a memorandum which Muirhead Bone sent to the Minister of Works. 'Rima' was several times defaced by paint over the years, twice by Fascists.

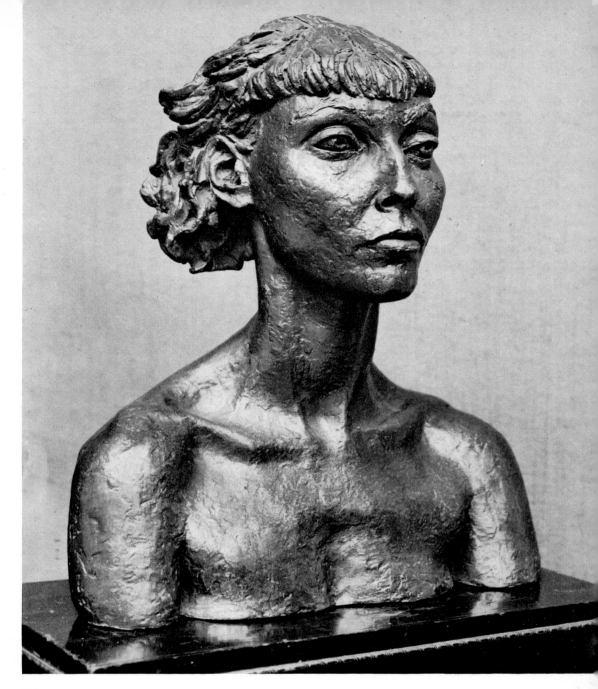

211 DUKE OF
  MARLBOROUGH

212 1ST PORTRAIT
  OF ORIEL ROSS

212

£400 was the fee paid for the Rima panel. It was the only public commission the sculptor received between the Oscar Wilde monument in 1909 and the figures on the Underground Headquarters Building in 1929.

'Finally', wrote Epstein, 'the protests died down. The "muck-rakers" grew tired of their fruitless journeys to the park, and the panel was left in its peaceful setting. The deserted spot could now be visited without alarm or interference. Grass grew again on the downtrodden soil.'

In 1925 it was two years since Epstein and the Duke of Marlborough had fallen out over the question of whether the Duke should be portrayed in modern clothes or in the classical convention; and the shrewdly observed head made in 1923 had remained shoulderless. Now the Duchess returned to the attack. A compromise was reached when 'it was agreed that the Duke should be depicted in his Robes of the Garter with the hands included'.

'Sittings for the BUST OF THE DUKE OF MARLBOROUGH were resumed in London and all went well.' As it turned out the sweeping draperies of the Garter robes added little to the Duke's portrait, and the hands were awkward.

Oriel Ross, a clergyman's daughter, was a beauty, an amusing woman and an actress. She later married Earl Paulett. After this FIRST PORTRAIT OF ORIEL ROSS, Epstein made two more studies of her.

[139]

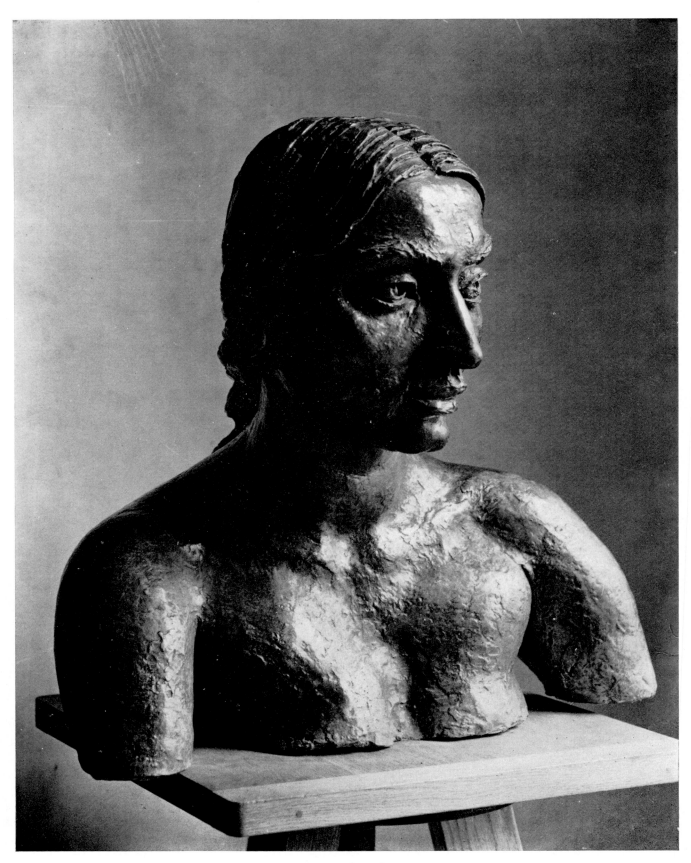

213

213 2ND PORTRAIT OF
SUNITA

214 ENVER

215 DRAWING OF
SUNITA AND ENVER

Amina Peerbhoy under the name of Sunita was to become perhaps the most famous of all Epstein's models. She and her sister Miriam Patel left their husbands and India to keep a stall of exotic artifacts at the Wembley International Exhibition, which was where Epstein first met them. The sisters and Enver, Sunita's son, moved in to live with the Epsteins so that the master might have models perpetually at hand. Between 1925 and 1933 Epstein would model four portraits of Sunita, one of Enver and one of Miriam, whom he called Anita. Sunita and Enver would also pose for the first 'Madonna and Child' (1926–7). Of Sunita alone Epstein would make countless drawings in pencil, charcoal or water colour; of Miriam-Anita alone several dozen; of Sunita with Enver a series of nearly a hundred; and of Sunita with Miriam-Anita perhaps as many again.

The 'First portrait of Sunita', a head, being very similar to the SECOND PORTRAIT OF SUNITA, a bust, also made in 1925, is not reproduced. In the bust Epstein has already seized on the brooding, tragic nature of the sitter's beauty, which was to create the dominant mood of the

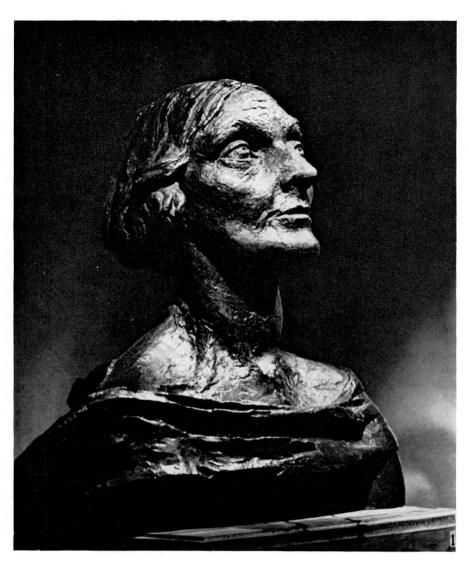

216 SYBIL THORNDYKE
217 PROFESSOR
SAMUEL ALEXANDER O.M.

'Madonna and Child'. Likewise the first head of ENVER, then aged five, can be seen in the light of that monumental bronze, as a first sketch for the infant Christ.

Sunita's first bust shows the top part of her arms and breast. Her head hangs forward, looking slightly to the left. Her smooth hair is parted in the middle; her face is a perfect oval; she has thick eyebrows, large, clearly defined and rather slanting eyes, a finely curved nose, straight chiselled lips and a small chin.

Sunita was a tall woman with a huge head, and far from madonna-like. She could find no food or drink fierce enough in taste, and used to put pepper in her whisky.

An outstanding success of the 1924–5 theatre season was Bernard Shaw's *Saint Joan*; and SYBIL THORNDIKE, who played the part of its heroine, came to sit for Epstein. He portrayed her gazing skywards, as if hearing voices, with the short bobbed hair she wore as Joan, but with the draperies of a *fichu* or part of an evening dress across her chest and flung round her right shoulder.

Next Epstein modelled the portraits of two distinguished old men from Lancashire. The bearded and patriarchal PROFESSOR SAMUEL ALEXANDER, O.M., was an Australian who became a Fellow and Philosophy Tutor of Lincoln College, Oxford, then Professor of Philosophy in Manchester. His retirement from the latter chair in 1924 was the occasion for the commissioning of his bust. C. P. SCOTT was the creator of the *Manchester Guardian* (now the *Guardian*), a paper of which he was Governing Director and which he had edited since 1872. He had also been a Liberal Member of Parliament and was a Governor both of Manchester University, for which the bust was commissioned, and of Manchester Grammar School.

In contrast to the aged Lancastrians, STEPHEN TENNANT, a younger son of Lord Glenconner, seems — as indeed he was — a sort of Dorian Gray. At this time a beautiful dilettante, he later developed into a serious writer, besides being a very individual water-colourist, with a speciality for nostalgic evocations of the low life of Mediterranean ports.

218

218 C. P. SCOTT
219 STEPHEN TENNANT

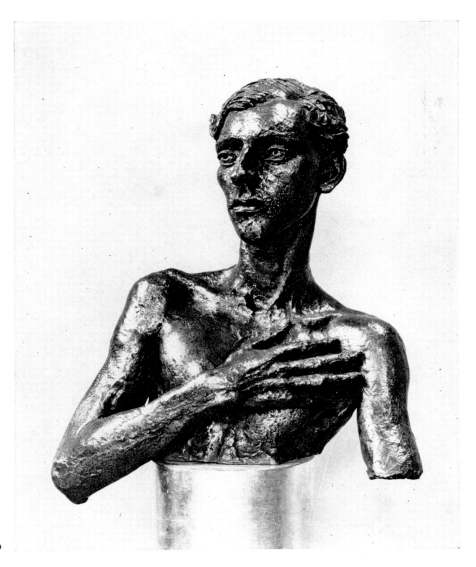

219

220. 221. 222
THE
VISITATION

220

[144]

We have seen how, following the 'Risen Christ', which he had exhibited and sold at the Leicester Galleries in 1920, Epstein considered making more than one large-scale religious composition: but neither the Deposition, nor the Annunciation, became more than intentions in the sculptor's mind. Now, in 1926, Epstein determined to make a Visitation. He had wanted it to be an Annunciation, but he changed its present title on realising a Virgin of the Annunciation could not be pregnant. (He later excused himself for this mistake on the grounds that Grünewald committed the same solecism.) Looking for a model who would serve for this figure of humility and resignation he found a willing sitter for the head and hands in the then secretary of the playwright John Drinkwater. With eyes downcast, the girl, with her hair in long plaits, makes, as if involuntarily, a nervous wringing gesture of the hands. Her dress with its skirt in long heavy folds, apart from recalling the inevitable uniform of Augustus John's dreaming Bohemians, suggests a comparison with Gothic sculpture, and the statue appears designed to stand in a niche: this Virgin is not a crowned Queen of Heaven, but an incredulous girl of our century humbled by the glory in store for her.

'In 1926 in Epping Forest I modelled a life-size figure which I intended for a group, to be called "The Visitation". I can recall with pleasure how this figure looked in my little hut which I used as a studio. I should have liked it to stand amongst trees on a knoll overlooking Monk Wood. This figure stands with folded hands, and expresses a humility so profound as to shame the beholder who comes to my sculpture expecting rhetoric or splendour of gesture. This work alone refutes all the charges of blatancy and self-advertisement levelled at me. When I exhibited the work at the Leicester Galleries, wishing to avoid controversy, I called it "A Study". By this disguise I succeeded for once in evading the critics, always ready to bay and snap at a work. A subscription was raised to purchase it, and I recall that Richard Wyndham gave the proceeds of an exhibition he was holding of his own work towards its purchase for the Tate Gallery. George Gray Barnard, who was passing through London at the time, came with me to the Gallery and was enthusiastic, and this from my old master moved me greatly.'

Barnard urged Epstein to work in America which 'held out so many more opportunities' for a sculptor. He also invited him to collaborate on 'a great Memorial Arch he was at work on'. 'I listened to him', wrote Epstein, 'but in the end decided I would rather do my own work. . . . In sculpture, although I had my first lessons from Barnard, we were poles apart in conception and execution.' Perhaps, though, Barnard's descriptions of the opportunities awaiting in America were one reason for his visit in 1927.

THE VISITATION now stands in the Tate Gallery. Another casting is on a Scottish moor.

K

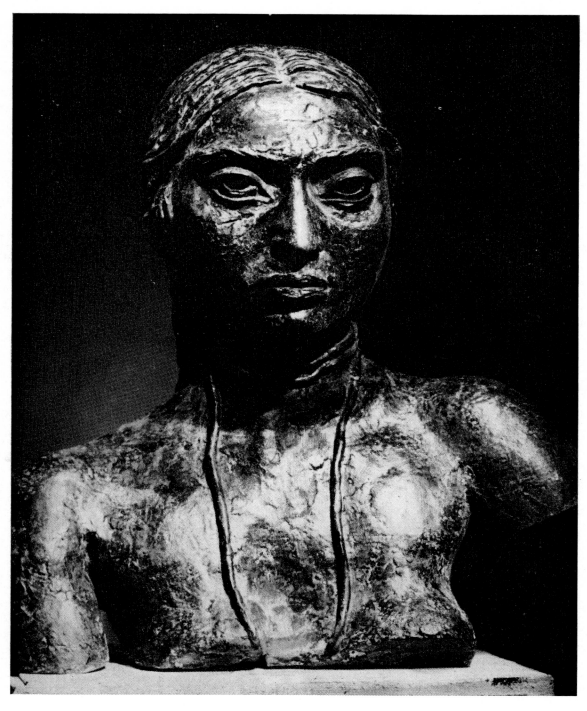

Epstein's second bust and THIRD PORTRAIT OF SUNITA WITH A NECKLACE had the same quality of musing melancholy as its predecessor, but was more tragic. The woman's features seem to have matured slightly even in a year; she now looks straight ahead of her; and she wears a snake-like rope of articulated metal wound twice round her neck and falling in a loop to emphasise the form of her chest. The sculptor has cut off her right arm below the deltoid muscle but carried the left down to the elbow, leaving a vestigial fragment of flexed forearm with an awkward result. This defiantly anti-classical habit of truncating an arm at an unexpected point was one of the tiresome gimmicks of Epstein's middle period. Like his rough surface it has since been copied by lesser artists unable to imitate his more essential characteristics.

When the Indian Poet RABINDRANATH TAGORE came to pose at the studio Epstein brought Sunita's son Enver to be introduced to him. 'Tagore', wrote Epstein, 'looked at him and asked: "A Hindu?" I said: "No, a Moslem", whereat Rabindranath lifted his eyes to the ceiling and

[146]

224

223 3RD PORTRAIT OF SUNITA
224. 225 RABINDRANATH TAGORE

passed on.' This may have been one reason that Epstein took a dislike to him: the proud, self-confident and humble artist treated all men as equals, whether dukes or beggars, and he could not bear people who put on side. ' "I am he that sitteth among the poorest, the loneliest and the lost," ' Epstein quoted from Tagore's *Gitanjali*, the book of poems which had won him the Nobel prize thirteen years before, and contrasted this line with his sitter's 'handsome, commanding presence' which 'inspired in his followers awe and a craven obedience'.

Sir Rabindranath Tagore, author of poems in Bengali and English, who set three thousand of his own songs to music and founded the International Institution called Visva-Bharati in Bengal, would himself take to the visual arts and become a painter three years later.

'He posed in silence and I worked well. . . . At the finish of the sittings usually two or three disciples, who waited in an ante-room for him, took him back to his hotel. . . . The manners of Tagore were aloof, dignified and cold, and if he needed anything only one word of command escaped him. . . . It has been remarked that my

225

226 1ST PORTRAIT OF RAMSAY MACDONALD
227 11TH PORTRAIT OF PEGGY JEAN (WITH LONG HAIR)

bust of him rests upon the beard, an unconscious piece of symbolism.'

Epstein modelled Tagore's head over life-size with big, bold strokes, so that the poet with his intense stare and flowing beard took on the monumental grandeur of a baroque apostle.

Epstein's FIRST PORTRAIT OF RAMSAY MACDONALD, the Socialist politician, a small bust, was made in 1926. In this study, which is almost too brilliant and 'effective', the sculptor brought out the eager aspiration — one hesitates to call it idealism — of that complicated character. MacDonald's lean and hungry look was to disappear when he became Prime Minister.

The ELEVENTH PORTRAIT OF PEGGY JEAN, aged $7\frac{1}{2}$, with long hair, shows her head leaning forward but looking up with an alert and interested expression.

[149]

228

We have seen how the Indian sisters, Amina-Sunita and Miriam-Anita, moved into Guilford Street so that they should always be at hand as models for the sculptor. Although Epstein made many drawings of the younger sister — some of which were published in *75 Drawings by Jacob Epstein*, with an introduction by Hubert Wellington, in 1929 — he only modelled one bust of ANITA. She was a less striking type than her elder sister,

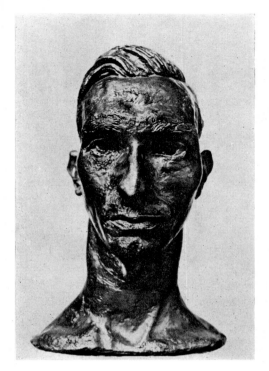

229

228 ANITA
229 JAMES KEARNS FEIBLEMAN
230 EDWARD GOOD
(MOSHEH OVED)
231 2ND PORTRAIT OF ORIEL ROSS

230

231

pretty rather than handsome. She married an American.

JAMES KEARNS FEIBLEMAN was a well-to-do American who commissioned this head of himself, and, two years later, one of his friend David Cohn, who had been brought up with him. It is easy to see that Epstein was interested in his intelligent and sensitive face.

Edward Good or MOSHEH OVED, a charming, fanciful and enthusiastic character and an admirer of Epstein's work, was the jeweller of 'Cameo Corner'. He used to lend the sculptor fantastic Oriental ear-rings and necklaces to adorn his models. In *Gems and Life* (Benn, 1927) he gave an account of the sittings for his portrait; and his strange *Book of Affinity* (Heinemann, 1933) had coloured drawings by Epstein in the latter's Old Testament style. His daughter and his second wife were also modelled.

The SECOND PORTRAIT OF ORIEL ROSS, a head, has a quizzical expression and was thought to resemble Leonardo's portrait of Ginevra dei Benci.

232

233

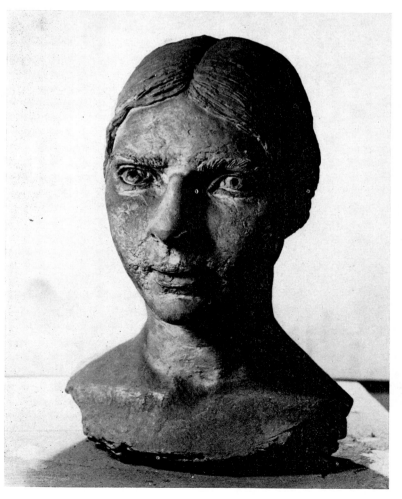

234

235

232 DRAWING OF ZEDA
233 ZEDA
234 PEARL OKO
235 DAISY DUNN
236 SKETCH FOR
GENESIS

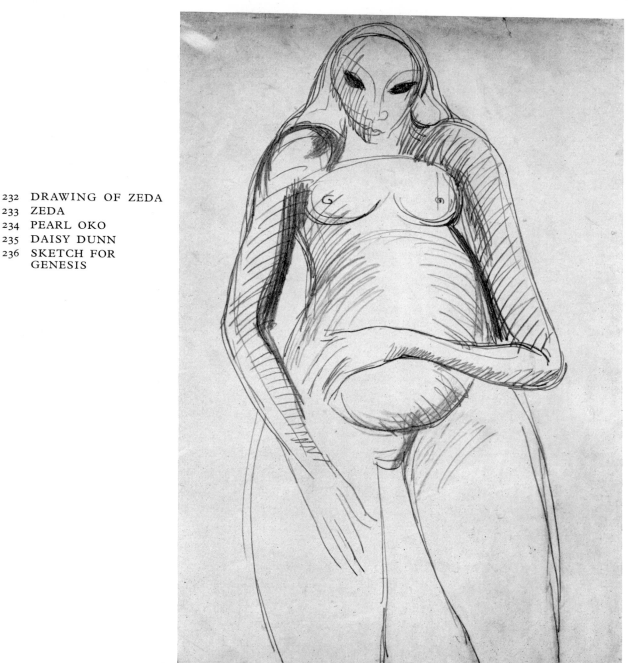

236

ZEDA was a Turkish model, of whom Epstein made many drawings and one bust. She combined a harem voluptuousness with an element of modern chic. Like the Indian sisters, she figured in the book of *75 Drawings* a few years later.

PEARL OKO was the daughter of Epstein's old friend Adolf Oko, of whom he had already made a portrait.

In 1925 London was taken by storm by the vitality and rhythms of the revue Florence Mills's *Blackbirds* from America. This was the first musical show with an all-Negro cast, and it seemed the epitome of that jazz music which had been born in the cabarets of New Orleans, early in the century and grown to be a vital influence on modern music and life throughout the Western world. DAISY DUNN was one of the original Blackbirds. Since his youth in New York Epstein had been attracted to coloured people: he modelled her leaning forward, lost in musing melancholy.

Epstein had bought a block of Serravezza marble in Paris, and it stood for a time in the shed in Epping Forest where he had carved 'Rima'. The idea of 'Genesis' — like 'Maternity' and the figure in Flenite another pregnant mother brooding on the child within her — came to him while he was working on 'The Visitation', and was as he

[153]

said, 'another facet of the same idea'. The carving, for which the first drawing is here reproduced, would not be finished for three years.

Epstein decided that Sunita's 'eternal Oriental type' was right for the Madonna. He began to model her with Enver as a MADONNA AND CHILD, and worked on this group for a year.

'When I had finished the head,' he wrote, 'the model remarked that she could not possibly "look as good as I had made her". She recognised that there was something eternal and divine in it and outside herself. Her boy . . . was another matter. He was restless. . . . My impatience at the time is responsible for the child's body being somewhat unfinished . . . its complex linear plan and very elaborate secondary motives were dominated by my original idea of presenting a massive group that would go into a cathedral or religious sanctuary.'

In the group the Virgin, in draperies, is seated with her knees apart, the young Christ standing between them. Her right hand rests on his belly and seems to hold his loin-cloth in place, her left clasps him round the chest. The child holds his arms before him, elbows bent, in a playful attitude: his attention has been caught by a bird in a tree or some incident which has made him thoughtful. As he looks up, so, over his left shoulder, his mother looks down, but without regarding whatever lies before her. She broods on the unknown terrors and glories of the future, on the destiny of mothers and sons.

The bronze is realistic, its chief distortion being a slight enlarging of the Virgin's lower limbs: her noble knees and large feet forming a strong base to the group and increasing its monumental character, while by enclosing the childish figure they convey the ideas of generation and protection. The gravity of Sunita's gaze is unforgettable. The group is remarkable for the way it combines realistic observation with a Byzantine or Romanesque

237

237 MADONNA AND CHILD
(detail)

238 MADONNA AND CHILD
(detail)

239. 240 (over)
MADONNA AND CHILD

238

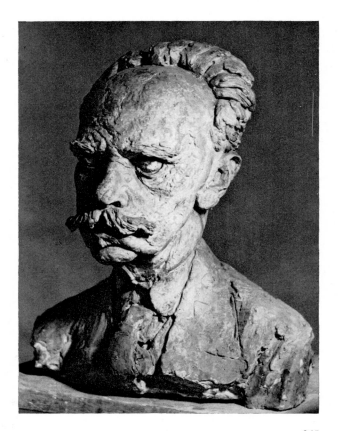

heart sank. There was no top light, but curtained walls, palms and chandeliers. The gallery proprietors were far from sympathetic, restricted the show to a fortnight's run, tried to charge the sculptor for every kind of expense including a woman publicity agent with vulgar ideas, and wanted to send the sculptures on a long tour of the States. From the risk of this last venture he had to be extracted by lawyers. Epstein shirked the *vernissage*. Nevertheless, his exhibition was a success and works were sold.

Epstein made three portraits in New York: those of PROFESSOR JOHN DEWEY, PROFESSOR FRANZ BOAS, the anthropologist, and the Negro singer PAUL ROBESON.

'The John Dewey portrait was a presentation to Columbia University, where it now is. The subscriptions were donated by students and admirers of Dewey who each gave five dollars. As a sitter Dewey was very sympathetic, and Joseph Rattner, a student of his whose idea it was to present the portrait, would come in and talk to him. They kept up a running philosophic conversation, and Rattner contrived at the same time to make coffee for the three of us. . . . Dewey's son-in-law . . . said that I

241 PROFESSOR FRANZ BOAS
242 PROFESSOR JOHN DEWEY

241

242

grandeur of composition. The surface is strangely rich.

Duveen, the famous dealer, saw the work in the foundry at Fulham. 'If you had in mind to do a Madonna and Child,' he asked Epstein, 'why did you not choose a beautiful model?'

The group was bought by Sally Ryan, the American sculptress, and lent to the Tate Gallery, London. She subsequently gave it to the Riverside Church, New York.

In 1927 came the offer of an exhibition in New York, and Mrs. Epstein decided to try the experiment of uprooting Epstein and transplanting him in the land of his birth. The lease of Guilford Street was given up, and the Epsteins set off with Peggy Jean. 'It was generally thought that I was shaking off the dust of England from my feet. That was not my intention. I had been away from America for twenty-five years.' His last short visit had in fact been twenty-two years ago. On board ship the representative of a Jewish paper asked him about his attitude to Zionism, and he replied that he had no attitude. At Sandy Hook the journalists came on board to interview him, and one asked if he had come 'to debunk sculpture'.

The exhibition, which included the 'Madonna and Child' and fifty other bronzes, was to be held at the Ferragill Galleries; and when Epstein saw the place his

243 PAUL ROBESON

had made him look like a "Vermont horse-dealer". This was not a bad characterisation, as Professor Dewey came from Vermont, and he pleased me with his Yankee drawl and seeming casualness. . . .'

'Professor Boas was also interesting to work from, his face was scarred and criss-crossed with mementoes of many duels of his student days in Heidelberg, but what was still left whole in his face was as spirited as a fighting cock. . . .'

Paul Robeson took Epstein round the Harlem dance halls and sang lullabies to Peggy Jean. His portrait, though, begun early in 1928, remained a sketch, for Epstein had come to the conclusion he could not live away from England and booked his passage home. Robeson's head, with its upward gaze, as if the singer were about to address God in the familiar language of the negro spiritual, has a noble, aspiring quality.

'I revisited the haunts of my youth — the dockland along the lower East and West Side of New York. I found it greatly changed. Gone were the wooden piers that had at one time jutted out into the river, the ancient warehouses with their strange spicy smells, the ship chandler shops with their heaps of cordage and tackle. . . . The Bowery was also sadly changed. These were prohibition days, and the saloons and the life of the old Bowery were gone.'

The sculptor found the New York artists were still under the spell of Paris, and 'absorbed the very latest "ism" long before the English artists did'. There was an American equivalent to Bloomsbury, the group which had rejected him and which he despised. On visiting the Art Students' League, his old school, he was surprised to see that 'all the work of the students was abstract or cubist'. He showed some of his bronzes there, and overheard one student remark, 'These Epsteins are dull. They bore me.'

'New York monuments were appalling to me,' wrote the sculptor, 'rivalling those of London in their commonplaceness.' Still, he enjoyed his stay. 'My flat overlooked Central Park, and in looking across it in the wintry landscape there was all the beauty of a Hiroshige. At night underneath my windows I could watch the myriad skaters glancing to and fro over the frozen ponds with

245 12TH PORTRAIT OF PEGGY JEAN (THE
     SICK CHILD)
246 12TH PORTRAIT OF PEGGY JEAN (THE
     SICK CHILD) (detail)

piercing shouts and gaiety. . . . The amazing skyscrapers
looked wonderful.'

Before leaving the United States Epstein saw a number
of fine pictures which had not been there in his youth. He
was thrilled with the Rembrandts and Cézannes at the
Metropolitan and even visited the great collection of
Impressionists belonging to the formidable Dr. Barnes of
Philadelphia, which was shown to few. He attended
concerts, of which he considered New York 'had almost
too full a fare'. And he gave evidence in court that a brass
'Bird' by Brancusi was a work of art, thus helping to
exempt it from customs duty.

The Epsteins returned to London; and while they
were looking for a new home and studio they were lent a
friend's house. It was here that the remarkable portrait of
Peggy Jean, aged ten, known as THE SICK CHILD, was

L

modelled. The girl leans forward listlessly, her arms stretched out on a table which is too high for her to eat off or draw on with comfort. The loop formed by the arms forms a base for the sculpture: without them the forward-hanging head would overbalance. Peggy Jean's long hair hangs down her back and is combed into a fringe in front. Her fingers seem to be holding both ends of an invisible pencil, which she is rapping idly on the table. The expression of a bored child (who is not allowed to read because she has an eye infection) is wonderfully caught. The title of the bronze reminds us of another remarkable work of art, 'The Sick Child' of Metsu: and Epstein in this sculpture does seem to have arrested time in a way which was the speciality of certain Dutch *genre* painters — one thinks of Vermeer in particular, and most particularly of his 'Maid pouring milk'. A moment is rendered classical.

Now in the spring of 1928 the Epsteins found a house with a big studio built out at the back, 18 Hyde Park Gate, which became their home for life.

Returning from America in January 1928, Epstein had met VISCOUNT ROTHERMERE, the proprietor of the *Daily Mail* and other papers, on board the *Aquitania*. Rothermere commissioned a bust of himself and came to sit in the new studio. 'The sittings ... began with a film company making a film of myself and the sitter at work, and altogether the proceedings went on, as it were, in public, as Rothermere liked company and conducted his various businesses in my studio. I did not mind this as it showed the sitter animated by subjects that really interested him. I have long ago been forced into the habit of ignoring those around me when at work and thinking only of the work in hand.... Rothermere was monumental and offered strange psychological problems to the artist. Also he possessed a natural sense of humour and did not expect me to flatter him. He jocularly remarked that I was not making an Ivor Novello of him. The work progressed, but my model had a disconcerting habit of leaving for foreign parts suddenly, and sending me a wire that he would turn up in about a week or fortnight and "join me in the clay bin", as he put it. This habit of the wire finally decided me to call it a day, and the bust was declared finished.... This bust, with its somewhat formidable character, seemed to have to be handled carefully, for when I proposed exhibiting it ... I was advised not to do so, as a general election was coming on and it might possibly exert some baneful influence on events....

'Lord Rothermere's secretaries seemed particularly upset by the work. This I take as a tribute to the sincerity and truth of the rendering of the character. What these "yes men" expected me to do, I do not quite know, but

248 A PORTRAIT (MRS. GODFREY PHILLIPS)

their hostility was expressed quite frankly. I think of the bust as one of my best portraits.'

Epstein often thought his last work was his best.

The sculptor next modelled the gaunt and interesting features of MRS. GODFREY PHILLIPS. She was the wife of a dealer. The bust, when exhibited, was known simply as 'A Portrait', and was still so-called when it came into the collection of the National Gallery of Modern Art, later renamed the Tate Gallery. In the bronze of Mrs. Phillips at the Tate her dress has an upstanding collar, which makes an interesting pattern with her page-boy haircut: the plaster, without a collar, is illustrated here.

In 1928 Charles Holden, who had employed Epstein on the British Medical Association building twenty years before, commissioned him to make two groups above the doors of the Underground Headquarters building in Westminster. The sculptor proposed to do 'Day' and 'Night'.

He had been considering the idea of carving a Pietà, and had made a tentative drawing for it. He decided to use this idea for 'Night', and tried out another drawing in which the seated figure had several sleeping children in

249

her lap. Then he made a small clay model, the MAQUETTE FOR NIGHT, which was later cast in bronze as being of interest in itself. 'Day' would be a father and son. In one of the drawings he made for it he introduced foliage, but this was eliminated.

Henry Moore, Eric Gill, A. Wyon, E. Aumonier, A. H. Gerrard and F. Rabinovitch were simultaneously engaged in carving sculptures representing the Winds high up on the tower. Moore's flying figure was very successful. Epstein was smuggled in anonymously by the architect, and introduced to the Clerk of the Works as 'the sculptor' for fear 'dark forces might upset things'.

'It was in this atmosphere of mystery that I began a six months' work, which took me through the entire bitter winter months of 1928, working out of doors and in a draught of wind that whistled on one side down the narrow canyon of the street. I invariably began work with a terrible stomach-ache, brought on by the cold. After I got over this I was all right and remained on the building until nightfall, having my lunch there, out of doors, so as not to lose time. I had to be oblivious of the fact that for some time tons of stone were being hauled up above my head, on a chain . . . of course my work astonished the men on the building, and many a facetious remark was passed. . . . I had a shed built round my work. . . .'

In his *Buildings of England Series: London* Dr. Nikolaus Pevsner describes the London Transport Headquarters as 'a bold building for its date and for London, even if in some ways keeping a retreat open to the broad Georgian road. The composition in blocks and their stepping back high up is entirely of the C.20. Functionally it is ingenious. The building had to combine the necessities of an under-

250

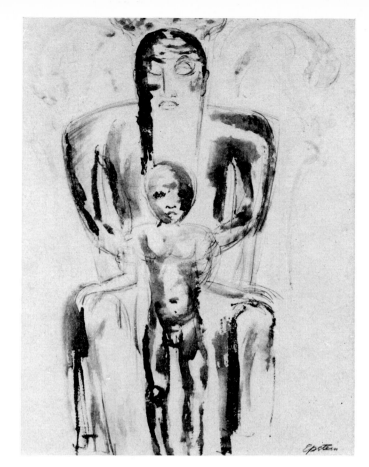

251

ground station with a large number of offices. So a large part of the area is one-storeyed. The centre is a tower 175 ft. high. . . . It has a square, gradually diminishing top. From the tower extend four spurs. What there is of sculptural decoration is of extreme interest. . . .'

DAY, over the eastern door to catch the morning sun, is a seated man holding a boy between his knees. The naked boy, with turned-out feet like a ballet-dancer, stands square on to the spectator, but he twists his head round to the left and his mop of bobbed hair swings back

249 DRAWING OF PIETA
250 SKETCH FOR DAY
251 SKETCH FOR DAY
252 MAQUETTE FOR NIGHT
253 EPSTEIN AND NIGHT IN THE SHED

252

253

254 DAY (PHOTOGRAPHED IN 1929)

as he stretches up his arms to embrace his father. The father's massive arms and shoulders are bare, his lower limbs draped. In spite of his flat-topped head and long curved Mexican nose, his face with its staring eyes, salient cheeks and undulant lips suggests a Greek tragic mask or the grotesque head which spouts water into a fountain. Yet there is little derivative about the group, which impresses with a startling unhesitant originality. The father is clearly a sun god — his face seems to radiate light from wide-open eyes, but he frowns too from the effort, or perhaps dazzled by his own effulgence, as he presents his son like a newly dawned day to the world.

Looking up at the statue from one or the other side, the spectator will notice the tremendous arc of the god's back, which is muscled like that of a professional strong-man; and also how the sculptor, reluctant to abandon his powerful verticals and yet obliged to bring the god's forearms slanting forward so that his hands can enclose the boy's thighs, renders the inward twist of the radius over the ulna with a distortion reminiscent of cubism.

NIGHT, facing north, is conceived, as we have said, as a Pietà. The seated goddess of darkness, with her draped head and closed eyes, bears a recumbent youth in her lap. She supports his hanging head in her right hand, and

255 NIGHT (PHOTOGRAPHED IN 1929)

with a tremendous gesture of her left, puts him to sleep. Her face is Chinese or Mongolian, and she emanates a Buddhist calm. Compare her with Michelangelo's early Pietà in St. Peter's, a similarly draped and seated mother carrying a limp and lifeless son, and it is clear she belongs to a far older mythology, to the Titans deposed by Zeus. She would have been at home in the grove where Keats's Thea found Saturn 'quiet as a stone'. So simple is the group, with its few incised lines to convey drapery, that it seems to be reduced to a face, a mood and a gesture. It may be thought that the sculptor has not solved satisfactorily the problem of the man's feet. In life the lower legs

would dangle and project, but Epstein did not want to detach them from the square bulk of the goddess's knees, so he doubled them back and under, giving to the arched feet a ripple which is out of keeping with the elemental grandeur of the group and recalls Art Nouveau.

The usual clamour arose in the Press, and an inquiry was held as to whether 'Day' should be hacked off the building. Was it because the child had no fig-leaf? In the *Evening Standard* R. H. Wilenski claimed that the two groups were 'the grandest stone carvings in London'.

This was the last commission for a public building received by Epstein until 1950.

[167]

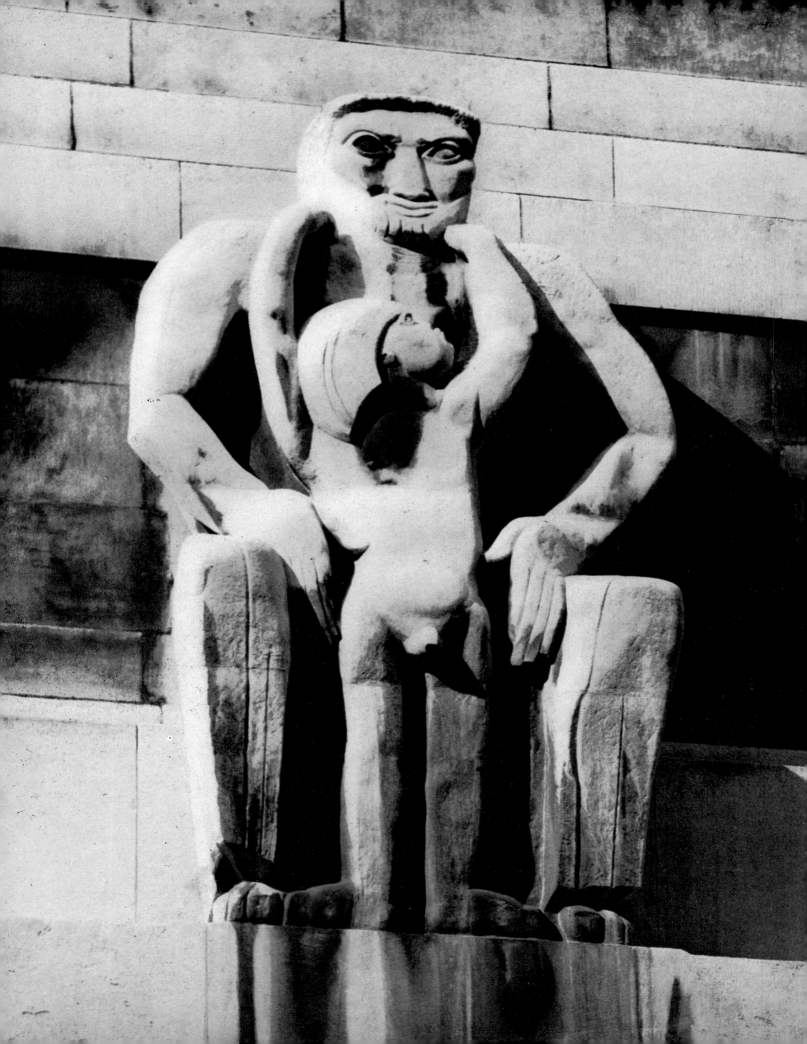

1930-39

MEN AND GODS

The 'twenties were over and Epstein had been in England for a quarter of a century. The last decade had seen the growth of the League of Nations, a General Strike, a total eclipse. *Ulysses* (1922), *The Waste Land* (1922), *A Passage to India* (1924), and *To the Lighthouse* (1927) had been published. Surrealism had happened. There had been great exhibitions of Dutch and Italian painting at Burlington House. Diaghilev's twenty-year reign had just ended with his death in Italy, where Mussolini was making the trains run on time.

Settled at 18 Hyde Park Gate, Epstein's life had now become one of steady routine. The execution of portrait commissions on which his livelihood depended in the absence of commissions for sculpture on public buildings, was varied with the making of studies of his family and of models who pleased him. Every Thursday night he took Kathleen out to dinner. Every year or so there was an exhibition. He would sometimes stay a few weeks in Epping Forest. Apart from a trip to Norfolk to model Einstein, and another to Paris to make notes for the backgrounds of his 'Fleurs du Mal' illustrations in 1938, and a third in the same year to receive his LL.D. at Aberdeen, I can find no record of journeys. No doubt he sometimes drove into the country on Sundays.

The stays in Epping Forest were responsible for a new departure: an immense output of illustrative drawings, landscapes and flower studies in watercolour. Exhibitions of Epstein's illustrations to the Old Testament were held at the Redfern Gallery in 1932, of landscapes of Epping Forest at Tooths and at the Redfern in 1933 and again at the Redfern in 1935, and of flower paintings at Tooths in 1936. Even in early New York days Epstein had been able to boast to Hapgood 'I could always sell my drawings'; and these series sold like hot cakes to a public which might have fled in terror from his sculpture. Though he turned out his landscapes and flower studies with immense facility and they sold well and proved a considerable addition to his income, it must be admitted that the majority were more effective than subtle. The interesting illustrations to Baudelaire, exhibited at Tooths in 1938, were less popular with the public.

To these series must be added those of nude studies of Sunita, Anita, Zeda and other exotic models, and the portrait sketches of Epstein's son Jackie, some of which were exhibited at the Leicester Galleries in 1939.

In 1931 appeared Arnold Haskell's record of his conversations with Epstein. By the end of the decade the sculptor would have written his autobiography.

The 'thirties would be a decade of monumental carvings, uncommissioned and at first sight unsaleable. 'Genesis' was exhibited at the Leicester Galleries in 1931 and greeted with derision; 'The Sun God' was completed and 'Primitive Gods' carved on its reverse and they were shown at the Leicester in 1933; 'Ecce Homo' was raised through the studio roof and transported to Leicester Square in 1935; 'Consummatum est' was shown in 1937 and 'Adam' in June 1939. All but the last of these returned unsold to the studio, and 'Adam' was bought for display in ignominious conditions.

Although Epstein threw himself wholeheartedly into any portrait commission he had undertaken and worked at it as if it were the last work he would ever do, it was inevitable, with a steady flow of sitters he did not know well personally and had not studied at leisure for long periods, that some of his heads should be much more interesting than others. What amazes us is that he maintained, with so large an output, the standard that he did. Among the outstanding portraits of the nineteen-thirties were those of Professor Donelly, Flaherty, Einstein, the 1935 Kathleen, Haile Selassie, Norman Hornstein and Betty Peters.

It must be remembered that Epstein stood outside the Bloomsbury group which ruled the left wing of the English art world, and whose prophet was Roger Fry. A tactless remark at a tea-party long ago had lost him the chance of becoming 'their' sculptor. Sickert he knew but rarely saw; though on one occasion they ran into each other at the Royal Academy and were followed round by an awe-struck crowd eager to catch their comments. Epstein and John had drifted apart. Only Matthew Smith remained a steady friend of the sculptor, and was so until his death. The double living-room at Hyde Park Gate was hung with glowing canvases by Smith, whom Epstein thought the only English painter with guts.

258 HANS KINDLER

HANS KINDLER, of whom at this time Epstein made a subtle, wide-eyed portrait, was a friend of at least ten years' standing. A cellist and the brother-in-law of Van Dieren, he later became director of an American orchestra.

He, Van Dieren and Cecil Gray had been with Epstein when in 1921 he first set eyes on Kathleen Garman, seated with her sister, reading Dostoevsky's *Brothers*, in the Harlequin Club.

[171]

259   ISOBEL POWYS
260   JOAN GREENWOOD (AS A CHILD)
261   TIRRENIA (MRS. GERRARD)

ISOBEL POWYS was the daughter of Powys, the architect, and niece of the three celebrated writers. Her family commissioned her bust, and T. C. Powys was eager to have one of himself too, but this was never realised.

Joan Greenwood, the daughter of a painter and professor of art, was a childhood friend of Peggy Jean and lived with her parents in the old studios of Manresa Road in nearby Chelsea. The 1930 portrait of JOAN GREENWOOD AS A CHILD may be compared with her later likeness (Plate 485).

The bust of Mrs. Gerrard, known as TIRRENIA, also made in 1930, is interesting as being the only portrait by Epstein in which the head hangs down sideways over one

261

259

260

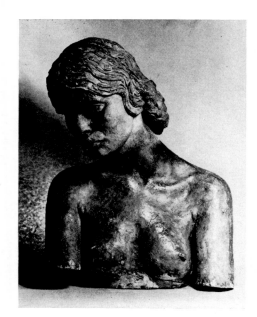

262

262 TIRRENIA (MRS. GERRARD)
263 LITTLE EILEEN
264 GERMAINE BRAS

263

shoulder. This mournful angle of the head, combined with the model's private-looking features, her wrapt expression and gently waving hair parted in the middle and gathered at the nape, give to the work an air of elegiac distinction.

LITTLE EILEEN, so-called to distinguish her from the bust of Eileen Proudfoot, was a girl who was temporarily adopted as a companion for Peggy Jean.

Of GERMAINE BRAS, a French sempstress, the sculptor made a head larger than life. His reason for magnifying her was probably that he saw in her some sturdy peasant quality which struck him as specially French; he saw her as Marianne, as France.

264

The *Blackbirds* revue had set a fashion for coloured entertainers. In 1930 Epstein modelled the portraits of two sisters, REBECCA and ESTHER, who were half Negro and half Jewish and worked in nightclubs. Rebecca, with her pigtails and her plaintive expression, seems a more introspective character than the sultry and provocative Esther.

In MAY GOLDIE, the mixture of Negro and Jewish blood produced a striking physiognomy, and the sculptor caught her expression of brooding and sensuous melancholy.

Of Lydia, yet another coloured girl, Epstein was to make three studies. The FIRST PORTRAIT OF LYDIA, free from overemphasis, is one of the best bronzes of this period.

265

265 REBECCA
266 BETTY (ESTHER)
267 MAY GOLDIE

266

In 1930 Epstein completed his carving 'Genesis', which had been begun in Epping Forest before his trip to America. While his bronze 'Visitation' had portrayed an ordinary woman glorified by wonder at the thought of her unborn child, and was treated realistically, the marble was to be a primeval Lilith hatching the world in her womb and she would be carved with a massive simplicity befitting the mother of mankind.

'I felt the necessity for giving expression to the profoundly elemental in motherhood, the deep down instinctive female, without the trappings and charm of what is known as feminine.... The figure from the base upward, beginning just under [*sic*] the knees, seems to rise from the earth itself. From that the broad thighs and buttock

267

97

268 1ST PORTRAIT OF LYDIA   [175]

269. 270 GENESIS

ascend, base solid and permanent for her who is to be the bearer of man. She feels within herself the child moving, her hand instinctively and soothingly placed where it can feel this enclosed new life so closely bound with herself. The expression of the head is one of calm, mindless wonder. . . . How a figure like this contrasts with our coquetries and fanciful erotic nudes of modern sculpture. At one blow, whole generations of sculptors and sculpture are shattered and sent flying into the limbo of triviality, and my "Genesis", with her fruitful womb, confronts our enfeebled generation.'

The mother's slit eyes and concave nose recall the African masks which Picasso had discovered in the Museum of Historic Sculpture at the Trocadéro in 1907 four years later than Epstein, and which had inspired the faces of the two right-hand women in his 'Demoiselles d'Avignon' and other paintings; and these elongations of African sculpture became the hallmark of Modigliani's art. Now, Epstein, who had been an enthusiastic collector of primitive carving for twenty years and had assimilated their lessons, combined in a single work the stark directness of Africa with the idealism and technical finesse of a Michelangelo. GENESIS with her masklike face, her stylised plaits of hair, her hunched back so finely rendered, her delicate arms ending in huge square hands, and her epic thighs, is indeed a daring mixture of the primitive and the sophisticated, the realistic and the monumentally symbolic: but the artist's genius carried him serenely through the shoals of danger, and he made a masterpiece.

When exhibited at the Leicester Galleries in 1931,

M

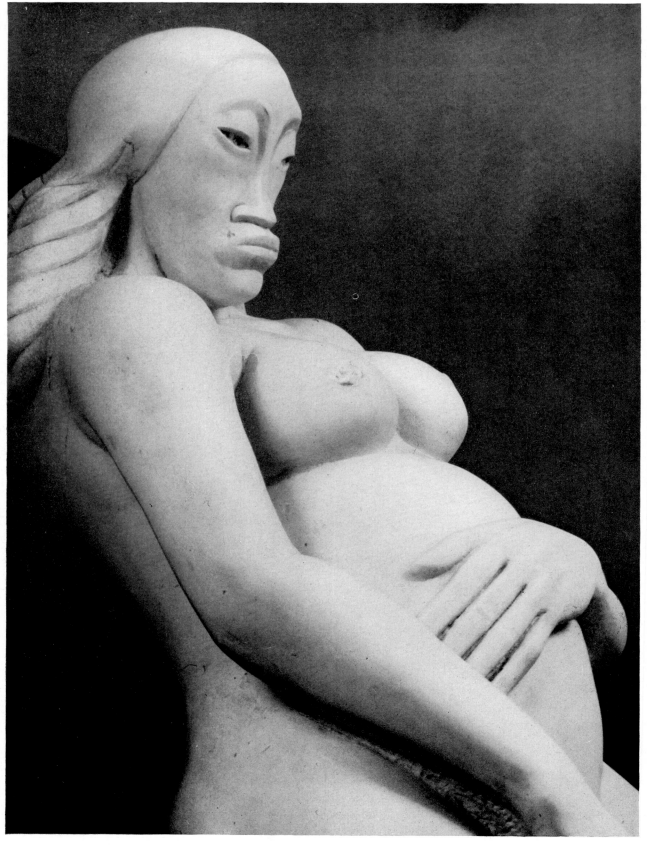

271. 272 GENESIS

274
ISRAFEL (SUNITA)

'Genesis' provoked a fiercer storm even than had become usual. 'Mongolian moron that is obscene. . . . Oh you white foulness!' — *Daily Express*. 'Epstein's latest and his worst' — *Daily Mail*. 'A statue unfit to show' — *Daily Telegraph*. Wilenski defended it in the *Observer*.

The statue was not sold at the show, and the Tate Gallery refused it as a loan. It returned to the studio. It was in c. 1931 bought by Sir Alfred (now Lord) Bossom, who offered it on loan to the Tate Gallery, who refused it. He made large sums of money for various good causes by showing it in public, then sold it again at Sotheby's for £4,200 in 1958. It was bought by Louis Tussauds of Blackpool. This firm already possessed 'Adam', 'Consummatum est' and 'Jacob and the Angel'. 'Genesis'

joined them in the basement room where they were shown to holiday-makers. The four carvings were bought by Lord Harewood and Mr. I. J. Lyons in February 1961.

In 1930 Epstein again modelled Sunita, this time calling her somewhat idealised bust ISRAFEL. Her expression is serene and angelic in contrast to her previous portraits, which were more tragic in mood. Her hair, now waved, falls down her back. Her neck is shortened to make her more masculine. Her eyes are scooped out hollows, with the result that she has a godlike rather than a human gaze. This work would twelve years later serve as a model for the big statue of 'Lucifer'.

In 1930 also after twenty years, Epstein began work again on his 'Sun God'.

[181]

273 SUN GOD (UNFINISHED)

The following year finds Sunita still a regular visitor to the studio, if not a resident in the house, and Epstein continued to make drawings and watercolours of her. In 1931 he modelled her half life-size in the nude and called the result RECLINING GODDESS. It seems possible that the sculptor intended to include Enver and make a group like one of his many 'Indian Mother and Son' drawings, for Sunita appears to be on the point of turning over in bed, and her big head lolls on her right shoulder as her eyes fix on something which was perhaps her son. Epstein broke off modelling just below her knees and added a sort of

wave — or is it a rug? — to finish the study off. The effect is perfunctory and awkward.

This is Sunita's last personal appearance in these pages, though her memory will inspire the tragic masks of 'Lucifer' and the seated Mother in 'Social Consciousness' years later. One of her exploits was to disguise herself as an Indian prince and come with a retinue to a restaurant where Epstein was dining with Kathleen Garman. She was curious to observe the Muse; and though Epstein and Kathleen watched her spectacular entrance, neither recognised her. Sunita fell in love with

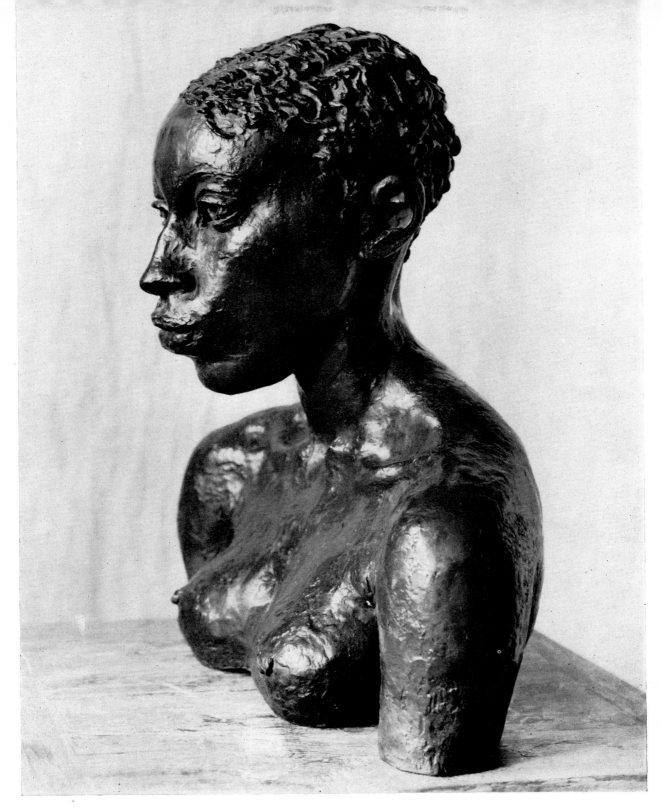

276 2ND PORTRAIT OF LYDIA

an illusionist who was supposed to have invented the trick of sawing women in half. She went on tour with him and was sawn in half all over the country. Finally she disappeared with the secretary of a maharajah into the heart of India, and nothing more was heard of her except a report of her death. Her great brooding eyes look down on Birmingham, Philadelphia and New York.

Epstein made a SECOND PORTRAIT OF LYDIA (SHINGLED), showing the pretty Negro model with a fashionable short haircut.

[183]

277
MRS. CHESTER BEATTY

278
MRS. SONIA HEATH

279
MRS. BETTY JOEL
(LA BELLE JUIVE)

280
DR. CRAMER

281
ELLEN JANSEN

282
MALCOLM BENDON

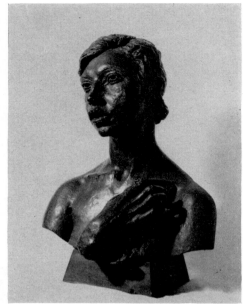

Now follow a mixed bag of portraits made in 1931.

MRS. CHESTER BEATTY was a well-known collector, whose collection of Impressionist and other paintings the sculptor went to see in Kensington Palace Gardens. When she commissioned her head he was pleased to think it would keep company with Van Gogh's 'Peasant in a Straw hat'. She bought other bronzes by Epstein.

The bust of MRS. SONIA HEATH with her right hand on her chest was commissioned by a London dealer and is now in the Walker Art Gallery, Liverpool.

The bust of BETTY JOEL, exhibited as 'La Belle Juive', was a work which worried Epstein and with which he was never satisfied. He tried adding earrings and elaborate necklaces in an attempt to give it something he felt it lacked, and the portrait went through several versions.

DR. CRAMER was engaged on cancer research. After his work he liked to sit in the Café Royal and talk to artists and their models. Epstein knew the doctor for some years before Cramer asked him to model his head.

The attractive catlike features of ELLEN JANSEN, enclosed in a helmet of bobbed hair, were modelled about the time her husband Maurice Browne directed *Othello* with Paul Robeson in the leading role.

The head of MALCOLM BENDON was commissioned by his mother, and Epstein enjoyed capturing the sitter's fine bone structure and noble proportions.

279   280   281

283 PROFESSOR LUCY DONELLY   [186]

284

285

The portrait bust of PROFESSOR LUCY DONELLY was one of the most successful Epstein executed at this period. The American Lucy Donelly, a distinguished scholar and essayist, was, from 1911 to 1936, a Professor of English at Bryn Mawr near Philadelphia, the most famous girls' school in the United States of America. Her bust was commissioned by Miss Edith Finch, a former pupil, who later became the wife of Bertrand Russell. The Professor recited poetry under her breath while posing, and when Epstein asked her what it was she replied 'Atalanta in Calydon'. The sitter's character is remarkably well conveyed; her wide, frank eyes which would be so quick to detect humbug, her fine hair parted in the middle and sweeping in natural waves back to her bun, the scholar's slight stoop, the capable patrician hand, the spirals of her blouse's silk sleeve — all these contribute a vivid impression of a likeable personality.

The face of MARY BLANDFORD interested Epstein as being like a Gothic saint or madonna, the possible starting for one of his religious groups.

The THIRD PORTRAIT OF KATHLEEN showed her in a wistful, dreaming mood. The sculptor has modelled a suggestion of the flower pattern printed on her light summer dress.

YOUNG PAUL ROBESON was the son of Paul Robeson.

284 MARY BLANDFORD
285 3RD PORTRAIT OF KATHLEEN
286 PAUL ROBESON JNR.

286

287 ELEMENTAL   [188]

288

In 1930 Epstein had written to Kathleen Garman from his cottage in Epping Forest, 'It is raining all the time. I have nothing to read except an old bible. I keep reading Genesis and have made some drawings.' This has been the beginning of his celebrated series of illustrations to the Old Testament, which were exhibited at the Redfern Gallery in 1932. In that year the sculptor rented Deerhurst, a larger cottage at Loughton; and the Forest, which was in the following years to inspire a great number of watercolour landscapes, also put into Epstein's head the idea of carving several primitive woodland spirits or demons. In this Forest which had been a forest since England was all forest, he heard ancient voices.

The first of these carvings, ELEMENTAL, though left rough and never quite finished, is impressive as a shape in alabaster and as a demonstration of how a mood —

290

almost a story — can be conveyed simply by the handling of masses. It reminds one of an anecdotal boss in a Gothic cloister, several times enlarged. There emerged from the stone a huddled, fearful creature, clutching his knees to his chin and keeping his eyes tight closed against the whistling winds of Hell.

Carved out of paler alabaster, CHIMERA was an even stranger conception. Was it intended as a gargoyle to be attached to a building? The disembodied neck and head, terminating in a mask of fearful surmise, seem to be eddying doubtfully and mindlessly round corners, like a fish among rocks.

In 1929, while Epstein had been carving 'Day' and 'Night' on the Underground Headquarters building, the thirty-one year old Henry Moore had worked on a successful flying figure representing one of the winds high up on the tower above. Epstein admired the younger man's work, and in April 1931 wrote a note in the catalogue of Moore's exhibition of sculpture and drawings at the Leicester Galleries. In the future they would go very different ways, but because of their mutual respect, perhaps because of the admiration for Mexican sculpture they had in common and because Epstein's 'Woman possessed', the third of his carvings made at Deerhurst in Epping Forest, was the only one of his works that could be mistaken for one of Moore's, their careers may

[191]

289. 290 CHIMERA

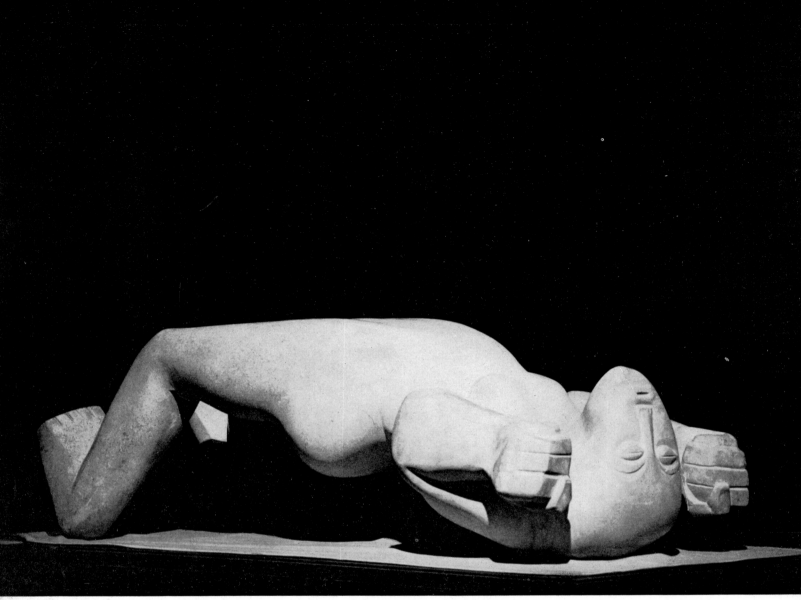

291

be said in 1931 and 1932 to have converged: so it is of interest to quote what Epstein wrote of Moore.

'Before these works I ponder in silence. The imagination stretches itself in vast disproportions, and by impressive outline throws the shadow of our fears upon the background of space; new shapes, growths of our subconsciousness, fill the atmosphere; robust expression of secret forces ready to burst forth on earth.

'If sculpture is truly "the relation of the masses" here is the example for all to see: Henry Moore by his integrity to the central idea of sculpture calls all sculptors to his side. What is so clearly expressed is a vision rich in sculptural invention, avoiding the banalities of abstraction, and concentrating upon those enduring elements that constitute great sculpture.'

Epstein owned several of Moore's carvings, two of which, the 'Mother and Child' in Cumberland alabaster (Hirshhorn Collection, New York) and the alabaster 'Suckling Child' (Herbert Marks Collection, London), were in the Leicester Galleries Exhibition.

Epstein's WOMAN POSSESSED was carved in Hopton Wood stone, a favourite material of Moore's. The woman, who seems to be consummating her union with a god, lies back clenching her fists, with body arched upward in a pose reminiscent of Lydia Sokolova at the climax of Massine's version of Stravinsky's 'Le Sacre du printemps'. Epstein had seen this ballet at Covent Garden in 1929. The features are incised in a way similar to those of Moore's 'Woman with upraised arms' of 1924–5, a figure which, even if she is only yawning, can be compared to Epstein's in that both are tensed and in the throes of some kind of physical abandon.

291. 292. 293
WOMAN
POSSESSED

294 1ST PORTRAIT
OF ISOBEL

It was natural that, once having met her, Epstein should be fascinated by the exotic features of Isobel Nicholas, a young art student. She had something of that Nefertiti look which he particularly admired. His FIRST BUST OF ISOBEL, though a fine work, now appears in the nature of a first sketch for the more resplendent and celebrated portrait he modelled in the following year.

In 1932 Epstein also made his THIRD BUST OF ORIEL. Apart from professional models and beauties, such as Dolores and Sunita, of whom he made numerous studies, Epstein would often find a woman who sat so well and so patiently and whose features presented him with such intriguing problems that he would want to work from her more than once. Of Oriel Ross, we have seen, he made

295 3RD PORTRAIT OF
      ORIEL ROSS

FOR COMPARISON
296. 297. 298
1ST, 2ND, 3RD PORTRAITS OF
    ORIEL ROSS

295

296

297

298

[195]

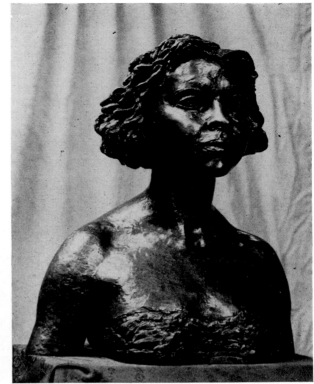

300

301

299 1ST PORTRAIT OF LOUISE
300 AHMED
301 HARRIET HOCHTER
302 1ST PORTRAIT OF ROMA OF BARBADOS

three portraits. He was demanding of his sitters, expecting them to be punctual and patient, in fact to give up whole periods of their lives in the cause of art. The good models were always sorry when sittings came to an end. But a girl only had to pose once for Epstein to become known as an 'Epstein model'. To be an 'Epstein model' between the wars was a claim to fame and a passport to publicity.

The FIRST PORTRAIT OF LOUISE, a bust, is most remarkable for the way the sculptor has caught her expression of melancholy brooding, as she chews over the cud of some problem in her mind.

AHMED, with her large placid features, her smooth hair and her draped shoulders, was an Arab dancer from Cardiff. Another individualistic dancer was the American HARRIET HOCHTER, of whom Epstein made a bust with bare shoulders in 1932. She did a 'rainbow dance' with floating scarves in coloured lighting, and was brought to the studio by Arnold Haskell, who admired her work. Roma was a coloured girl who posed professionally. The FIRST PORTRAIT OF ROMA, a head, showed her looking up wraptly, like Paul Robeson.

[198]

304

305

303 FOURTEENTH PORTRAIT OF PEGGY JEAN (JEUNESSE)
304 ROSE
305 ARTHUR NICOLLE
306 2ND PORTRAIT OF ROMA OF BARBADOS

In 1932 Epstein made the FOURTEENTH PORTRAIT OF PEGGY JEAN, a bust with arms. At fifteen the much modelled eldest daughter had become a buxom jovial woman. As in 'The Sick Child' she holds her arms out before her, but they no longer form the base to a drooping head.

ROSE was a mulatto girl, discovered in the chorus of a little coloured revue at the Chelsea Palace. She had a sweet, mournful expression and sang Negro Spirituals.

A successful commission of 1932 was the bust of ARTHUR NICOLLE, a Jersey landowner, whose aristocratic features clearly appealed to the sculptor. He has in his possession a letter from Epstein written in the following year asking to borrow the bust for an exhibition as he reckoned it among his best pieces and relied on it to 'confound the critics'.

In 1933 the sculptor modelled a SECOND PORTRAIT OF ROMA, this time a bust showing the top part of the arms. Her scooped-out eyeballs gaze leftwards. Her high cheek-bones give her face a peculiarly satisfying form.

306

307

307 ROBERT FLAHERTY
308 EPSTEIN WITH
   ROBERT FLAHERTY
309 MAN OF ARAN
   ('TIGER' KING)

308

It was while he was making the film *Man of Aran* that
ROBERT FLAHERTY asked Epstein to model his head.
The director was also something of an explorer and he
had in common with the sculptor an interest in so-called
'primitive' peoples. The portrait turned out to be one of
Epstein's subtlest — and at the same time grandest —
heads; and this is the more remarkable in that Flaherty,
though he had a powerful personality, was a fat man, and
the character of his face would be so much harder to
search out. It is a heroic portrait, the portrait of a
visionary, the portrait of an Irishman.

When the Irish fisherman, 'Tiger' King, came to
London for the showing of Flaherty's film, in which
he had been the principal character, the director brought
him to Epstein to be modelled. The resulting work,
called MAN OF ARAN, was a fine rugged study.

[200]

309

310

310 PRIMEVAL GODS
311 SUN GOD

311

When the shed in Emerald Street, Bloomsbury, near the old Guildford Street house, was about to be pulled down, Epstein had moved the big block of Hopton Wood stone containing the unfinished SUN GOD to Hyde Park Gate, and begun working on it again after twenty years. Seeing the block standing free in the space of a large studio and having an innate dislike of a blank surface, he was seized with the urge to carve the reverse side also. The resulting relief he called PRIMITIVE GODS, and it was carved in his 'primitive' style. It represented a male deity, nearly three-quarter length, with squarish, flat-topped head and incised Mexican-style features (like 'Woman possessed'), — huge hunched shoulders and hands clenched outwards. Across the belly of this impassive being there tumble two squat little godlets, their legs and arms extended in circular loops which might suggest ballet if their tubular limbs were not squashed into a stylised pattern more reminiscent of Fernand Léger at his crudest.

Meanwhile the more elegant SUN GOD, on the obverse, was finished at last. The reliefs were exhibited in 1933 at the Leicester Galleries, and are now in the garden of Miss Sally Ryan's house, High Perch Farm, George Town, Connecticut.

A severe, commissioned portrait of the film magnate ISIDORE OSTRER led to this sitter ordering a head of his friend LORD BEAVERBROOK. 'The Canadian peer entered my studio one morning very like the stage hero in a musical comedy, dramatic and breezy. . . .'

Also modelled in 1933 was the handsome BASIL BURTON, a nephew of Lord Rothermere, in whose bust, with its bare chest and shoulders, Epstein, always eager to try something new, extended the left arm from the body, cutting it off just above the elbow.

A bust of JOHN GIELGUD, then enjoying his first great success in 'Richard of Bordeaux' was commissioned by a female admirer. A photograph of this turned up recently, but both plaster and bronze have been lost sight of.

The sculptor had thought his third portrait of Kathleen made her look too sad, so in 1933 he determined to make a FOURTH PORTRAIT OF KATHLEEN, this time smiling. The strange work cannot be called unsuccessful, but it verges on the grotesque.

NEANDER was a model from the Middle East.

BELLE CRAMER, the artist wife of the cancer researcher whom Epstein had modelled two years before, was a colourful contrast to her saturnine-looking husband.

312

314

312   ISIDORE OSTRER
313   LORD BEAVERBROOK
314   BASIL BURTON

313

315 JOHN GIELGUD
316 4TH PORTRAIT OF KATHLEEN
317 NEANDER
318 MRS. BELLE CRAMER

315

316

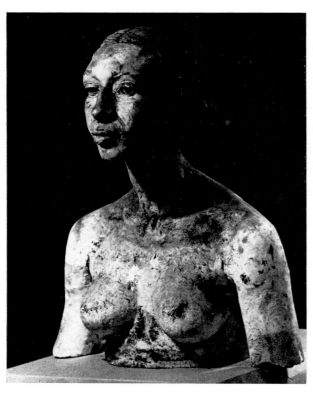

317

318

In 1933 Epstein modelled the portraits of two famous Jews. Of DR. WEIZMANN, the architect of the new state of Israel, he made a powerful bust whose scooped-out eye-sockets seem to hold more than mundane vision; while of ALBERT EINSTEIN he made a head which was little more than a mask, though it proved one of his most extraordinary portraits. Both works were executed in the sculptor's bold impressionistic manner.

Einstein had left Nazi Germany, fearing assassination, and come to England, where Commander Oliver Locker-Lampson provided him with a retreat in a camp near Cromer. Epstein was sent for to make a portrait of him. From Cromer the sculptor 'was driven out to the camp situated in a secluded and wild spot very near the sea'.

'Einstein appeared dressed very comfortably in a pull-over with his wild hair floating in the wind. His glance contained a mixture of the humane, the humorous and the profound. This was a combination that delighted me. He resembled the ageing Rembrandt. . . .

'I worked for two hours every morning, and at the first sitting the Professor was so surrounded with tobacco smoke from his pipe that I saw nothing. At the second sitting I asked him to smoke in the interval.

'Einstein watched my work with a kind of naive wonder, and seemed to sense that I was doing something good of him, . . . but, as so often happens, the work had to be stopped before I had carried it to completion.'

Not only did the illustrious model resemble Rembrandt: in none of his works was Epstein more Rembrandtesque.

319   DR. CHAIM
       WEIZMANN

320   PROF. ALBERT
       EINSTEIN

319

320

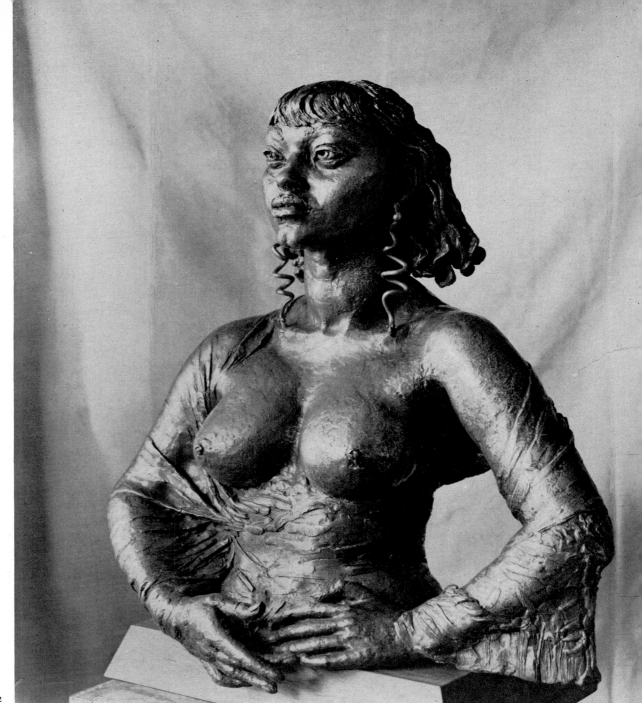

321. 322
2ND PORTRAIT
OF ISOBEL

321   322

In 1933 Epstein made the bust of a girl which, with her exotic features, her bare breasts, her flamboyant pose, her Spanish shawl and her corkscrew ear-rings — in fact with all the stage properties of a vulgar painter who turns out souvenirs of Spain for tourists who will never go there — might well have been an artistic disaster: but the SECOND PORTRAIT OF ISOBEL was a triumph.

The sculptor's mastery shows itself in the way that, observing narrowly every minute gradation of plane and outline, he knows by instinct or experience just where to exaggerate the curl of a lip, the length of a neck, the elegance of a waist or wrist, the outward jut of a breast. Isobel's asymmetrical shoulders, the interesting gap between her body and her left elbow, her hands with which Epstein had taken more trouble than usual, the crazy ear-rings, and the fringe which recalls Dolores — all contribute towards a picture of savage sophistication.

Isobel Nicholas married in turn Sefton Delmer, the political journalist, and the composers Constant Lambert and Alan Rawsthorne. She became a painter of repute and designed two ballets, 'Tiresias' (1951) and 'Madame Chrysanthème' (1955).

o

323 BERNARD SHAW

Of the portrait of BERNARD SHAW, the sculptor wrote 'I think that there are in it elements so subtle that they would be difficult to explain.

'Shaw sat on condition that I was commissioned to do the work. He thought I ought to benefit materially and not just do his bust for its own sake. Orage arranged a commission for me from Mrs. Blanche Grant, an American. Shaw sat with exemplary patience and even eagerness. He walked to my studio every day, and was punctual and conscientious. He wisecracked of course.

324 2ND PORTRAIT OF
     RAMSAY MACDONALD

In matters of Art he aired definite opinions, mostly wrong.

'Throughout my life in England, Shaw was an outspoken champion of my work . . . I will not say that he understood what I have made. He seemed deficient in all sense of the plastic, but had a lively notion of how stupid the newspapers can be over new works. . . . He was generous to young talent.'

After reading Epstein's autobiography, Shaw wrote him a long letter which began by describing his previous sittings to Rodin, Paul Troubetskoy, Jo Davison and Strobl. 'Your first sketch,' he wrote, '. . . is a brilliant thumbnail version of me as I am. Then you went on to perform marvels of modelling on lips and cheeks and mouth with all the mastery that makes your busts precious. But you had also to introduce your theories with which you are obsessed; and here you are recklessly mendacious. I became a Brooklyn navvy in your hands. . . . My wife . . . said that if that bust came into our house she would walk out of it. . . .'

A casting of the head without the shoulders is reproduced here, and it has been mounted with a backward tilt which results in a more spiritual expression. In the bust the head was set squarely on the bare shoulders.

By the time Epstein modelled the SECOND PORTRAIT OF RAMSAY MACDONALD, the sitter had become the first Socialist Prime Minister, had grown fatter and lost his eager look. The sculptor was surprised to learn that MacDonald carried a 'fountain pen' filled with vitriol to use against possible assassins.

[211]

'Sometimes', wrote the sculptor, 'the sitter impresses his or her own conception of themselves upon the artist. This can never result in a successful work — one that renders the character of the model.' HUGH WALPOLE was apparently one of these. 'He insisted on sitting for me like a Pharaoh, with head held high and chin stuck out. In reality, Sir Hugh was the most genial of men with sparkling, twinkling humour in his eye, and his mouth wreathed in a kindly and genial smile. But with the rigidity of Sir Hugh's pose I could do nothing. . . . It was Sir Hugh Walpole in the role of Benito Mussolini.'

The author of the *Rogue Herries* saga and of so many popular novels had a number of Epstein works in his collection. He had signed a petition to prevent 'Rima' from being removed from Hyde Park.

Two other sitters in 1934, eminent in the world of the arts, were MICHAEL BALCON, a pioneer of British film production (whose daughter Jill would also be modelled by Epstein in 1948), and EMLYN WILLIAMS, already famous as an actor and for his play *The Corn is Green*. He would later write in *George* one of the most remarkable autobiographies of his generation. Epstein modelled with verve but without overstatement the eager, intelligent features of the young Welshman.

325

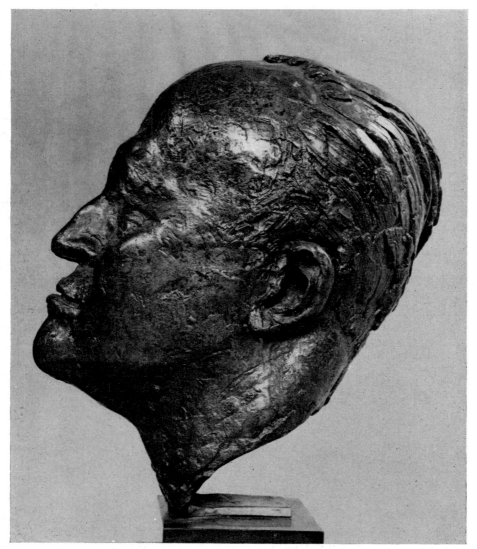

325 MICHAEL BALCON
326 HUGH WALPOLE
327 EMLYN WILLIAMS

326

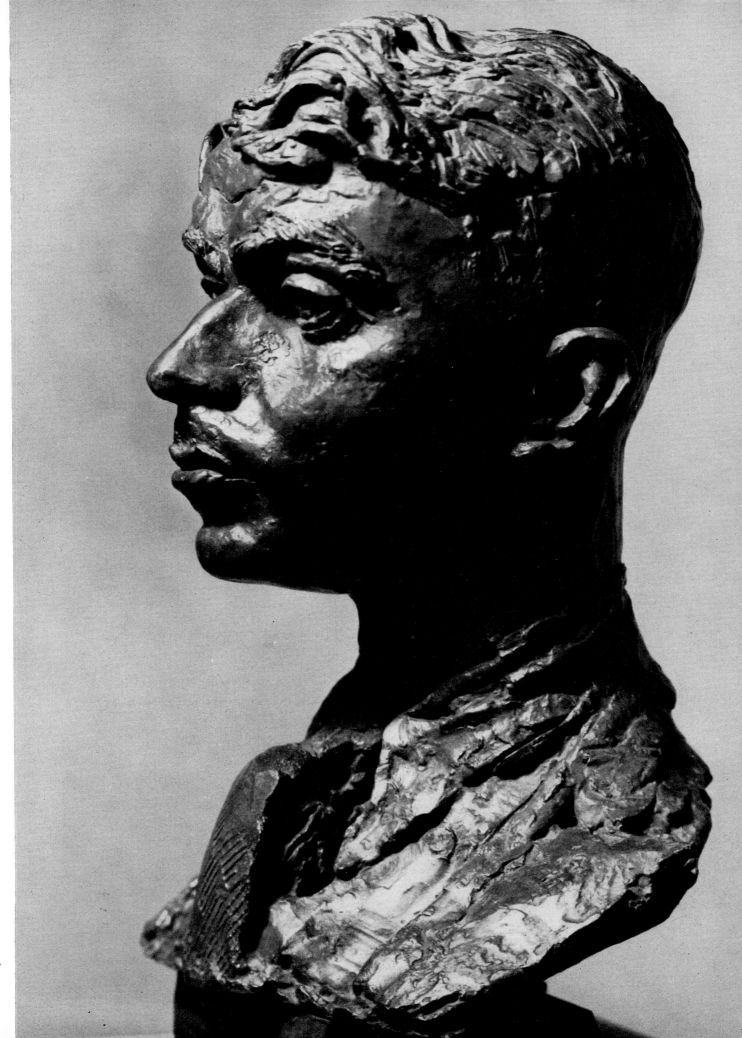

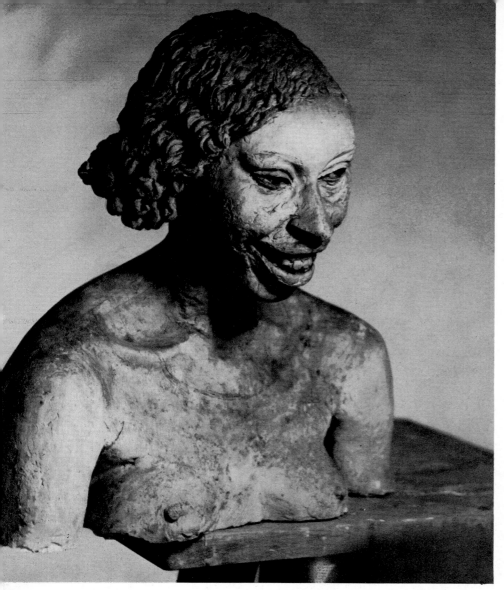

328   3RD PORTRAIT OF LYDIA
329   OLIVE
330   RANI RAMA

328

If Roman or rococo sculptors could portray the face in movement as well as the body, Epstein was confident that this difficult skill — to model features distorted by laughter or tears — was not beyond his power. We have seen how in 1923 he made 'The Weeping Woman', and brought off a striking work, though it bordered on the grotesque. He had made in 1932 the curious smiling portrait of Kathleen; and was throughout his life to try to catch the fleeting moods of children, from laughter to gravity. In the THIRD PORTRAIT OF LYDIA (LAUGHING), a bust, he came near to the absurd. The gentle features of the Negress are contorted by a tremendous toothy grin.

Another coloured girl, the sweet-faced OLIVE, was about eleven when her parents brought her to the door as a prospective model, and Epstein made a careful head of her, looking down.

Of the Siamese mannequin and dancer RANI RAMA, with her downcast eyes and pomegranate mouth Epstein made a nude bust which seems lapped around by the scented calm of the seraglio.

329   330

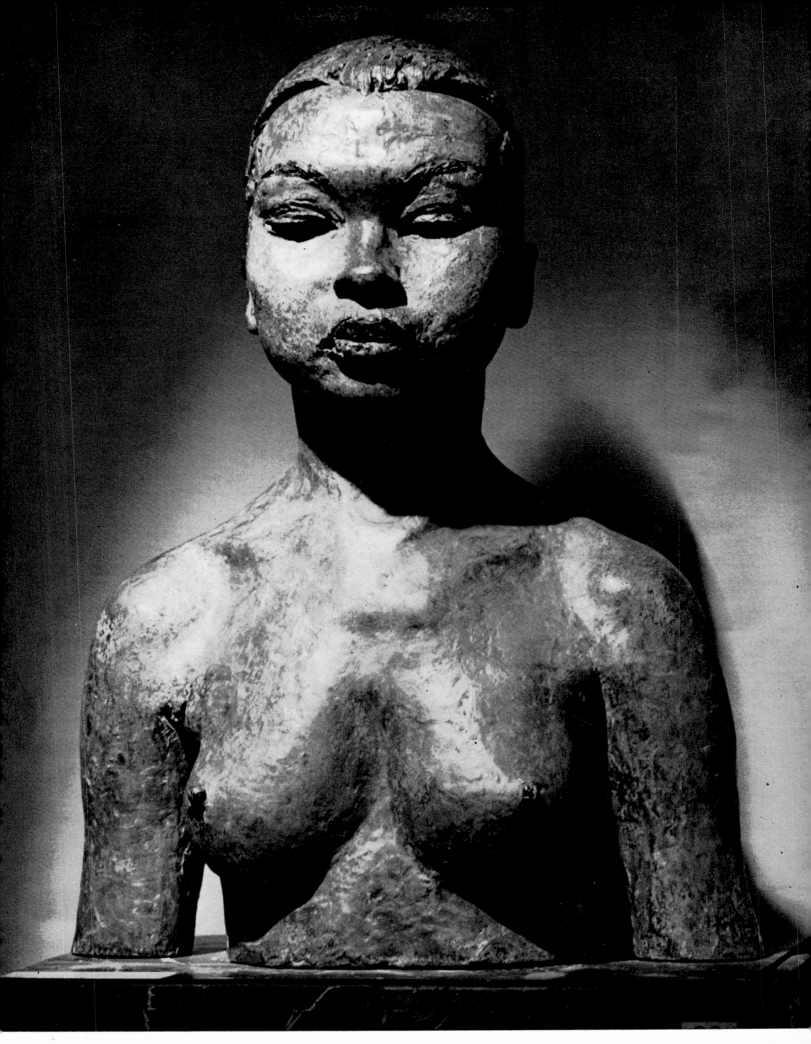

331

331 M. S. MYERS
332 HIRAM HALLE

332

[216]

The stockbroker M. S. MYERS was so pleased with the portrait bust Epstein made of him in 1933, wearing a carnation in his buttonhole, that he ordered several copies of it for his friends.

HIRAM HALLE was an American oil magnate of a kindly genial nature. At the time his portrait, a small bust without shoulders, was made, Epstein found himself more than usually hard up because of spending more than he could afford on his collection of primitive sculpture; Hallé offered to lend him some money and never asked for repayment, though the sum was paid to his heirs after his death. The sculptor loved his portrait of Hallé and had a copy made for himself. Studying it he would exclaim 'What humanity in his face! Rembrandt would have worked from him.'

Throughout 1934 and into 1935 Epstein was working on what was to be his biggest and possibly greatest carving — ECCE HOMO.

'At the stone-yard I see a tremendous block of marble about to be sliced up and used for interior decoration. When I see these great monoliths lying ready for the butcher's hands, as it were, I instantly have sentimental feelings of pity that the fate of a noble block of stone should be so ignominious. Knowing that this stone could contain a wonderful statue moves me to purchase it and rescue it, even though at the moment I have no definite idea for it. . . . This Subiaco block of marble, when I carved it, I found the toughest, most difficult piece of stone I had ever tackled. All the tools I had broke on it, and it was only after trying out endless "points", as they are called, with different toolmakers that I finally hit upon a "point" that resisted, and began to make an impression on the stone. I wished to make an "Ecce Homo", a symbol of man, bound, crowned with thorns and facing with a relentless and overmastering gaze of pity and prescience our unhappy world. Because of the hardness of the material I treated the work in a large way, with a juxtaposition of flat planes, always with a view to retaining the impression of the original block. Matthew Smith on seeing the statue in my studio said: "You have made a heavy stone seem heavier" — a profound comment. The plastic aim was always of paramount importance and the "preaching" side secondary, or rather, the idea, the subject, was so clear and simple to me, that, once having decided on it, I gave myself up wholly to a realization of lines and planes, what our critics are fond of calling "the formal relations" . . . I look at the work and feel that it confronts time and eternity.'

The statue is most impressive when seen full on from the front: looking at it from a distance of, say, thirty feet, one is amazed at the way the sculptor has contained his

333 EPSTEIN WITH 'ECCE HOMO'

image of suffering in the exact shape of the stone block. Only two nicks at the sides where Christ's waist is suggested below his elbows interrupt the outline of the rectangle. The contrast between the immutable simplicity of this monolith and the drama created by the deep shadows where the marble is cut away under the chin and hands is the chief reason for 'Ecce Homo's' powerful impact; and this contrast between the figure's architectural, columnar nature and its human pathos is the most surprising and novel thing about it. The figure, seen from the front, is an oblong relief ready, so to speak, to be framed, yet the head and hands project, carved in the round. The price to be paid for this paradoxically brilliant effect is that the figure loses its meaning when seen in profile. A criticism levelled at Epstein's big carvings is that they are not conceived in the round, and only make sense from one side. This is true in some cases, and the defect is no doubt a legacy of the Strand statues commission, and of 'Day' and 'Night', all works which adorned the face of buildings. Epstein might have admitted this fact to himself, just as he owned that he had not allowed for enough length at the base, so that the legs and feet of the figure are unduly compressed and only perfunctorily suggested. 'Ecce Homo' would be best shown in a gap in a wall.

I wrote of 'Night' that it was reduced to a face, a mood and a gesture. The same could be said of this 'Ecce Homo'. The hands bound with cord are symbolic, like the

[218]

hushing hand of 'Night'; the mood induced is that of catharsis, a purging by pity and terror; the face is a mask of tragedy. Christ's lips are stiff with pain, but his eyes, beneath the contracted brow and the crown of thorns, are wide with compassion for the sufferings of generations yet unborn. Criticism fades into silence before the gaze of this rocky Christ, who could only have been conceived by an artist of supreme genius.

After being exhibited at the Leicester Galleries in 1935, the statue returned unsold to the studio. It was still there at the time of the sculptor's death.

In 1958 the rector of Selby Abbey, Yorkshire, wrote to Epstein asking him to leave the sculpture to Selby in his will. Epstein saw no reason to wait till his death to give his work to the church: he travelled to Selby, was delighted with the Abbey and agreed to present 'Ecce Homo'. The Council for the Care of Churches were unanimously in favour, but a Mr. Wigglesworth, Chancellor for the Abbey, was opposed. A petition against the work was organized and the grand plan failed.

In 1935 Epstein made the last study of his eldest child, FIFTEENTH PORTRAIT OF PEGGY JEAN, a bust, and his earliest study of his latest born child, FIRST PORTRAIT OF JACKIE, a bust with dancing arms.

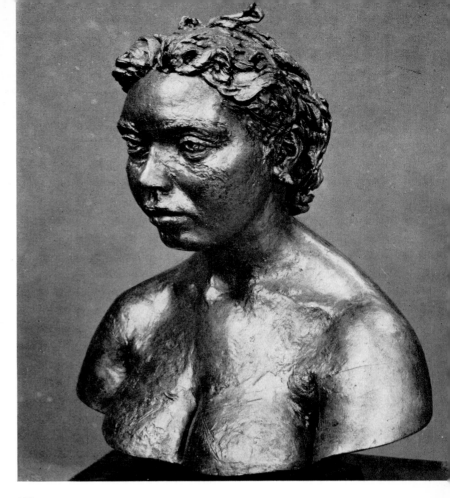

337

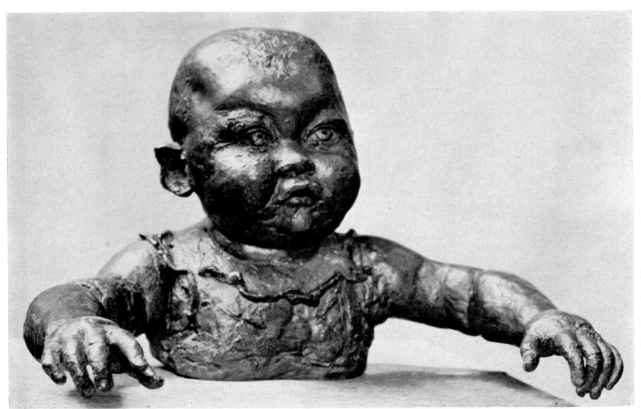

336 ECCE HOMO
337 LAST PORTRAIT
     OF PEGGY JEAN
338 1ST PORTRAIT OF JACKIE

338

Epstein was thinking of the FIFTH PORTRAIT OF KATHLEEN, surely one of his greatest works, when he wrote the following account of the way he set about a new and exciting task:

'The sculptor is to model a bust and the beautiful sitter has arrived. . . . Imagine him then in a state in which critical analysis of the form and emotional exaltation are present, at the same time. To the exclusion of all else his vision is concentrated on the model, and he begins (a state of high nervous tension). His searching and loving eye roams over the soft contours of the face and is caught by the edges of the brow enclosing the eyes, and so to the cheek-bones, and then downwards past the mouth and nose. The mask is lightly fixed and the salient points established. This mask is arrested by the twin points of the ears. Behind, the mass of hair from above the brow and falling to the shoulders is then indicated by broad and sketchy additions of clay, without particular definition, merely a note to be taken up later. Return to the mask, the expression of the eyes, and the shape and droop of the upper eyelid, the exact curve of the under-lid is drawn. Here great care is exercised and the drawing must be of hairbreadth exactness. The nostrils are defined, and for this a surgeon's sharp eye, and exactitude of observation and handling, are necessary; a trembling sensitiveness, for the nostrils breathe; and from thence to the contours of the lips and the partition of the lips. Then the contours of the cheeks, the faintest indication of cheek-bones, and the oval of the head never exactly symmetrical, must be shown, and when so much is achieved — a halt. A sonnet of Shakespeare, or Faust's invocation to Helen comes to mind. Return to work. Inward fire must be translated to clay. The mind and hand of the sculptor must work together. . . . From the model who sits quietly, unconscious of the absorbed worker, the sculptor draws out wizard-like the soul, and, by a process almost of incantation, builds up the image. Now the head is formed and takes on life, by ever so slight gradations. The movement of the head is finally resolved on, and by ceaseless turnings of the stand, the planes are modelled and related. The subtle connections between plane and plane knit the form together. The forms catch the light, emphasis is placed, now here, now there, the shapes are hunted, sought after with ardour, with passion. . . . Now the shoulders are formed, they are related to the cheeks, the back is studied, the arms and hands come into being, the hands flutter from the wrists like flames, a trembling eagerness of life pulsates throughout the work. What a quartet of harmonies is evoked in this bust! Head, shoulders, body and hands, like music. Turn the stand, pace round the clay, study from a thousand angles, draw the contours, relate the planes, evoke the immortal image — sculptor of eternal images.'

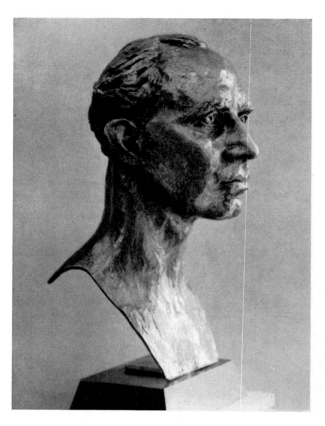

342 BENN LEVY
343 W. H. COLLINS
344 SIR ALEC WALKER

In 1934 Epstein made portraits of BENN LEVY, the playwright, of W. H. COLLINS, a benefactor of the Middlesex Hospital, and of SIR ALEC WALKER of Johnny Walker's whisky.

MORNA, whose bust was modelled in 1936, was the daughter of Judge Sir Lewis Stuart and she married Judge Nicholas. She was the author of the play *Traitors' Gate*. Her aquiline features, the heavy held-back hair, the flat chest with the delicately modelled breasts across which some transparent material is tightly drawn, contribute to an unusual and arresting image.

'Haile Selassie had arrived from Jerusalem an exile, and Commander Locker-Lampson asked me to do a study of the Emperor which might be used to further the cause of Abyssinia. The Commander fondly believed that I might do a work which in reproduction would be popular and raise funds for the heroic struggle. As it turned out, my bust had no popularity, and was only a matter of great expense to myself.

'I knew Haile Selassie's appearance from photographs,

345 MORNA

P

but when I saw him advancing through the rooms of the
house next door to the Abyssinian Legation, at which I
worked, I was astonished at his calm air of dignity . . . on
our meeting we delivered deep bows to each other, and
without further preliminaries, Haile Selassie ascended
the box and I started to work. . . . His fine handsome
features were lit by a pair of melancholy eyes which
seemed tired and strained. . . . All his movements were
distinguished and firm. It was strange to me to be, as it
seemed, at an African Court when in mid-Kensington.
His people on approaching him prostrated themselves
to the ground. . . . The Emperor's hands especially
attracted my attention. They were fine, even feminine. He
was altogether delicately fashioned, although this delicacy was tempered with a Semitic virility. I made what I
considered an interesting study, although an unfinished
one.'

Of the remarkable portrait of HAILE SELASSIE,
EMPEROR OF ABYSSINIA, the half-finished head in clay is
reproduced here, as well as the ultimate three-quarter
length figure in bronze with the heavy vertical draperies
which make it so distinctive.

346

346 CLAY HEAD OF
H.I.M. HAILE SELASSIE
EMPEROR OF ABYSSINIA

347. 348
H.I.M. HAILE SELASSIE
EMPEROR OF ABYSSINIA

347   348

349   ROSEMARY

350   MRS. ADOLPH OKO

351   3RD PORTRAIT OF BERNARD VAN DIEREN

349

350

In 1935 Epstein made the bust of a young American actress called ROSEMARY, who was brought to England by her mother to pose. With her close-fitting, short-sleeved bodice buttoned up to a high neck, her mop of short curls and her elfin features, she seems a particularly modern type; and the artist has caught her expression of a startled deer.

MRS. OKO was the second wife of Epstein's childhood friend, the scholar Adolf Oko. Oko had already been modelled in 1923 and his daughter Pearl in 1927.

Epstein's friendship with Bernard Van Dieren had lapsed in recent years, but, in 1936, shortly before the composer's death, the sculptor made another likeness of him. Of the sittings for his THIRD PORTRAIT OF VAN DIEREN Epstein wrote: 'He was very ill, and by turns hot and cold, and very faint, and yet he had a noble emperor's air which is in the bust. There is bitterness in the head, frustration. A genius neglected, misunderstood. One whose work will have to wait in our welter of vulgarity, noise and opportunism, before it comes to be understood, for qualities that our age does not care for.'

ELSA was one of many aspirant models who came to the door in the hopes that Epstein would find their faces

351

352 ELSA

353 SIR FRANK FLETCHER

of interest to him. He would look them over and say yes or no. It was rather like having a film test. The sculptor found in the face of this young photographer's assistant flaming, seraphic qualities, and I believe, though there is no evidence to confirm my opinion, that she may without knowing it — and perhaps without the artist knowing it too — have contributed her 'flashing eyes' and 'floating hair' to the great angel who would emerge from a block of alabaster, wrestling with Jacob, in five years time.

The bust of SIR FRANK FLETCHER was commissioned in 1936 when he retired from being Headmaster of Charterhouse. Epstein went down to the school to see it in position. He noticed a small boy looking at the bust and asked him whether it was like the Headmaster. The boy replied 'I don't know, sir. I never dared look at him.'

Of J. B. PRIESTLEY, the best-selling author of 'The Good Companions', now launched on a successful career as playwright, Epstein made a bust which seemed to fix admirably the notoriously 'rugged' and 'North Country' aspects of the sitter's character: but Priestley later took a dislike to the work and put it up for sale.

[230]

354 J. B. PRIESTLEY

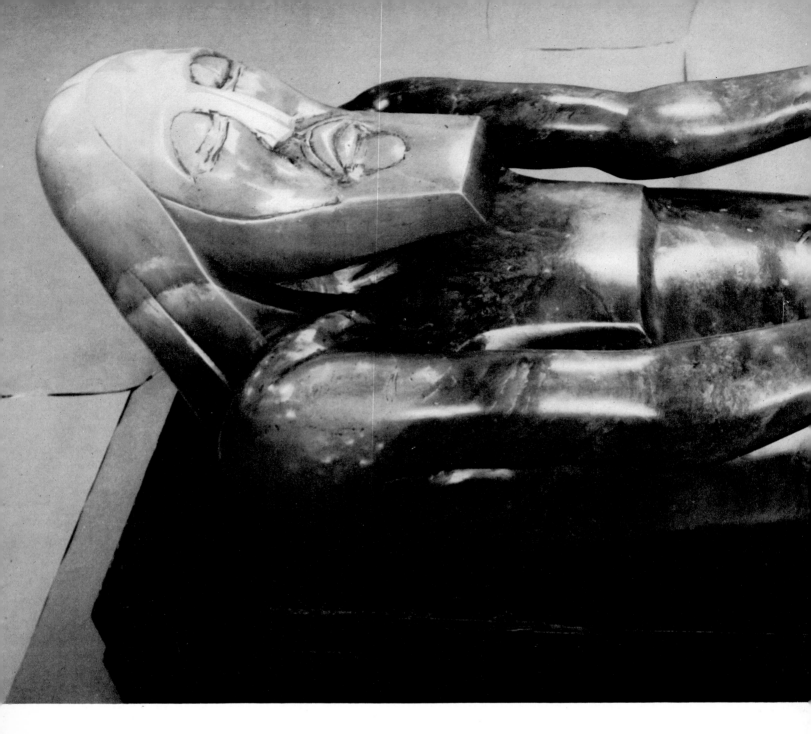

Of CONSUMMATUM EST, the first of three big carvings in alabaster and which he began in 1936, the sculptor wrote:

'The unworked alabaster block lies in my studio for a year. While I work at other things I look at it from time to time. The block lies prone in its length, and I consider whether I should raise it, but decide to leave it where it is. I can conceive any number of works in it. I can conceive a single figure or a group of figures. I have been listening to Bach's B Minor Mass. In the section Crucifixus I have a feeling of tremendous quiet, of awe. The music comes from a great distance and in this mood I conceive my "Consummatum Est". I see the figure complete as a whole. I see immediately the upturned hands, with the wounds in the feet, stark, crude. . . . I even imagine the setting for the finished figure, a dim crypt, with a subdued light on the semi-transparent alabaster.'

The words 'It is finished' were, of course, spoken by Christ from the cross: but in this work, following two years after the defiantly tragic 'Ecce Homo' with its feeling of suffering transformed into the creative force of pity, Epstein was making a sequel or epilogue to the

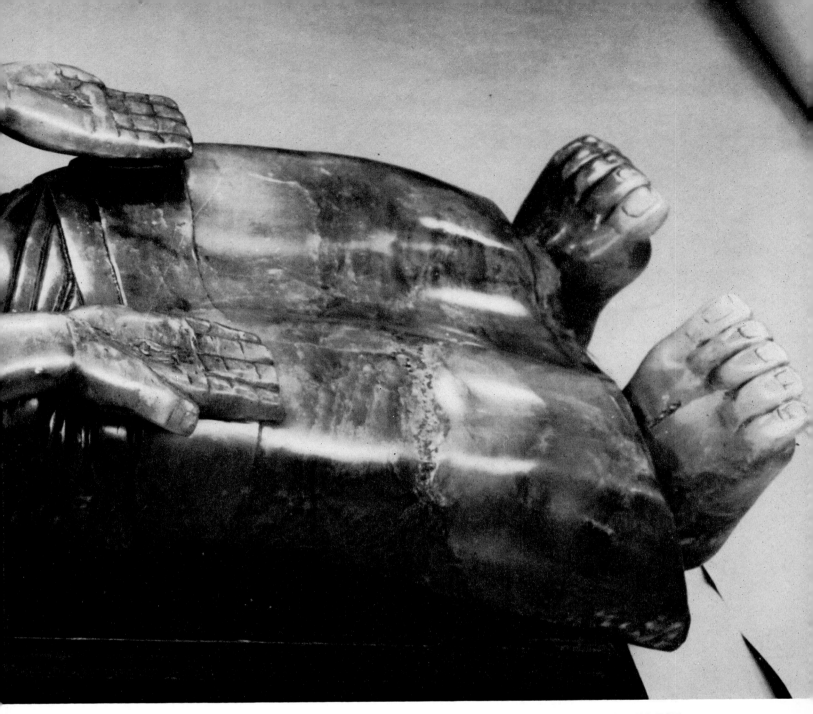

greater carving. Here lay the defeated shell of the Man-
God's invincible spirit, to which his children-murderers
had done their worst.

> 'Envy and calumny and hate and pain,
> And that unrest which men miscall delight
> Can touch him not and torture not again.'

Perhaps it is impossible to make the image of a dead
man project a powerful emotion. This writer feels that
the stiff rectangular statue is not one of Epstein's most
successful inventions.

[233]

356. 357
1ST PORTRAIT OF
NORMAN HORNSTEIN

357

Norman Hornstein, an American of Russian-Jewish descent, studied medicine in Edinburgh. He was to become a doctor and marry Peggy Jean in 1938. In the FIRST PORTRAIT OF NORMAN, a bust without shoulders also known as 'The Young Communist', the sculptor gave him — or perhaps recognised and rendered in clay — that superb air of nobility mingled with high-minded intelligence which shines particularly from certain portraits of Titian's youth, such as Lord Halifax's 'Man with a glove' or the 'Man in a red cap' in the Frick Collection.

In October 1937 'Consummatum est' was exhibited at the Leicester Galleries with twenty-one bronzes. 'The Young Communist' was among these, and so were portraits of Kathleen, Peggy Jean, Morna, Sally Ryan, J. B. Priestley, Sir Frank Fletcher and Ramsay Macdonald, besides two commissioned works which are not here reproduced, the studies of Sir Alec Martin of Christie's and Edward Goldston. In a review in the *New English Weekly*, which Epstein disliked sufficiently to include as an appendix to his autobiography, Hugh Gordon Porteous wrote: 'Many of us will turn with relief [from the carving] to the contemplation of Mr. Epstein's miraculous portrait busts.'

Another commissioned portrait shown in the exhibition was that of the young American sculptor Sally Ryan. She was an admirer of Epstein's work. (A bust by Rodin of her grandfather, Thomas Fortune Ryan, who built the Canadian Pacific Railway, is in the Tate.) She bought the big bronze 'Madonna and Child' which had been shown in New York in 1927. After lending this for some years to the Tate Gallery she transferred it to the Museum of Modern Art, New York, then gave it to Riverside Church in the same city, in a garden outside which it stands

[235]

358

359

358 SALLY RYAN
359 LEONA
360 TANYA
361 RITA ROMILLY

360

361

362 JACKIE
363 COUNTESS
     CASTLE STEWART

362

today. SALLY RYAN also bought the 'Sun God', with
'Primitive Gods' on its reverse.

LEONA was a somewhat stylised head of the model who
had posed four years earlier for the bust of 'Neander'.

A more voluptuous and catlike model was TANYA, a
girl of Belgian and Russian parents, of whom the sculptor
made a curl-crowned portrait, which might illustrate
T. S. Eliot's lines about Grishkin: 'Uncorseted, her
friendly bust Gives promise of pneumatic bliss.'

RITA ROMILLY, whose head with its wide eyes and
smooth centrally-parted hair the artist also portrayed in
1937, ran a night-club, but put her work aside to pose.

In 1937 the sculptor made his SECOND PORTRAIT OF
JACKIE (WITH LONG HAIR).

COUNTESS CASTLE STEWART was born Eleanor,
daughter of S. R. Guggenheim, the patron of modern
art, whose spiral museum by Wright adorns Fifth
Avenue. She was for some years Chairman of the East
Sussex Federation of Womens' Institutes. Epstein tried
out another version of her head wound round with a veil,
but this was only cast in plaster.

363

364

365

In 1937 he also made a striking bust of the gaunt POLA GIVENCHY, a Polish girl who was later to pose for 'Resurrection Study'; a beaming head of a dancer from Vienna, POLA NERENSKA, with arched eyebrows and curiously outlined lips; and a bust of the Jewish financier DAVID MORRIS.

In 1938 Epstein made his SECOND PORTRAIT OF LOUISE, also called 'Berenice', a heavier bust than the first. He met a new model who was to pose devotedly for him, the Negro MARIE TRACY and made a bust of her. This long, elegant and attractive woman would be the subject of a number of figure studies during the war.

366

364   POLA GIVENCHY
365   POLA NERENSKA
366   DAVID MORRIS
367   2ND PORTRAIT OF LOUISE
       (BERENICE)
368   MARIE TRACEY

367

368

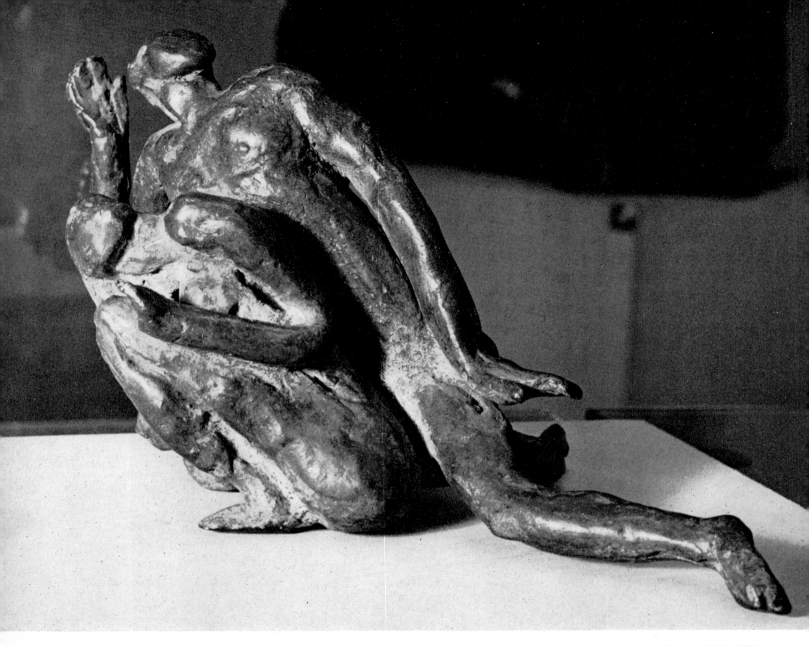

Since that wet night in 1930 when Epstein wrote from his cottage in Epping Forest to Kathleen Garman that he had nothing to read but an Old Testament, the sculptor's mind had been continually preoccupied with biblical themes. To the pregnant goddess in marble whom he had been working on at the beginning of the decade he gave the name 'Genesis'. She had been followed by a series of illustrations to the Old Testament in pencil and wash, with such subjects as 'The Spirit of God moving upon the face of the Waters', 'Lot and his daughters' and 'Moses with the tables of the Law'. In 1938 Epstein was already working on his great statue of 'Adam' and the close of the decade would see the beginnings of 'Jacob and the Angel'.

It was the sculptor's habit throughout his life, if the idea for a group came into his head, to sketch it out rapidly and roughly in plasticine. Such inspired 'jottings', probably never intended to be cast in their rough state, were the ADAM AND EVE and the BURIAL OF ABEL of 1938. These maquettes, so fortunately preserved, are of extreme interest, constituting as they do the equivalent of a line scribbled down, white hot from heaven, in one of Victor Hugo's notebooks, which might become the theme of a canto in 'La Légende des siécles', or of a bar of music recorded by Beethoven, destined to flower into the slow movement of a symphony.

In the first group Adam, concealing the crouching Eve beneath his body, with left leg extended and head up-turned to God, is saying 'I heard thy voice in the garden, and I was afraid, because I was naked; and I hid myself.'

[240]

In the second group a standing Adam, with head sunk on his breast carries at arm's length and seems about to place in a grave the dead body of Abel, whose right arm trails on the ground; while a stooped and mourning Eve follows behind. The dead son in the T.U.C. Memorial of nearly twenty years later (see Plate 644) would perhaps be a reminiscence of this Abel. The dramatic group is Rodinesque: and it is the more tragic that this and other moving compositions were never realised, because 'Social Consciousness', the biggest and most elaborate composition Epstein did complete (in 1953: see Plate 590) until his posthumously cast group for Bowater House, suffered from a tricky subject and a lack of unity.

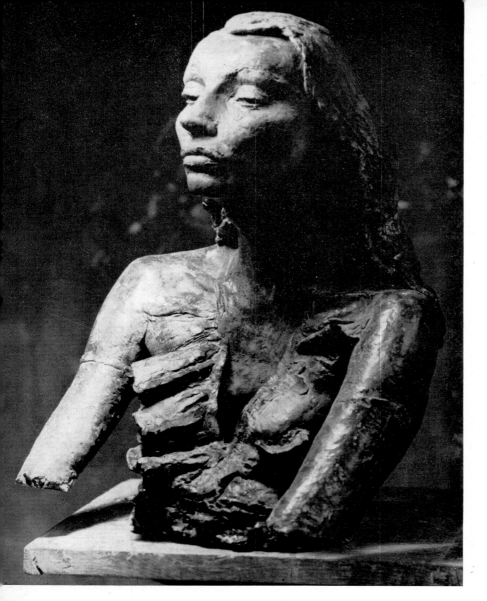

373

371

374

375

371 BETTY CECIL
372 TI-YI
373 DAVE
374 ELLEN BALLON
375 IVAN MAISKY

Other portraits of 1938 were the bust of BETTY CECIL, with her flowing fichu hair, and aloof expression; the commissioned head of an aspiring young opera singer with Satanic eyebrows, known as TI-YI, which Epstein never liked; the nude bust of the Negro boxer known as DAVE; and the bust of ELLEN BALLON, a friend of Sally Ryan's, who was portrayed with outstretched arms, playing the piano — her right hand resting on the invisible treble keys, her left raised to execute a thumping chord in the bass.

Sally Ryan had not yet bought the 1927 'Madonna and Child' when in 1938 Ivan Maisky, the Soviet Ambassador was brought to the studio by Victor Gollancz. He and his wife 'were especially struck with this group. Madame Maisky thought the Soviet would be interested in it, although the title did not accord with the Soviet "Ideology" .' Nothing came of this.

Of IVAN MAISKY, with his round, smiling face, shrewd but genial, Epstein made a lively head.

376. 377
ADAM (BEFORE POLISHING)

376

In 1938 Epstein began work on another even bigger block of alabaster over seven feet high which had lain for several years in his studio. This was to become ADAM. 'The conception, fairly clear in my mind in its general outlines, developed a law of its own as it proceeded, and I managed to get a tremendous movement within the compass of a not very wide, upright stone. The movement lies not in flung-out forms, but in an inner energy, comparable to a dynamo.... Into no other work had I merged myself so much, yet an Australian said to me: "It is as if a people had done this work and not just an individual." I feel also that generations spoke through me....'

The great figure is man rising from the earth and aspiring to the stars; or it is Prometheus; or it is the birth of a nation. Striving to retain the monolithic mass of the block while at the same time bringing it to life, and reluctant to cut away any more of the delicate pinkish alabaster than he must, Epstein gave to the upturned head, braced arms and climbing legs of his figure a primeval animal bulk, as if Adam, the first man, were still partly a beast. At the same time the uninhibited but

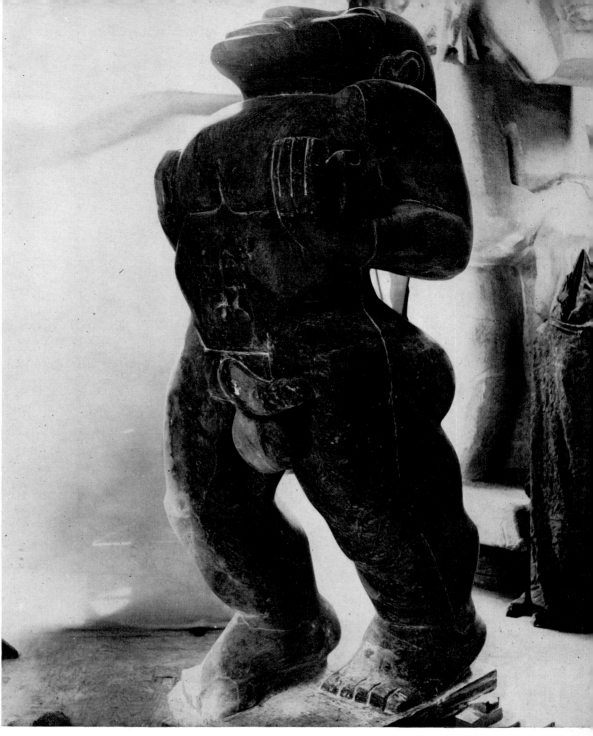

377

innocent-minded sculptor gave him sexual organs on a heroic scale, carving the virile member as if swung to one side by the vigorous upward motion of the giant. This was undoubtedly the reason why Messrs. Brown and Phillips of the Leicester Galleries were for long reluctant to show the statue in Epstein's 1939 exhibition, fearing a scandal, and why, courting one, Stafford the showman who bought 'Adam' and toured him round the fairgrounds of the country before selling him to the owners of the wax-work display at Blackpool, made a fortune. Never before had private parts won such publicity.

In 1940 'Adam' was shipped to America, and shown to the public at the Fine Arts Gallery, 57th Street, New York, and elsewhere at 50 cents a peep. The New York *Daily Mirror* reproduced a photograph of the carving, but with polka-dot underpants painted over its middle. The critic asked 'Why not just bomb Berlin with Adam?'

Still, after the sniggers and the denunciations have died down the statue remains, crude, Whitmanesque, a symbol of sublime endeavour. The statue is at present in the Exhibition Rooms at Harewood House, Yorkshire. It should stand on a mountain top in America.

[245]

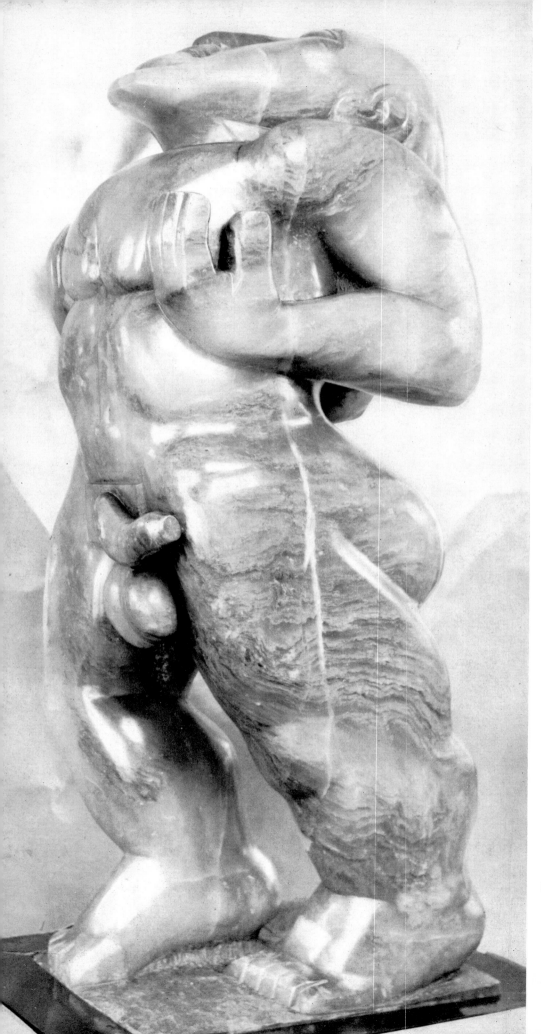

378. 379 ADAM

378

379

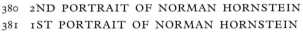

380 2ND PORTRAIT OF NORMAN HORNSTEIN   380
381 1ST PORTRAIT OF NORMAN HORNSTEIN

The SECOND PORTRAIT OF NORMAN HORNSTEIN, a
nude bust with the beginnings of outstretched arms, was
called 'Ishmael'. This was presumably in reference to
his son-in-law's voluntary exile from the United States.
Whether the mood was only temporary or not, Norman
Hornstein seems to have undergone a change of temper
since his head was first modelled two years before. The
serene and serious young man looks tragic and em-
bittered.

381

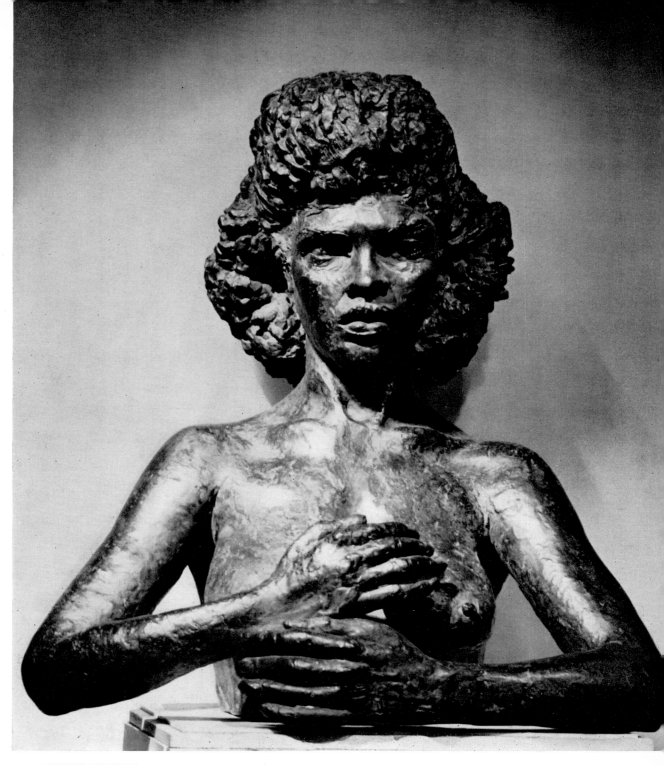

382 BETTY PETERS

The sculptor and Kathleen Garman saw the Negro BETTY PETERS in the street as they came from dining in the Ivy Restaurant, and asked her to pose. She kept a hostel for coloured seamen in the East End. The girl's puffed-up hair and mobile arms form a dramatic frame for her little wary provocative face: and this is one of Epstein's most brilliant studies.

From his student days Epstein had loved the difficult task of modelling babies and very young children. (We have seen how the only surviving sculptures of his years in Paris were two heads of a baby, and how almost the first portrait he made in London was that of young Romilly John.) The birth of Peggy Jean had provided the impetus for a harvest of *putti*. Of his younger children the most portrayed during the 'thirties was Jackie.

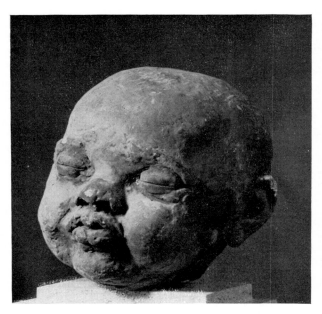

383

383 1ST PORTRAIT OF LEDA (AT 2 MONTHS)
384 MRS. PEARSON
385 AFRICAN MOTHER AND CHILD
386 RABBI STEPHEN WISE
387 2ND PORTRAIT OF LEDA (AT 4 MONTHS)
388 3RD PORTRAIT OF LEDA (AT 6 MONTHS)

384

But by 1939 Epstein had a grandchild, the firstborn of Peggy Jean and Norman Hornstein, and he made of her a head and two little busts with arms. The FIRST PORTRAIT OF LEDA (AT TWO MONTHS) is a head of her sleeping. In the SECOND PORTRAIT OF LEDA (AT FOUR MONTHS) the girl's head is turned to the left and looks slightly downward, and her elbows are bent, her fingers

385

386

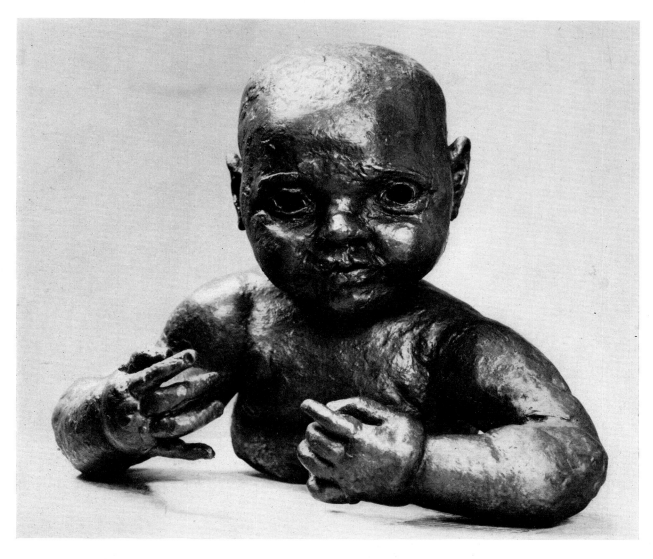

clutching loosely at the air. In the THIRD PORTRAIT OF
LEDA (AT SIX MONTHS) she looks up happily with parted
lips and opens her arms in the attitude of the infant Christ
welcoming the Magi.

As mentioned above, the four-months old Leda, tilted
backwards, became the baby in 'African Mother and
Child'. The model for the mother in AFRICAN MOTHER
was a student called NAMTANDA JABERWU, who had
already posed for a series of nude drawings when she was
pregnant. Her fine head is beautifully modelled, but the
gaping holes where the sculptor cut off her arms above
the elbows are distracting.

MELINDA PEARSON, whose head was modelled in the
same year, was the wife of Lionel Pearson, a partner of
the architect Charles Holden, who had commissioned the
Strand Statues and 'Night' and 'Day'.

In 1939 the sculptor was commissioned to make a
portrait head of RABBI STEPHEN WISE, who travelled
from New York to sit for him.

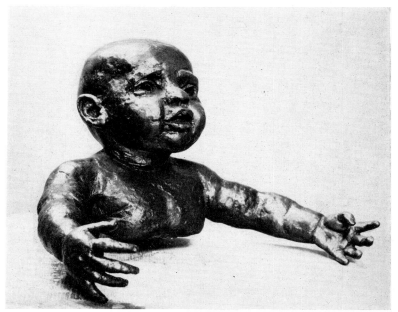

1940-49

CHILDREN, WARRIORS AND NUDES

The student of Epstein's huge output of sculpture must constantly be on the look-out for new developments in style which will allow him to divide the artist's work into 'periods' and read some story into the cornucopian flow. He will continually be thwarted in his generalisations by the sculptor's ability to work in several different ways at the same time.

Furthermore the student will be tempted to pronounce judgement, if only for his own satisfaction, on the panorama of Epstein's career. Did he get continually better and better, or gradually worse and worse? Were his commissioned portraits on the whole inferior to his private ones and therefore best forgotten? Were the carvings a mistake?

At the beginning of a four years course of study, it may not come amiss to record, the present writer found himself growing extremely interested in some of the early portraits and simultaneously in the latest of all, done in the nineteen-fifties. The classic repose of 'Marie Rankin' and the reticent modelling of 'Mrs Epstein in a mantilla' seemed as wonderful on the one hand as the subtlety of 'Lady Anne Tree' and the psychological profundity of 'T. S. Eliot' on the other. It was tempting to relapse into a facile assumption that Epstein, through misanthropy, the desire to amaze or shock, overproductivity or the wish to turn out strikingly effective portraits, fell, in the nineteen-twenties, into self-indulgent habits of mannerism, of which he only began to cure himself in old age.

I was not long in emerging from this state of error. In the 'thirties, for instance, Epstein certainly executed a number of commissioned portraits of eminent men, some of whose faces interested him more than others: but did he not also model the lustrous 'Isobel', the noble 'Norman' and the great mysterious portrait of Kathleen with serpentine arms? One evening, during the time this book was shaping, the writer found himself in the underground bar of the Cambridge Theatre during an interval, and saw that Emile Littler's casting of the bust of Betty Peters (which he knew well, having borrowed it for the Edinburgh Exhibition) was displayed at the far end of the room, cunningly and softly lit. Joining a small group of spellbound spectators he was at once convinced (as he had been on looking at many other individual works of Epstein on many other occasions) that the bronze before him, in this case the living, breathing and thinking portrait of a Negro girl was the sculptor's masterpiece; and renewed his conviction that while a few sculptors had equalled Epstein, none had ever excelled him in bringing clay to life.

During the 'forties Epstein would model his last and perhaps most extraordinary portrait of Kathleen, and portraits of her daughters, of which one, the 'First Portrait of Esther', he considered his most perfect work.

So much for a foolish attempt to dismiss Epstein's middle period. Still, a new trend in his modelling began to manifest itself during the second world war which would lead to the extreme 'smooth' style of the nineteen-fifties. Epstein took to spending more time on what he called 'pulling together' his clay. The relationship of planes had always constituted for him the essence of sculpture, and at one time he had been content to allow the planes to stand out in clear contrast from each other, leaving a vibrant and sometimes raw surface. Now he began to cover over the transitions to achieve a subtler effect. This work was often done in the afternoons during the sitter's absence.

In the course of the decade the sculptor was to model two monumental bronzes, 'Girl with Gardenias' and 'Lucifer', besides carving 'Jacob and the Angel' and 'Lazarus', two of his most mysterious and original inventions.

The war was not allowed to interrupt his work or to alter his way of life. German bombing did not drive him from London. And Kathleen remembers how, one night, the sight of a conflagration gave him an idea for a group of Shadrach, Meshak and Abednego in the burning fiery furnace.

During the war Epstein made a number of nude studies from Betty Peters and Marie Tracy. He also made some commissioned portraits of war leaders, culminating in the famous (though unfinished) study of Winston Churchill, done in 1946.

More carefully observed portraits of children would be executed in the nineteen-forties; and the first of these was another study of Peggy Jean's daughter, the FOURTH PORTRAIT OF LEDA (WITH COCKSCOMB).

389 4TH PORTRAIT OF LEDA
(WITH COCKSCOMB)

390 PICCANINNY

391 3RD PORTRAIT OF
JACKIE (LAUGHING)

390

The model for PICCANINNY, made in 1940, was the adorable daughter of Marie Tracy, with her knobbly curls and straggling pigtail. In this head, with its satisfying surface, as in the 'Victor' of 1949, Epstein conveyed something of that wondering angelic quality which is peculiar to Negro children.

The THIRD PORTRAIT OF JACKIE (LAUGHING) also known as 'Ragamuffin', is the portrait of a grin and verges on caricature, but is nevertheless entirely successful.

The episode in the Book of Genesis of Jacob wrestling with the angel is a mysterious one. After twenty years away from home, Jacob was preparing to meet his brother Esau, whom he had wronged. He sent his family and his animals ahead over the ford Jabbok, intending to pass the night alone; but 'there wrestled a man within him until the breaking of the day'. When this man saw that Jacob was a match for him 'he touched the hollow of his thigh' and put it out of joint. Then he said, 'Let me go, for the day breaketh.' But Jacob would not let him go until the man had blessed him. And the stranger said, 'Thy name shall be called no more Jacob, but Israel: for as a prince hast thou power with God and with men, and hast prevailed.' When the stranger refused to say who he was Jacob assumed that he was God. Next day Jacob

[254]

391

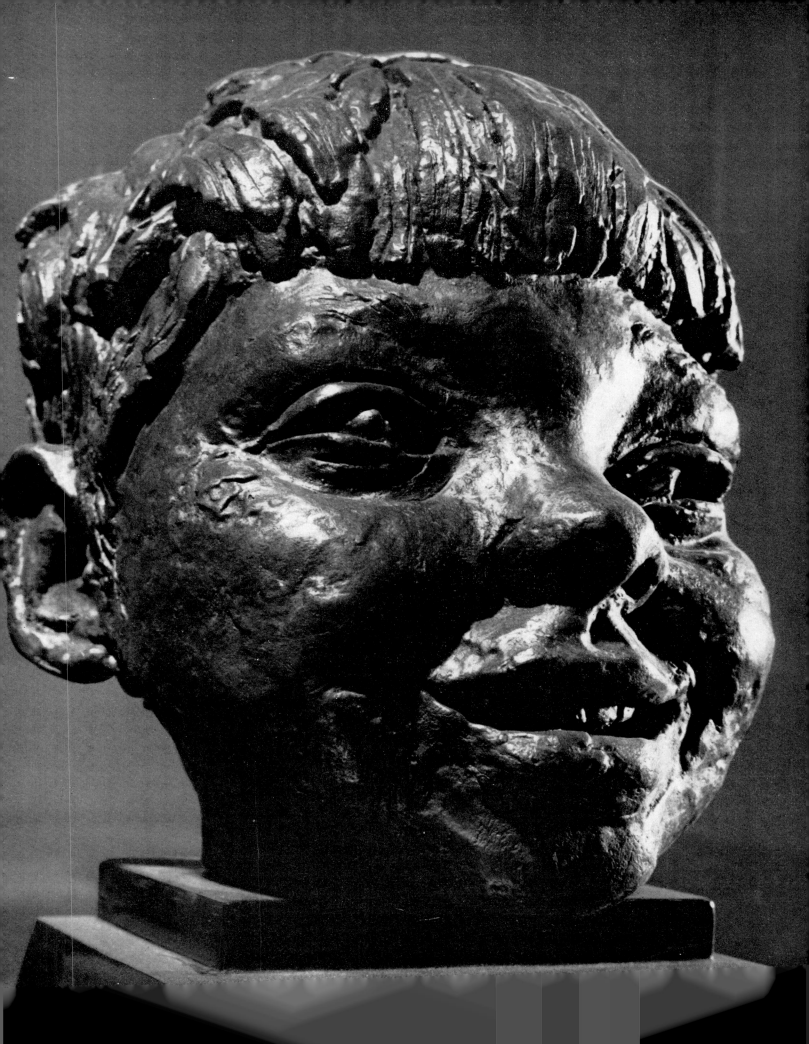

393

humiliated himself before Esau and offered him all his   392
possessions, which the forgiving brother refused. But
Jacob's thigh remained shrunken as a reminder of the
encounter, and he limped for the rest of his life.

The story may have an origin in folklore, and the
Jewish historian may have turned an old tale to the purposes of religion. Then, Fraser relates that there was a
primitive belief that rivers disliked being crossed, so the
stranger may once have been an angry river god. The
most satisfactory construction seems to be that of the late
Dr. S. R. Driver, who read the wrestling match as a
battle between Jacob's carnal and spiritual natures, a
turning point in his life when he realizes he can no longer
live by the flesh, and which results in his making repara-
tions to Esau and becoming a more spiritual man.

That Epstein left no explanation of his aims in carving
the group of JACOB AND THE ANGEL, as he did with other

394–400 JACOB AND THE ANGEL

396

monumental works, is not altogether to be regretted, for he had no great gift for expressing himself in words, and his notes are often confusing. Studying the figures, we may guess that several ideas, like superimposed negatives, fused in the dark room of his mind to produce this strange conception.

We notice first the squatness of the figures, the result of Epstein's desire to respect his noble block of alabaster and retain as much as possible of its monumental bulk for his creatures — the angel's slab-like wings and the square base also mark the old boundaries of the stone. We see that the exhausted Jacob is hanging limp in the

[259]

arms of the angel, whose hands clasp him behind the back. We note the vivid contrast between the two faces, juxtaposed like those of lovers. Jacob, with curved nose and a cap of woolly hair seems the more boyish and human for his pursed mouth and upstrained chin. The angel's flowing lucent locks proclaim his divine origin;

he has a long straight nose, lips imperially curved and wide eyes whose stare is like a searchlight. What exactly is going on? and how are we to interpret this embrace, from which an element of sex, clearly, is not excluded?

Perhaps the sculptor's mind worked something like this. Love is a battle and prayer is a battle: the aim of

400

both is ecstatic communion. Why not represent the divine intercourse in human, that is, sexual terms? When God came to Jacob as he meditated, prayed or slept, having long ago singled him out for favour, he came to change his life, as the realisation must often assail men in their middle years — 'Nel mezzo del cammin di nostra vita' —

that the time has come to think of other things than physical pleasures and wordly gain; and He decided to make the revelation or conversion a terrible, wonderful and unforgettable experience (in the way that He would later blind St. Paul). The struggle, which was of course a struggle in Jacob's mind, culminated in a sudden blind-

[263]

401. 402
1ST PORTRAIT OF
DEIRDRE

401

ing vision of God and a momentary understanding of the whole purpose and order of creation; and this the sculptor has represented by showing Jacob at the pinnacle of sexual fulfilment. After this crucial night by the brook Jacob would have sciatica for the rest of his life to re-member it by.

At the beginning of the war the Epsteins engaged an exceptionally pretty girl called Deirdre as cook-house-keeper. Her talents in the kitchen turned out to be negligible and she was called upon to pose as a model. This, it appeared, was what she had all along intended to happen. Though hungry for immortality, Deirdre was reluctant to expose her naked body — Epstein was congen-

itally incapable of understanding such modesty — and her shyness probably accounts for the fact that in the three portraits the sculptor made of her she is either holding her arms in front of her breasts or leaning forward in a huddled and self-deprecating way.

The FIRST PORTRAIT OF DEIRDRE (WITH ARMS), because of its graceful gesture, is the most rococo of the sculptor's works, and brings to mind certain Bavarian wood carvings of the mid-eighteenth century. The model's long curly hair tumbles onto her shoulders; her eyes look down, dreaming; a wistful half-smile flickers on her lips; and her slender arms are arrested in move-ment as if she were about to fold them over her breast.

[264]

402

403
  2ND PORTRAIT OF
  DEIRDRE

404
  SLAVE HOLD

405
  SKETCH FOR
  SLAVE HOLD

404

The SECOND PORTRAIT OF DEIRDRE (WITH A SLIP) is perhaps an even more delightful work than the first. Her hair falls forward over the left shoulder to where the shoulder-strap of her slip is only just holding it on; and the curve of the slip slanting across her breast continues a crescent frame to the face which the hair began.

It is hard to see how Epstein's drawing for the 'Slave Hold' could have been realised in sculpture except as a relief; and in fact his project got no further than a double bust. In the SLAVE HOLD the man, who is modelled down to the pelvis, clasps his hands above his head, while the woman in front of him seems to shield her eyes. Are they dazzled by a sudden light, like the released prisoners in *Fidelio*? The chain round the man's wrists is an unfortunate addition.

405

The SIXTH PORTRAIT OF KATHLEEN was the top half of the full-length statue called 'Girl with Gardenias'; with the difference that there are no gardenias.

GIRL WITH GARDENIAS is an anomalous work with certain wonderful qualities, but doomed from the start to give only partial satisfaction to the spectator. The thought often occurs to a student of Epstein's sculpture that, working in isolation as he did and being scornful — or fearful — of advice and criticism, he inevitably embarked from time to time on projects which a friendly circle of sympathetic fellow-workers — such as so often springs up in France — would have reasoned him out of attempting.

Having decided to do a full-length female nude, life-size or rather larger, the first for many years, Epstein clearly thought there could be no better model than Kathleen, whom he found beautiful in all weathers. But Kathleen was by now middle-aged: and although her figure was still girlish her face bore the badges of character and experience which the young have not earned. The anomaly of this nude statue is not that Kathleen's face has the wisdom and fascination of an older woman, but that her body has remained youthful. A middle-aged or pregnant or old or even ailing nude is justifiable artistically in certain circumstances, but a young

[268]

408. 409 GIRL WITH GARDENIAS

nude with a middle-aged face takes a bit of explaining.

Kathleen is running gently. Her hands sketch a gesture similar to that in the 'First Portrait of Deirdre'; an odd flimsy garment hangs down behind her left leg which extends backwards, the foot turned out; the bent right leg is advanced and the weight taken lightly on the ball of the right foot. She holds one gardenia in her left hand, four more fall down the front of her body and one lies on the ground between her feet. The finest modelling is in the right leg: the arms are disappointing.

410

Epstein had in mind to make a Resurrection group, and he modelled a RESURRECTION STUDY of Pola Givenchy, holding her hands parallel before her face as if groping her way back to life. LALAGE LEWIS was an actress. JUANITA FORBES posed in 1942 for her bust, and three years later for a study in the nude. ROBERT SAINSBURY, Quaker, grocer and collector of works of art, notably African sculpture, was another sitter of this year. His wife Lisa also posed.

The American-born COUNTESS OF BERKELEY took time off from her war-work with the W.V.S. to sit for her portrait, and the sculptor made a fine head of her. Thinking nostalgically no doubt about her villa overlooking Assisi, she suggested to Epstein that he might make a statue of St. Francis to stand on the hill above the town. Nothing came of this but the HEAD OF ST. FRANCIS.

411

412 LALAGE LEWIS
413 JUANITA FORBES
414 ROBERT SAINSBURY
415 ST. FRANCIS
416 COUNTESS OF
        BERKELEY

412

413

414

s

415

416

417

418

419

417. 418. 419 GEORGE BLACK
420 ALEXANDER MARGULIES
421 CHIA PI

420

421

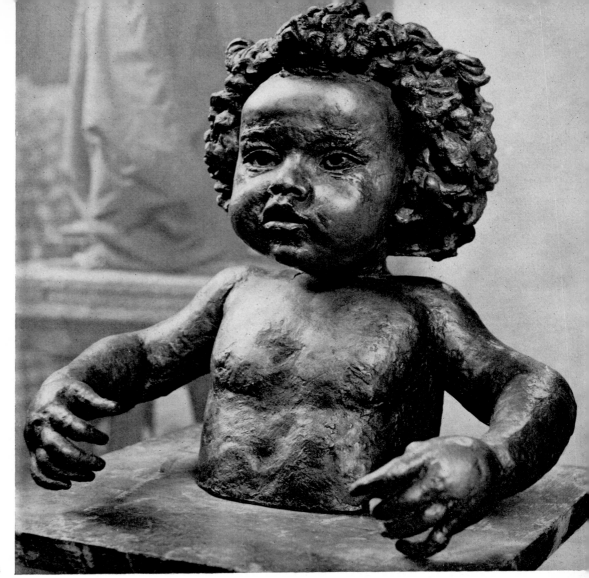

422 IAN (OSSIAN)

423 3RD PORTRAIT
OF DEIRDRE

422

Two commissions in 1942 were the busts of GEORGE
BLACK, ophthalmologist, of Leeds, who was modelled in
his white overalls, and of the jeweller ALEXANDER
MARGULIES, whose daughter Judith was also to pose in
1942, and whose fine collection of modern paintings is
destined for Israel.

The wife of a Chinese diplomat whom the change of
regime threw out of work, CHIA PI (Precious Flower)
posed in a high-necked sleeveless dress, for a serene bust
with arms which was shown in the 'Aid for China' exhibition at the Wallace Collection.

Epstein made in the same year a portrait of his grandson, younger brother of Leda and child of Norman
Hornstein and Peggy Jean. IAN was modelled with open
arms, but his head with its mop of curls was also cast
separately.

The THIRD PORTRAIT OF DEIRDRE (LEANING FOR-
WARD), like its two predecessors, was modelled with
subtlety, besides being a happy conception. Shortly after

423

424
GENERAL SIR ALAN
CUNNINGHAM

425 ERNEST BEVIN

it was made, having achieved her ambition of posing (not once, but three times) for Epstein, Deirdre went to work in the War Office, married an officer and left with him for Australia.

The commissioning by the Ministry of Information of several portraits of eminent war leaders was heralded by Epstein's Cockney maid, who announced 'The Ministry of Inspiration is on the phone'.

'Although the fees offered were nominal,' wrote Epstein, 'I was interested to undertake the work. The first of this series was Sir Alan Cunningham, the victorious commander of the Abyssinian campaign. As he took his place on the stand he came face to face with my portrait of Haile Selassie. "Good heavens!" said the

General, "I thought I'd seen the last of him." I remember the General's impassive expression as my plaster moulder, who was in the Home Guard, regaled him with a dramatic description of the epic defence of Putney Bridge by himself and his comrades one Sunday morning. Perhaps the flicker of a smile passed over my sitter's face. Far from being bellicose, I was impressed by the gentle courtesy of a man whose chief ambition at that moment was to grow roses and "cultiver son jardin".'

The portrait of GENERAL SIR ALAN CUNNINGHAM, with his clipped moustache and open bemedal-ribboned bush shirt, besides being a soldierly image, conveys the quality of sensitiveness which Epstein saw in the sitter.

Next Epstein made a vivid head of ERNEST BEVIN. 'At

426 FIELD MARSHAL
EARL WAVELL

427 AIR MARSHAL
VISCOUNT PORTAL

the end of his sittings, however, he looked at it long and seriously and remarked "Epstein, you know I'd have hardly recognized it".'

The critic is often impelled to compare Epstein with Rembrandt: either for his humanity, for the simplicity of his life combined with a princely expenditure on works of art, for his love of 'failures' like Old Smith and Old Pinager, even for his technique — if a sculptor's technique can be compared to a painter's.

Epstein could portray the gentleness and dignity, just as Rembrandt might have done, in a face such as that of GENERAL EARL WAVELL, which to the superficial observer must have seemed commonplace and plain. A lesser artist — an academician, say — might faithfully have rendered the mask of an ugly man: or might have flattered him. Epstein by his combined instinct, knowledge and manual skill could manipulate the planes and give just the accent, exaggeration or distortion necessary to bring out the essence of a good man with elements of greatness. Wavell had just published his anthology 'Other Men's Flowers', all of which he said he knew by heart: sculptor and soldier talked about poetry.

AIR MARSHAL VISCOUNT PORTAL, on the other hand, was a handsome man.

[278]

427

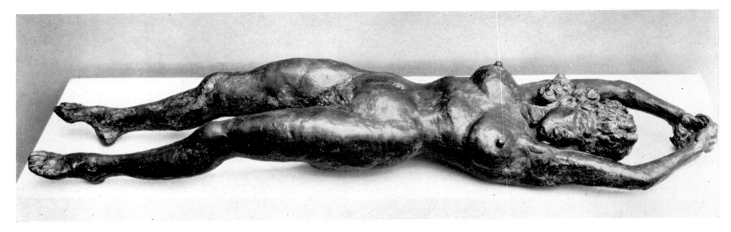

428

429

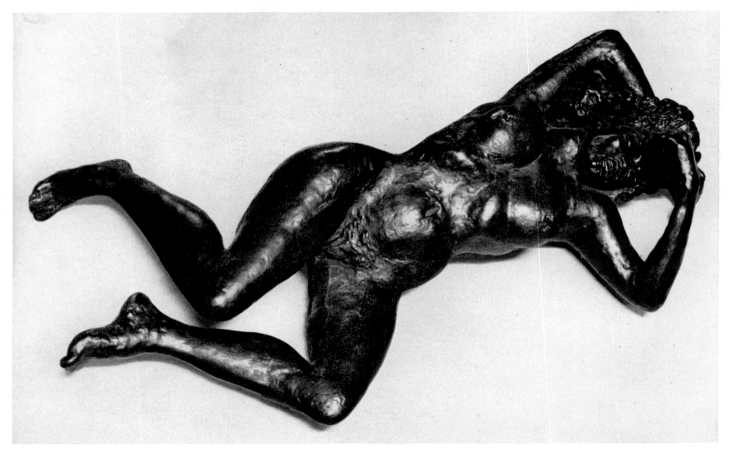

430

428   NUDE STUDY A
429   NUDE STUDY B
430   NUDE STUDY B
431   NUDE STUDY C
432   NUDE STUDY C
433   NUDE STUDY D

431

432

Betty Peters posed for many NUDE STUDIES in the following months, of which five, together with one of Marie Tracy, are here reproduced.

Whether because he had been lucky enough to find ready models, or because of the outbreak of war, or because of a sudden urge to go back to school, Epstein set himself for the first time since his student years, to make study after study from the nude. Once he got started on a subject — drawings of Sunita or Jackie, illustrations to the Old Testament or to Baudelaire, or watercolours of Epping Forest — he would continue with it compulsively as if in pursuit of some irresistible spoor. This is no stranger than that Monet should paint endless variations on his cathedrals or waterlilies, or Picasso on 'Las Meniñas' or 'Le Déjeuner sur l'herbe'. Of Betty and Marie he made perhaps more than a score of painstaking studies from life, and eighteen of these were cast for exhibition at the Leicester Galleries in 1947.

Epstein's aversion, when a student, from learning anatomy from corpses and his unwillingness to accept tuition from academic professors had hindered his acquiring a complete knowledge of the human body. Through-

433

434 NUDE STUDY G   436 NUDE STUDY I

435 NUDE STUDY H   437 NUDE STUDY J

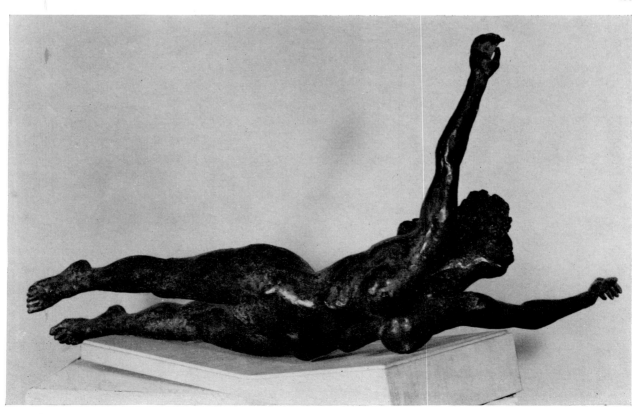

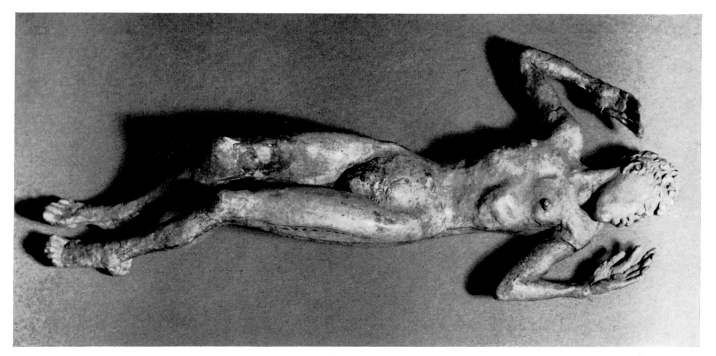

out his life he relied on his eagle eye to carry him through when the science was lacking; and it seldom let him down. It would be true to say that between the careful realism of these small nude studies from life made at the beginning of the second world war and the stylisation of such monumental nudes as 'Lucifer' and 'St. Michael', which were made after it, he was never to seek or find a middle course. The idealism of Praxiteles or Michelangelo which he had approached in his first London years when he made the Strand Statues and the 'Garden figure' was now something to which he could no longer subscribe.

The voluptuous Betty, sprawling on her stomach clasping an invisible cushion under her head, splayed in somnolent or sexual abandon, childishly clasping her breasts, or clinging to an unseen rail — all Danaë to some sadistic executioner — seems like a denizen of the seraglio imagined by Delacroix for Sardanapalus. The elegant, attenuated Marie is perhaps Zobeïda, Shah Shahriar's queenly favourite wife, too proud to yield to the scimitars of slaves.

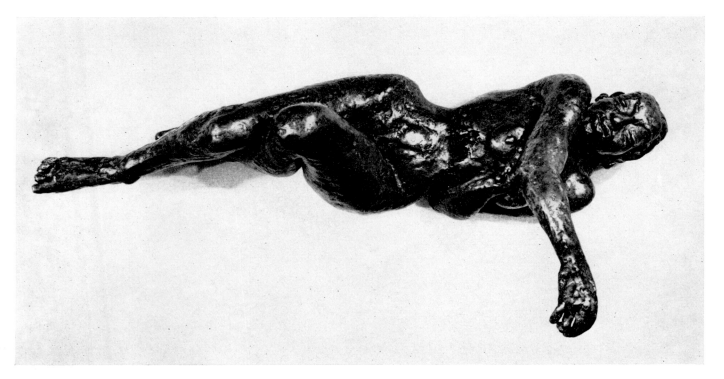

438 YEHUDI MENUHIN   [284]

439 GIRL FROM BAKU
440 5TH PORTRAIT OF
LEDA (POUTING)

439

Since early days in New York, when he heard Wagner and Italian opera from the gallery of the Metropolitan, Epstein had been a concertgoer and liked to have music on Sundays in his home. YEHUDI MENUHIN was not the first musician he portrayed and would not be the last. Epstein exaggerated the size of his eyes and gave him the look of an angel from Buddhist mythology.

In the GIRL FROM BAKU he found something of that 'Nefertiti look' he had descried in Dolores, in Kathleen and in Isobel. He modelled her with head held high, conscious of her beauty, a torrent of hair falling behind her shoulders: the naked torso, with arms at her sides, is cut off just above the navel.

The sculptor's granddaughter was now four. In the FIFTH PORTRAIT OF LEDA (POUTING) she has a mass of curly hair and a pensive expression rather like that of her

440

441 PRINCESSE DE BRAGANZA
442 DRAWING FOR LUCIFER
443 DRAWING FOR LUCIFER
444 SATAN, BEELZEBUB AND BELIAL

442

mother Peggy-Jean when she was modelled as 'The Sick Child' twenty-four years before.

The PRINCESSE DE BRAGANZA, an American married to a Portuguese, was modelled with head held high and bare torso.

Epstein, himself a rebel angel, was always fascinated by his predecessors. In 1943 he began to make sketches inspired by the first book of 'Paradise Lost'. Should he model a single figure? or a group or a relief?

Before modelling a small group of three figures, which he called SATAN, BEELZEBUB AND BELIAL, he made a drawing of Lucifer with wings unfurled and tragic hand to brow, then a wash drawing of the heads and shoulders of three rebel angels, of whom the centre one is more or

443

444

less a self-portrait. This reminds us that there is often an autobiographical element in Epstein's imaginative works.

Then he decided to model a panel in relief: THE FALL OF LUCIFER. The unfinished composition is dominated by the surging, defiant central figure of Lucifer, hand to brow, based on the first drawing. He rises from a snake-pit of tormented companions, who clutch themselves as they burn in 'that inflamed sea'. Above, to right and left, are good angels, flying upside down, aërial police who have escorted the damned to their destination.

It is a pity the relief, which might have turned out a noble work, was never finished: but the sculptor went on impatiently to model during 1943 and 1945 the great figure of LUCIFER for which these drawings, the maquette and the relief had been only a preparation. Meanwhile his thoughts about the rebel angel and the way he should be represented had undergone an unexpected change.

Lucifer, with wings upstretched, is shown alighting in Hell. His right foot has overstepped the precipice on which he stands, and is about to be drawn up to join the left. His hands, still arched to repel the fiery air, will soon fall to his sides. His eyes full of 'the thought Both of lost happiness and lasting pain' gaze down on a scene of horror, but his look, unexpectedly (after the defiant drawing and relief), is one of compassion. His face — how mysterious! — is the first Madonna's — Sunita's.

It is a strange work. Sunita's idealised features, with waved hair unruffled by flight; stiff conventionalised wings; an expressionistic torso, narrower at the chest than at the pelvis, and bound round with a band which constricts the chest and seems almost to be holding the wings on; realistic arms but hands bent back at an exaggerated angle; realistic legs draped with a skirt which magically now covers, now reveals them, which is there and not there. All these contradictions were doubtless necessary to achieve the desired result of drama and solemnity. The figure was cast with a golden patina.

'I had worked on this', wrote Epstein, 'with great concentration for the greater part of a year and showed it at an exhibition of my work at the Leicester Galleries where it remained unsold. Some time later Professor Lawrence (brother of Lawrence of Arabia and then at Cambridge) wrote to me proposing to purchase the statue from the Seven Pillars of Wisdom Trust and to present it to the Fitzwilliam Museum, Cambridge. . . . To his astonishment the gift was rejected. . . . I suggested the V and A and the offer was again rejected, this time on the grounds that this museum did not exhibit works by living artists. He next turned to the Tate Gallery with its large bare sculpture hall. This time the gift of the statue was unanimously rejected by the Board of Trustees, and this, being reported in the Press, brought several requests from provincial galleries. I was visited by the Lord Mayor of Birmingham and the Director of the Art

447. 448
LUCIFER

450

Gallery, Mr. Trenchard Cox, who asked that Birmingham should be honoured with the gift.

The Seven Pillars of Wisdom Trust gave £4,000 for 'Lucifer', the highest price yet paid for an Epstein.

In 1944 Epstein's youngest daughter, then aged 15. sat for him for the first time. The FIRST PORTRAIT OF ESTHER (WITH LONG HAIR) could be justly considered the most wonderful of his bronzes.

Esther's hair, cut in a straight fringe in front, is swept heavily back from her bare shoulders to fall down behind; and the way it is arranged as well as the stringy almost artificial way the sculptor has handled it gives her somewhat the look of a bewigged Egyptian princess. Her head is thrust slightly forward, and when seen in profile, the diagonal of the neck, the length of which is exaggerated, is echoed and emphasised by the slanting cataract of hair. Esther's nose is sensitive and noble; the sculptor has exaggerated the passionate pout of her lips. Impossible to analyse one feature in isolation from another: but perhaps the bust owes its magic quality — both as the portrait of a human being and as a piece of sculpture, for in it human and sculptural values are indivisibly fused by the master's art — to the modulated sweep of the oval cheeks and to the way the eyes with their scooped out pupils are set within them.

Epstein said, 'If I had to be judged by one work I should choose this. It has all the qualities I most value in sculpture. I could not have done it better.'

[293]

451   452   453   454   45

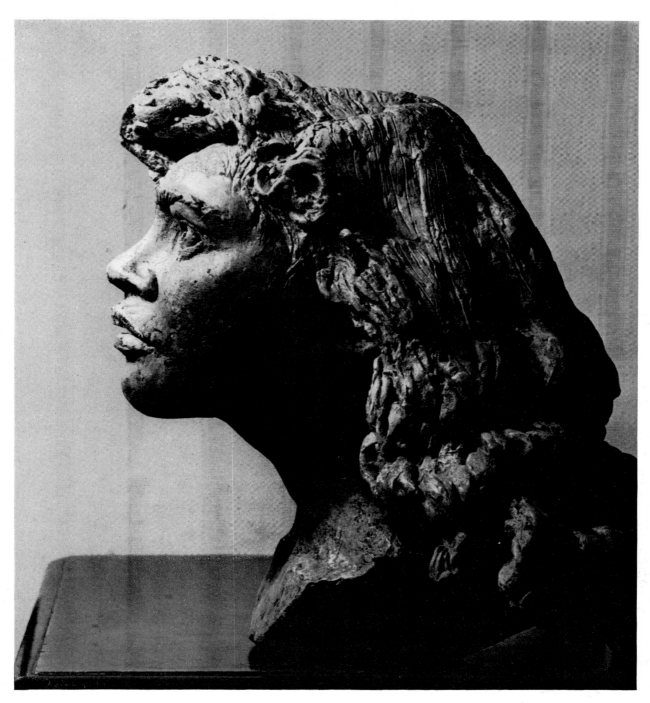

1ST PORTRAIT OF KITTY (WITH CURLS)

This extraordinary head, the expression of whose features changes with different light from wistfulness to sorrow, projects a mood of voluptuous reverie, like Debussy's 'L'Après-midi d'un faune', and seems destined to become a legendary image, like the Berlin bust of Nefertiti or Leonardo's Mona Lisa.

In 1944, too, Epstein made a head of his second daughter. The FIRST PORTRAIT OF KITTY (WITH CURLS) was a lyrical work. During the war, as if to compensate for other shortages, women made the most of their hair, wearing it long on their shoulders and sometimes puffed up on their foreheads like poodles. Kitty's tumbling curls

458 1ST PORTRAIT OF KITTY

459   GIRL WITH A BOW

are the distinctive feature of this portrait. She leans forward eagerly, huge eyes gazing upward and full lips slightly parted, listening, aspiring. One lock of hair falls over her right brow — her eyebrows are rendered like plaited ropes and the delicate drawing of her cheeks is set off by the dancing hair, which seems to be growing visibly and will surely overflow the room to unfurl, like Mélisande's, out of the window.

The plaster cast of GIRL WITH A BOW was one of the few Epstein ever parted with, though he lost or destroyed several. It is the property of Sir Leon Bagrit, the pioneer of automation.

[299]

VISCOUNT WAVERLEY, who as Sir John Anderson had been Home Secretary during the war, filled among other offices that of Chairman of the Port of London Authority; and it was this body who commissioned his portrait. When he came to sit his wife said to the artist, "His face has two aspects, that of a butler and that of a Roman emperor. I wonder which you will bring out." Besides conveying the somewhat dour character of the distinguished statesman and his intellectual power, Epstein — as a friend of Waverley's pointed out to this writer — was able to suggest his latent sense of humour, a characteristic which was probably only evident to his intimate associates. A casting of the shoulderless bust constitutes a memorial to Lord Waverley in the church of West Dean, Sussex.

NUDE STUDY OF JUANITA was the last of the series of reclining nudes which had preoccupied Epstein during part of the war.

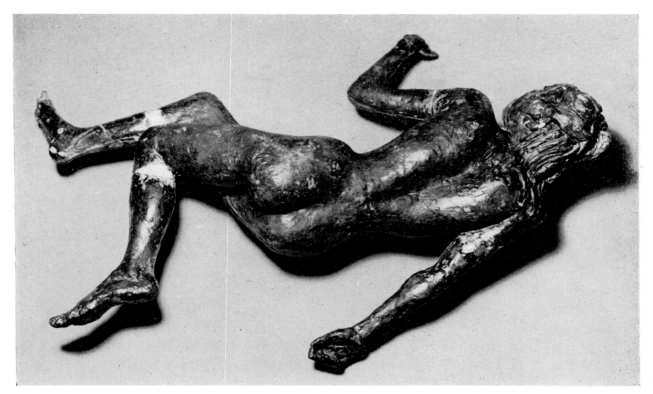

461

462

461. 462 NUDE STUDY OF JUANITA

463

Of his head of WINSTON CHURCHILL Epstein wrote: 'The Ministry of Information were naturally eager for me to work from Churchill but the opportunity did not come until after the war when he was living opposite me. He arrived at my studio complete with secretary, and a plain clothes man who planted himself at the door intending to remain on guard throughout the sitting. I offered this gentleman a chair whereupon Churchill abruptly dismissed him. Lighting his cigar, with his secretary seated behind me for dictation, we were all set for a fair start.

After an hour this secretary was dismissed and a second appeared for further dictation to the accompaniment of a second cigar. After three somewhat restless sittings Churchill decided to stay at Chartwell where he gave me three further sittings. Unfortunately it was winter and the light far from ideal and I felt that I had made no more than an interesting character study. . . .'

Sketch or not, it is the finest portrayal of Churchill in existence. Who is the happy warrior, if not he who has an artist of genius to fix his features in paint or bronze?

[302]

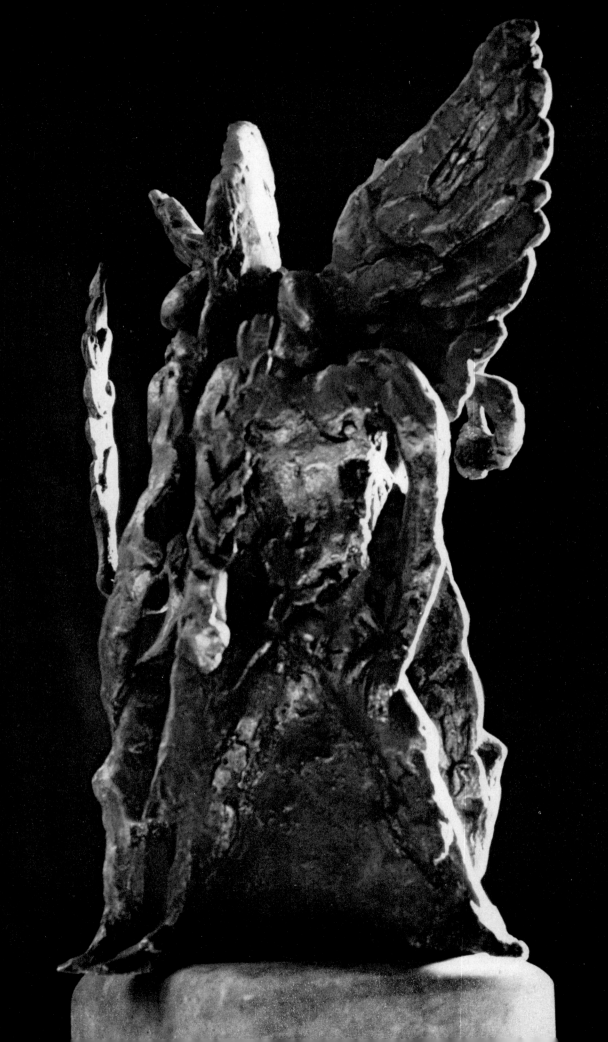

466

In 1946 the sculptor made several small maquettes or projects for monumental works. These were cast in bronze and exhibited at the Leicester Galleries in the following year. 'Pasiphaë', 'Jupiter and Semele', 'Narcissus' and 'Nightfarer' are not illustrated here.

GUARDIANS OF PARADISE was a striking conception: three winged angels standing back to back, with flaming swords. If Epstein had made a big group from it, however, he might have had difficulty arranging the six wings in such a way that they looked well from every side.

BIRD IN FLIGHT, also called 'Lovers on an eagle's back' was an idea for a carving in marble. With a few deft movements the sculptor twisted his sticks of plasticine into an arabesque of nude lovers embracing.

[305]

465 GUARDIANS OF PARADISE
466 BIRD IN FLIGHT

u

467

468

469

467 MYRA HESS
468 ANNA FRANKEL
469 RONALD DUNCAN
470 YMIEL OVED
471 SKETCH OF PANDIT NEHRU

Epstein had attended several of the lunch-time concerts organised by MYRA HESS during the war: he was
pleased to make her portrait at the request of the Griller
Quartet. The piano was brought into the studio, and he
modelled her as she played.

Epstein had met the composer Benjamin Frankel on a
train, and he modelled his wife ANNA FRANKEL in 1946.
Her portrait and that of RONALD DUNCAN, the poet and
playwright, were among the few to be exhibited with the
nude studies at the Leicester Galleries in 1947.

YMIEL OVED was the daughter of Epstein's old friend
Mosheh Oved, the jeweller (see Plate 230). She studied
dancing and her bust was made, with arms vaguely in a
ballet position, in exchange for a gold Moroccan necklace.

The FIRST SKETCH OF NEHRU came into being as a

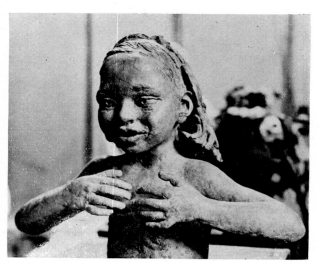

470

471

result of Pandit Nehru's telephoning, during his visit to England for the Commonwealth Conference of 1946, to ask if he might visit Epstein's studio. The sculptor was eager to model his head, and for the three remaining days of his visit Nehru came at 9 a.m. for one hour.

In 1947 the sculptor's second daughter Kitty was married to LUCIAN FREUD, and in the same year Epstein made a bust of his new son-in-law. A grandson of the great Sigmund, the inventor of psycho-analysis, Freud was one of the most gifted and original of a group of young English artists, including Keith Vaughan, John Minton and John Craxton, who came into prominence during and immediately after the war. In his portraits — and he made a number of Kitty — he showed a microscopic observation which had about it an element of Germanic ruthlessness. Lucian and Kitty Freud had two daughters whom Epstein was later to portray. The painter was modelled looking down and slightly to the left with a somewhat menacing expression, his bare arms detached from his sides and cut off above the elbow. The head was also cast separately.

DR. WILLIAM WHITTAKER, a composer and musicologist, collector of North Country folk songs and editor of

472

473

474

472 LORD
LINDSAY
OF BIRKER

473 DR WILLIAM
WHITTAKER

474 ISAAC
MYERS

475 LUCIAN
FREUD

475

Bach and Handel, was another sitter in 1946. The head went straight up north without ever being exhibited in London. Comparatively unknown (and certainly never illustrated until now), this is only one of many studies, which, if it were the only work of its author to survive, would still earn for him a place among the world's most illustrious sculptors.

How different to the humane but tragic and Hardy-esque features of Dr. Whittaker are those of the bland, optimistic Socialist, LORD LINDSAY OF BIRKER, the retiring Master of Balliol, whose portrait the college commissioned in 1947.

ISAAC MYERS, another commission of 1947, was a tobacco magnate from the deep south of America.

476

The British Museum, Epstein's old haunt, was open again after the war. 'I was in the Greek room', he wrote, 'when I noticed the rapt interest of two small dark-eyed boys who, with their peasant-like mother, were examining the antique works. I asked her if she would bring them to my studio to pose for me and she joyfully assented, much to the glee of the children. I worked from the younger one called ANTHONY while the older one aged about eight

476 ANTHONY IN A BALACLAVA HELMET
477 ANTHONY

477

478 LAZARUS

immediately rolled up his sleeves and started making clay vases as if from some age old inheritance.' After modelling the Greek boy's head, the sculptor, as was often his habit, tried out a second version of it, wrapping plasticine round it to form a Balaclava helmet. He had experimented with this kind of decorative addition to the head of the Old Italian Woman he met in Bloomsbury forty years before.

In February 1947 Epstein exhibited his portrait of Churchill — for which, ever since, the demand has far exceeded the limited edition of ten castings — at the Leicester Galleries: it was incongruously surrounded by eighteen of the small nude studies on which he had worked intermittently throughout the war.

It must have been soon after this, probably in the spring of 1947, that he carved LAZARUS out of a tall block of Hopton Wood stone which stood in the studio.

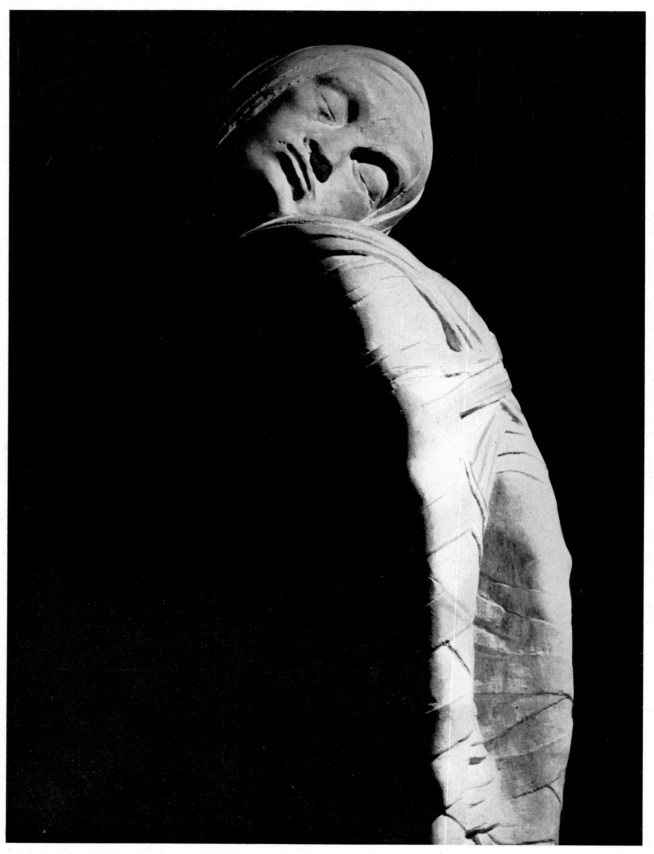

479. 480 LAZARUS

479

480

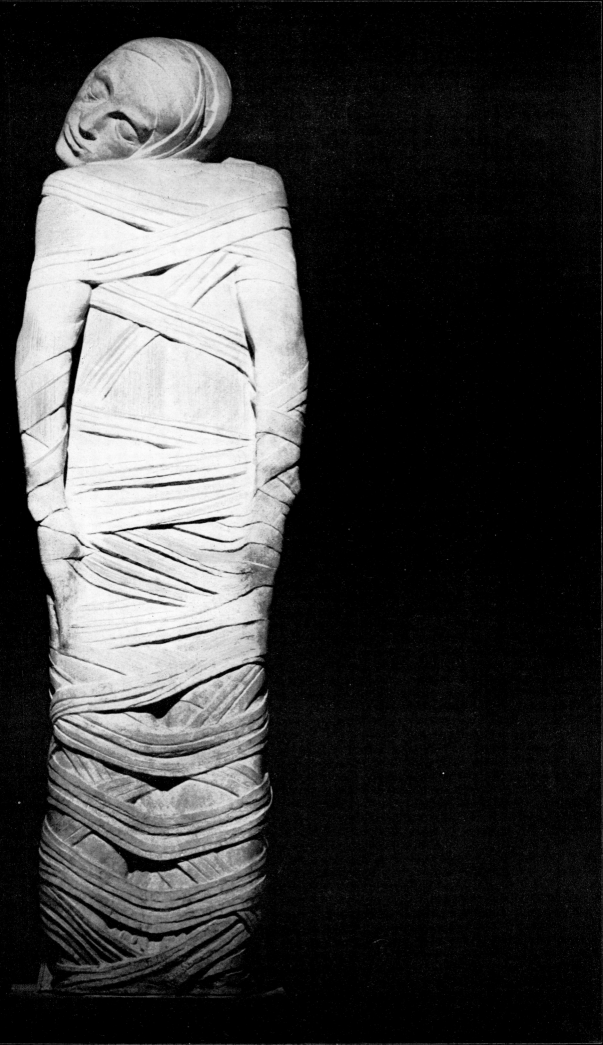

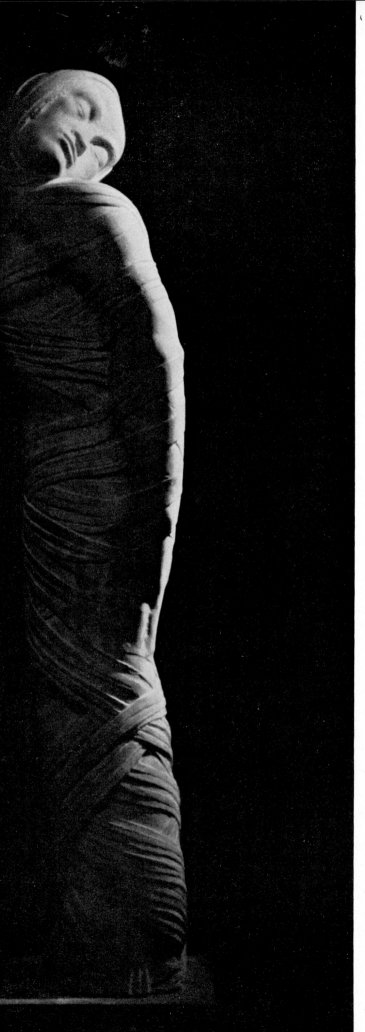

481 LAZARUS

482 2ND PORTRAIT OF
ESTHER

483 HELEN ESTERMAN

'This work,' he wrote, 'suggested by the gospel account of Lazarus being raised from the dead, was the outcome of an idea which had haunted me for many years.'

Emerging from the petrifaction of death, a column coming to life, Lazarus, bound with criss-cross cerements, twists his head stiffly to the left and tries to open his eyes.

I think Epstein intended the principal view-point to be from behind the back of Lazarus, as it was from here he had the statue photographed and he eventually placed it in the ante-chapel of New College in such a way that its back was visible to the congregation during services. But from this angle the constricted shoulders seem too narrow for the big leaning oval of the head and the statue seems subtler and more interesting when the body is seen in left profile. How marvellously rendered is the grimace of a man emerging reluctantly through layer after layer of sleep! To match this for strangeness as well as for skill we must go to Donatello's Magdalen in the Baptistery of Florence, on whose features remorse, love and abjection are so incredibly blended.

Lazarus was finished in 1948: two years later it was exhibited at the Leicester Galleries, received much unfavourable comment and returned unsold to the studio. In 1951 it would be exhibited in an open-air show of sculpture in Battersea Park, and in 1952, as will be related, bought by New College, Oxford. The Warden and Fellows of New College allowed the carving to travel north for the Epstein Memorial Exhibition at the 1961 Edinburgh Festival.

The SECOND PORTRAIT OF ESTHER, also a bust, of which only the plaster is illustrated here, was an attempt at the impossible, that is to better the first on its own terms.

In the third portrait made a year later Epstein would approach his subject in quite a different way and score another triumph; but the second portrait suffers from comparison with its predecessor. This time the thick hair flows more cloudily as if it had just been washed and is fluffed out in a bang over the eyes. It may be that the artist, having first made a portrait of which the predominant mood was melancholy, wanted to model his daughter looking more cheerful — just as after the sad Kathleen of 1933 he felt impelled to catch her laughing. The full lips turn up at the corners, instead of down. The whole eyes, not just the pupils, are hollowed out. In bronzes cast from this plaster the bust ends beneath the shoulders.

HELEN ESTERMAN said she had walked from Ayot St. Lawrence, where Shaw had refused to receive her. She was married to a professor of literature, wrote poems and called her children Dante and Homer. The only bronze of this head, with its torrents of post-war hair, is in the Winnipeg Art Gallery.

482

483

484

485

486

484   LINDA CHRISTIAN
485   JOAN GREENWOOD
486   JILL BALCON
487   FRANKLYN DYALL

Four portraits of the year 1948 enable us to make a page of actors. Epstein used to frequent the Caprice Restaurant in Arlington Street, whose proprietor Mario Gallati collected his sculpture. It was here he saw LINDA CHRISTIAN, liked her face and asked her to pose. The Mexican-born film actress was then the wife of Tyrone Power.

JOAN GREENWOOD had, of course, already posed for Epstein as a child (see Plate 260). She was now making her name as an actress.

JILL BALCON, whose father had been modelled by Epstein in 1934 (see Plate 325) tells the story that she was embarrassed that the sculptor was only modelling her out of politeness, as the head was not a commission; but was put at her ease when Epstein, fearing she might be losing work by sitting for him, offered to pay her by the hour. She later married the poet Cecil Day Lewis.

FRANKLYN DYALL was an old friend. He had once taken Epstein to see Yeats in his rooms behind St. Pancras Station. Yeats told Epstein he was lacking in one of the four elements — earth, fire, air or water; and the sculptor replied 'Stick to poetry!'

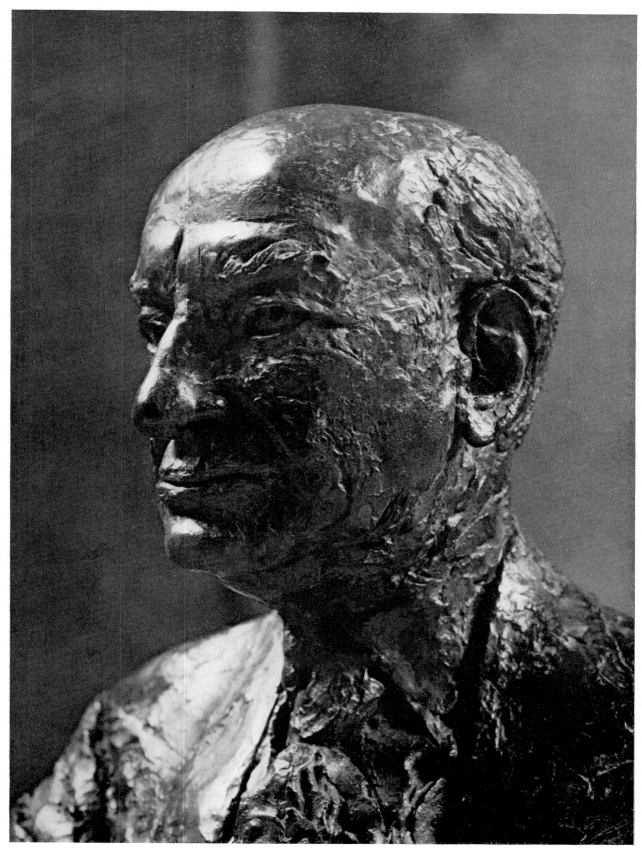

[317]

488. 489
PETER LAUGHING

490
7TH PORTRAIT
OF KATHLEEN

488

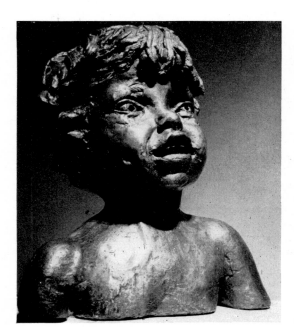

489

PETER LAUGHING was a commission. Having decided to model the child laughing, Epstein deputed to Kathleen Garman the job of keeping him amused, and for several days the studio became a circus. The upward and sideways tilt of the head with its irregularities, the untidy hair, the parted lips, the dimples and the fascinated eyes whose pupils are simply pierced holes — all contribute to an impression of dancing vivacity.

Now, in 1948, Epstein came to model his SEVENTH PORTRAIT OF KATHLEEN, which would also be his last. It was a tall bust showing the body down to the waist in a draped dress whose loose diagonal folds made interesting patterns to complement the arms which were crossed over — but not touching — the chest. Kathleen leans slightly forward but holds her head up. Her hair, which

[319]

491

1921   1922   1931

THE SEVEN
PORTRAITS OF
KATHLEEN

493   494   495

491. 492
7TH PORTRAIT
OF KATHLEEN

492

lies in a heavy fringe over the forehead, is combed behind the ears to fall straight down and break into a foam of curls on the shoulder-blades, like water tumbled on to rocks. From the smooth eighteenth-dynasty face with its salient cheek-bones the seeing eyes, so meticulously placed and drawn beneath their heavy brows, dream forth; the petal lips are about to part — to comment or console.

Epstein's first portrait of Kathleen (1921) had been that of a dreaming girl with the world before her — he had nicknamed it 'Joan of Arc'; his second (1922) was more sultry and sensuous — an afternoon portrait; then came Cassandra (1931); the laughing Kathleen (1933) was an experiment; the great portrait (1935), with arms, seemed to combine the qualities of the previous two in an extraordinary image of *das Ewig-Weibliche* — Circe; in the next (1941), the top half of the 'Girl with Gardenias', she was thoughtful; and now (1948) Kathleen was the Sibyl who like Eliot's Tiresias had 'foresuffered all.'

1933   1935   1941   1948

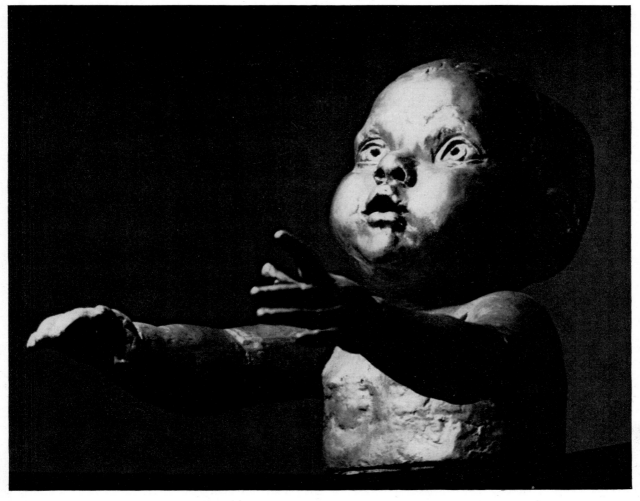

501

500   VICTOR
501. 502   BABY WITH ARMS

In 1949 Kathleen engaged a West African cook. She
arrived at the door of 18, Hyde Park Gate, with five suit-
cases and her little son dressed entirely in white satin.
The boy's name was VICTOR; and Epstein made of him
one of his most delightful heads. Negro children are often
more attractive than white ones: and the sculptor, in
modelling the planes of the boy's head, has conveyed
both a quality of sturdiness and an air of expectancy.
Epstein thought him a handsome model, and wrote, 'It
was a good thing that there was something to compensate
for his mother's culinary defects.'

BABY WITH ARMS, a daughter of Michael Stewart, was
one of the sculptor's most appealing studies of children.
Less than a year old, the girl looks up as if bewildered at
some bright object which is being dangled before her,
and her hands stretch out to grasp it, the fingers splayed
at funny awkward angles.

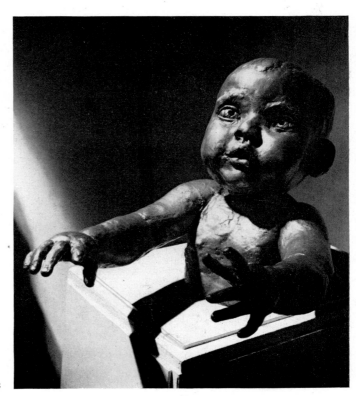

503 PANDIT NEHRU   [324]

It was a year since PANDIT NEHRU had given the sculptor three brief sittings. He now returned to England and Epstein carried on where he had left off, completing a portrait bust. 'At this time, so soon after the assassination of Mahatma Gandhi, Nehru seemed burdened with the cares of office and it was in this mood that I conceived this sombre portrait.'

Epstein, who seldom went to parties, accepted an invitation to meet ERNEST BLOCH, but missed the composer, who had 'hurried off to a rehearsal of his "Sacred Service"'. 'However, when he heard that I had been there to meet him he came to my studio unannounced one Sunday morning as I was leaving for the country.

Cancelling my plans I at once put him on the stand and started his portrait. I am told that the whole house resounded with the ensuing conversation, carried on in a resonant mixture of several tongues. Nevertheless the portrait developed rapidly, assisted by Bloch's complete lack of self-consciousness and what might be truly called a dynamic personality. His conversation was a series of eruptions alternating between despair at his chequered career and wild hilarity. He invited us to hear him conduct the rehearsal of his music for a recording . . . I greatly enjoyed these somewhat stormy sessions with Ernest Bloch. . . .' It is the plaster cast of the head of Bloch which is reproduced here.

LADY MADELEINE LYTTON, a Chelsea friend of Kathleen Garman's, was another sitter during 1949. She had also posed, holding orchids, for a Steuben glass vase.

Wide-eyed SIOBHAN with her wavy hair was a commission. And so was straight-haired JUDITH MARGULIES with her bow and party frock. Her father Alexander Margulies, the collector, had posed for Epstein during the war.

The sculptor's youngest child Kitty, the wife of the painter Lucian Freud, was by now the mother of a daughter. The SECOND PORTRAIT OF KITTY shows her with short hair combed forward, looking up with a wondering expression. It is a curious experiment, in that the upper eyelashes are modelled in relief on the underneath of the overhanging brow. Eyelashes are seldom rendered in sculpture, though the Charioteer of Delphi had them.

The last 'Esther' is as different as possible from the first, and in its way no less successful. It is also surely among the most elegant portraits ever made. How strange the contrast between that first brooding, sultry

505 LADY MADELEINE LYTTON
506 SIOBHAN
507 JUDITH MARGULIES
508 2ND PORTRAIT OF KITTY

509–511
3RD PORTRAIT
OF ESTHER

509

510

and mysterious image with its lank Egyptian wig, and this THIRD PORTRAIT OF ESTHER, the bust of a girl poised, serene and adorned for an evening in society. She wears her glamour with an eighteenth-century nonchalance, like a Tiepolo goddess or one of those worldly personifications of the Virtues with which Serpotta adorned the white oratories of Palermo.

In his old age Epstein was evolving a new 'smooth' style of modelling which was to be perhaps his supreme technical achievement. In his early days in England, before he developed the 'rough' impressionistic technique for which his portraits of the 'twenties and 'thirties were famous, he had modelled heads with a smooth surface such as those of Romilly John (Plate 16) and Marie Rankin (Plate 78). But the smoothness of those heads had been of a monumental character, and sprang from a wish to render a portrait ideal and timeless as a carved Buddha. Just as Epstein had insisted in the 'twenties that his rough texture was not 'finish' applied at the last moment, but something which grew from within, so this new smoothness of his later heads was the rough surface of the middle period carried a step further.

511

512

513

512 PRINCESS DESTA
513 PRINCESS MENAN
514 BRACHA ZEFIRA
515 ELIZABETH TINDALL-LISTER

514

515

516

PRINCESS DESTA and PRINCESS MENEN (of whom the sculptor made a second study with ear-rings not reproduced here) were the half-Belgian nieces of the Empress of Abyssinia. At the time Epstein modelled their handsome heads they were sharing a room at the St. Martin's Hotel with their mother and a small nephew who was later to become celebrated in France as the pop singer Johnny Halliday.

BRACHA ZEFIRA, also modelled in 1949, was a Yemenite singer.

When asked for biographical details to be included in these notes, ELIZABETH TINDALL-LISTER, whose swanlike neck Epstein evidently admired so much that he exaggerated its length, replied modestly that her only claim to fame was to have posed for Epstein.

The CHINESE BOY was only half-Chinese. Epstein chose him as the model for his statue 'Youth Advancing' commissioned for the Festival of Britain.

516. 517 CHINESE BOY

517

1950-57

LATE HARVEST OF COMMISSIONS

The last decade of Epstein's life was probably the happiest, but it was marked by more than one personal tragedy.

Margaret Epstein had died in 1947. Her force of character and faith in the sculptor's genius had played an important role throughout his career; and her supervision of financial matters and indeed of almost every aspect of his life outside the studio continued to the end. Theo, who at the age of five had posed for the boy's figure in the group 'Day' on the Underground building, had grown up devoted to the father he only saw on certain days of the week. But from 1950 he suffered increasingly from the illness which would destroy him in 1954. Nevertheless, he had developed into an unusually talented painter, and in the foreword to the catalogue of his Redfern Gallery exhibition in 1949 Matthew Smith spoke of 'the intoxication caused by these lovely and impressive paintings'. When Theo fell ill Epstein offered to take him as a pupil in his studio. He had no understanding of illness, thinking the practice of sculpture could cure anything: and he did not understand why his offer was rejected.

'Day' and 'Night', carved in 1929, had been the last sculptures Epstein was commissioned to make for a public building. For twenty years architects and public bodies had been too scared of the publicity which his imaginative works invariably attracted to give him a job. Then suddenly the tide turned, and he was generally accepted as the grand old man of British sculpture.

The commissioning in 1949 of 'Youth Advancing' by the Arts Council for the Festival of Britain had been the first sign of the tide's turning. Orders for the Cavendish Square 'Madonna and Child', for 'Social Consciousness', for 'Bishop Woods', for 'Christ in Majesty', for the 'Liverpool Giant', for 'Smuts', for 'Blake', for 'St. Michael and the Devil' for the T.U.C. War Memorial, for 'Lloyd George' and for the Bowater House group followed in rapid succession. Setting aside the three posthumous portraits, these may be divided into three categories. First, modelled figures in movement (in the style of 'Girl with Gardenias' and 'Lucifer') verging on the realistic: such were 'Youth Advancing', the 'Liverpool Giant' (more stylised) and 'St. Michael'. Second,

static 'Byzantine' images, in which an idealised face was framed in formal, architectural drapery: such were the 'Madonna and Child', and the 'Llandaff Christ'. 'Social Consciousness' fell half-way between these two styles. Thirdly, carvings; of these there was only one, the T.U.C. Memorial, and like all Epstein's big carvings it was in the neo-primitive style.

Epstein was supremely self-confident and incapable of playing for safety. Just as he had shocked the low-brows with the massive carvings of his middle age, so, growing more fascinated by that will-o'-the-wisp of sculptors, the portrayal of movement, he was to throw himself open to ridicule from a new generation of high-brows who had grown up to admire nothing less abstract than the immutable landscape-figures of Henry Moore.

The demand for Epstein's portraits was as steady as ever. He was called upon to model some of the eminent and interesting men of his day; and not a few of these commissioned portraits, far from being turned out perfunctorily, were among his best works.

Although in the 'fifties Epstein made portraits in several styles, he tended increasingly to give his heads the smooth finish at which he had begun to aim in the 'forties. The subtleties arrived at as a result of this 'pulling together', which was sometimes accompanied by a drawing on of little lines, leads me to call this his 'psychological' manner.

During the 'fifties Epstein would make two trips to America, and as his health grew worse would be persuaded into holidays in Scotland, Italy and France: but most of his time was spent working steadily in Hyde Park Gate, where Kathleen at last came to look after him, and it was in this same house where he had lived since 1928 that he died.

*　　*　　*

GWEN, LADY MELCHETT, of whom the sculptor made in 1950 an unusual head with the right hand holding back her flaxen hair, was the widow of the second Lord Melchett, herself a collector of works of art, and a friend of Epstein and Kathleen.

[332]

518 GWEN, LADY MELCHETT [333]

Of RALPH VAUGHAN WILLIAMS, the composer, who came to sit in 1950, Epstein wrote 'Here was the master with whom no one would venture to dispute. [How many people in the past must have thought that of Epstein himself!] He reminded me in appearance of some eighteenth-century admiral whose word was law. Notwithstanding, I found him the epitome of courtesy and consideration and I was impressed by the logic and acuteness of everything he discoursed upon and was made aware of his devotion to an art as demanding as sculpture. . . . We were received with charming hospitality by the Master at his country home in Dorking, from where we went at his invitation to hear his annual performance conducting the Bach St. Matthew Passion.'

519. 520 RALPH VAUGHAN WILLIAMS

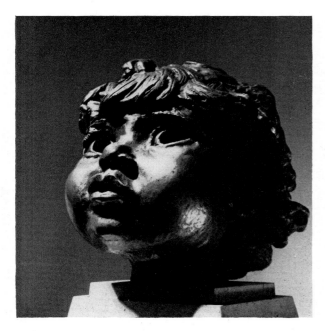

522

In his powerful rendering of the composer's head, Epstein reverted to his 'rough' style of modelling. This may have been because he saw him as a rugged giant or because he chose to break off at a moment when he had caught what he was aiming at and feared to lose it by imposing a smoother finish. This became one of the sculptor's most sought-after bronzes, a rival in popularity to those of Einstein and Churchill.

A pictorial genealogical tree could be made of Epstein's family from Epstein's drawings and sculptures of them. He had drawn, modelled or carved all his children, Peggy Jean, Theo, Jackie, Kitty and Esther; he had portrayed Peggy Jean's husband Norman Hornstein, and their two children, Leda and Ian; and had modelled Kitty's first husband Lucian Freud (and would model her second) and now he made a head of Kitty's elder daughter ANN FREUD. With her parted lips and upturned wondering eyes, Ann seems intended as a *pendant* or sequel to the 'First Portrait of Kitty (with curls)'.

DIANA COPPINGER HILL came from Suffolk to pose. Epstein placed her head, with its intelligent quizzical expression, on the end of a long neck to allow for the looped-up braids of hair at the back to make a good pattern.

ROLAND JOFFÉ was the son of Mark Joffé, author and publisher, who lived abroad, and he became an adopted member of the Epstein household.

521. 522 ANNE FREUD
523   DIANA COPPINGER HILL
524   ROLAND JOFFÉ

523

524

526

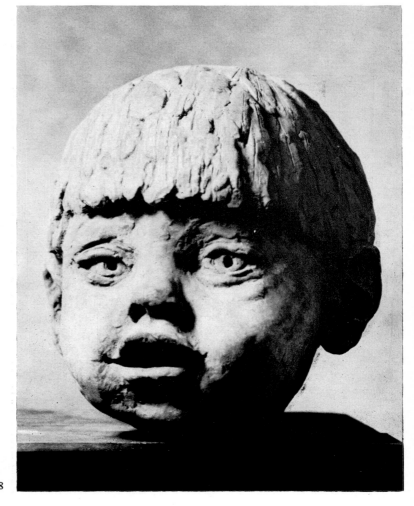

527

525 ISOBEL HUGHES
526 PENELOPE HUGHES
527 CHRISTINE HUGHES
528 CHRISTOPHER HUGHES

It was Matthew Smith who introduced Mr. and Mrs. Peter Hughes to Epstein, as he thought the sculptor would be attracted to their four-year-old youngest daughter Isobel, who had a chubby face full of character and long curling hair. The introduction led to all four Hughes children being modelled.

The head of ISOBEL HUGHES, one of the sculptor's finest portraits of children, was destined to inspire one of the cherub's heads on the doorhandles Epstein gave to the Convent of the Holy Child Jesus and to Coventry Cathedral. Of Isobel's two elder sisters PENELOPE HUGHES with her amused, musing look and short swept-back hair, and the more serious CHRISTINE HUGHES, and of their brother CHRISTOPHER HUGHES, with his fringe and open mouth, Epstein made lively portraits too. Notice how loose strands of hair have been drawn or scratched over the forehead, and how, though the modelling is infinitely delicate and smooth, the sculptor felt it necessary to leave a squarish patch of roughness below the left brow.

The bust of LORD SAMUEL, with its benign but shrewd expression was commissioned by a Liberal admirer for presentation to the Reform Club.

DR. BETHEL SOLOMONS, a well-known Dublin personality, was a fox-hunting doctor and head of the Rotunda gynaecological hospital in Dublin.

Another portrait Epstein made in 1949 was that of the GAEKWAR OF BARODA, whose small son would sit three years later.

PROFESSOR PATRICK BLACKETT, the eminent physicist and Nobel Prizewinner, had a handsome rugged head, and the sculptor made a striking portrait of him. How is it we can tell by looking at it that the Professor is a tall man?

In March 1950 Epstein exhibited 'Lazarus' with some bronzes at the Leicester Galleries. Shortly after this he received an exciting commission.

The Society of the Holy Child Jesus, an order of nuns, occupied the two handsome pedimented Palladian houses in the middle of the north side of the square, which had been built about 1770 on a site where the Duke of Chandos had once planned for himself a palace never erected. The houses were separated by a lane, and after taking them over the Society decided to span this with a bridge. The architect appointed to build this was Louis

529

529 LORD SAMUEL
530 DR BETHEL SOLOMONS
531 GAEKWAR OF BARODA

531

530

532 PROFESSOR PATRICK
BLACKETT

532

Osman, who designed a windowless bridge recessed from the square, framed by Corinthian pilasters and topped by a balustrade. He planned to have a group of sculpture pinned to the flat wall of this bridge, which would thus become the focal point of a grand architectural unit; and was determined that Epstein should make it. The story of how the nuns were persuaded, how Epstein was interested, how Sir Kenneth Clark on behalf of the Arts Council contributed and of various vicissitudes which befell is too long to tell here. Suffice it that Louis Osman had the daring, determination and diplomacy to commission Epstein, unknown to the nuns; to insist that the work should be a monumental bronze, not a carving;

to keep the whole thing secret so that the sculptor could work tranquilly, unprovoked to any violent excesses by Press or public; to persuade the Society to accept Epstein as a sculptor; and to raise money to pay for the group.

The sculptor joyfully undertook this first commission for twenty years to adorn a building, though the fee was only a thousand pounds. In his little maquette he made clear his intentions. The group would have a formal vertical composition, but slightly lozenge-shaped, the better to dominate the empty wall. In the sketch the Virgin's head was based on that of Kathleen: it resembles her last portrait. The nuns approved the design, only asking that the Madonna's expression be more resigned.

[341]

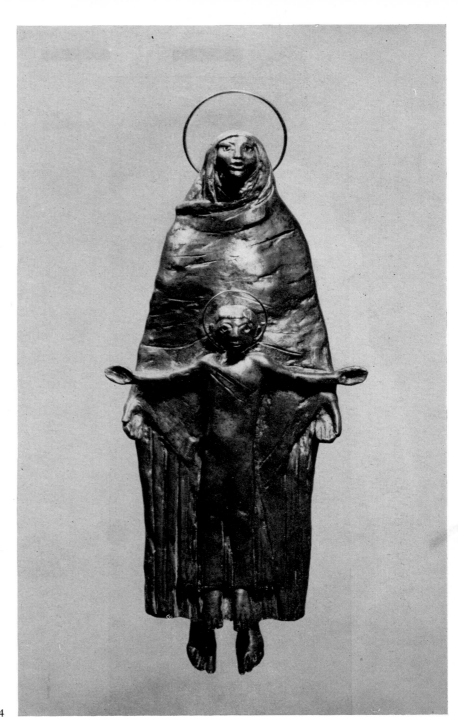

533 MARCELLA BARZETTI

534 MAQUETTE FOR THE
CAVENDISH SQUARE-
MADONNA AND CHILD

534

So whereas the MAQUETTE FOR THE CAVENDISH SQUARE MADONNA AND CHILD has Kathleen's features, the finished statue would have those of another woman.

Earlier that year an Italian pianist, MARCELLA BARZETTI, had come to London with an introduction to Kathleen Epstein. Kathleen met her by appointment at a shop in Wigmore Street, where she was practising, kept the taxi waiting nearly an hour while Marcella played Busoni's 'Fantasia contrappuntistica', then took her home to play for Epstein. The Italian girl had a pinched and private-looking face, so Kathleen thought, and her looks were not improved by a bad cold. Nevertheless the sculptor saw right through to her bones, and insisted on modelling her on the spot. When the nuns made their comment on his maquette Epstein decided to adapt his head of Marcella for the Virgin. Not only was she to become the Madonna and hang in Cavendish Square a few yards from where she had first played Busoni to Kathleen: she was later to be the right hand gliding figure of Death in the Philadelphia group.

[343]

535 A. H. SMITH
536 YOUTH
   ADVANCING

536

Early in 1951 Epstein was commissioned to make a bust of A.H. SMITH, Warden of New College. 'I...was reminded when working from him of one of the great humanist scholars of the Renaissance. It must have been during the third sitting after an unusually quiet spell, for he was a great talker, that the Warden said, contemplating the "Lazarus" — "How wonderful that would look in our cloisters at New College!" ' We shall see later what came of this project.

The sculptor had been working since 1949 on YOUTH ADVANCING, an over-lifesize figure, commissioned by the Arts Council for the Festival of Britain, and in 1951 the finished bronze was set up by a pool on the South Bank site. This realistic male nude, with the Chinese Boy's head (see Plates 516 & 517) was clearly meant as a symbol of ecstatic optimism. The head thrown back with its long hair, the nostrils dilated to sniff the spring, the clenched fists, the right foot dancing forward through the air — are intended to convey a feeling of youth exulting in its own strength and potentialities. But it is all a little too much. Looking at 'Youth Advancing', we think of *Kraft durch Freude* and are embarrassed.

[345]

535

537

The Fairmount Park Trust of Philadelphia invited
Epstein to make a big group to stand on the terrace
behind the Philadelphia Gallery of Art, so he travelled
to the United States, visited Philadelphia and spent a
short holiday at Cape Hatteras with Peggy Jean and her
family. Norman Hornstein was the only doctor on the
island and Peggy Jean used to deliver all the children
born on it. Epstein observed giant turtles in a swamp,
collected odd-shaped stones and pieces of driftwood on
the beach and delighted to watch the storms and rough
seas through which ships had to make their way, bound
to or from the naval base of Norfolk, Virginia. It was
half a century since he had cut ice and watched sunsets
with Bernard Gussow on Greenwood Lake, New Jersey.

The subject of the Philadelphia Group was to be
'Social Consciousness' — an awkward title, if a noble
theme. Epstein made three tentative sketches in plasticine, later cast in plaster: a WARRIOR WITH SWORD, a
MOURNER, and a MAQUETTE FOR THE SEATED MOTHER.
The last of these was the only one he followed up in the
final work.

[346]

538

537 WARRIOR WITH
SWORD
MOURNER

538 MAQUETTE FOR THE
SEATED MOTHER

539 LADY ANNE TREE

539

The bust of LADY ANNE TREE is an extreme example of the sculptor's late smooth style and of the supreme technical accomplishment at which he arrived in old age. So skilled was he that he no longer had to break up, to exaggerate or to distort in order to achieve likeness and vitality. Houdon could not have modelled the girl's features more tenderly. As ever the artist pays attention to the individual quality of the hair, rendering it in an attractive chunky way: and one would think the sitter's hairdresser, being also a plastic artist of a kind, must have been flattered to see his or her work touched with the wand of immortality.

During the summer of 1951 'Lazarus' was exhibited in an open-air show of sculpture in Battersea Park. That winter Epstein modelled T. S. Eliot.

The sculptor had long wanted to portray the poet,

[347]

like himself an American by birth, though born into a milieu which was the antithesis of his own. What had the Bostonian and the Polish Jew from Hester Street in common but language, their adopted British nationality, and the fact that their works, at once revolutionary and traditional, had inspired a whole generation? The present writer remembers with what especial passion, as a schoolboy, he discussed the latest poems of Eliot with his companions, and as vehemently defended the sculpture of Epstein from the sarcasm of his aunts.

Ashley Dukes, the playwright, who had been a friend of Epstein's since the days of Hulme, Orage and the Vortex, and who had put on Eliot's first play, 'Murder in the Cathedral' at his Mercury Theatre, brought the poet to the studio and commissioned the bust. 'I was very impressed', wrote Epstein, 'by the grave courtesy of his bearing frequently lighted up by a smile at once genial and ironical. Eliot himself seemed most interested in the development of the work and on one occasion came with me to the foundry where my large "Madonna and Child" was being cast in lead and seemed profoundly impressed. I look back on those sittings with pleasure.'

Epstein modelled T. S. ELIOT with head hanging forward in an attitude of polite attention to his muse. He has the air of a benevolent bird of prey. The planes are juxtaposed with extraordinary subtlety; the marks of time are faithfully charted; and the sitter lives, reflects, waits, listens. Few of our poets have been portrayed so well.

How different and yet how successful in their diverse ways are the busts of Warden Smith, of Lady Anne Tree and of Eliot, all made within a year. The high-minded scholar with his aspiring look, the carefree young woman and the pensive poet are remarkable from whatever angle they are surveyed. And yet so learned an authority on modern art — notably on the Impressionists and Picasso — as Douglas Cooper could write after the sculptor's death that posterity may well be grateful for 'Epstein's portraits of our leading contemporaries, even if it finds that many of them look alike and does not rate Epstein highly as a sculptor.' The same critic argues that Epstein's works can be looked at only from one side (which is true of certain carvings, and sometimes, of course, intended), and claims that with the bust of Eliot 'the profile view is the most significant and expressive', though this does not make it 'less two-dimensional'. The photographs reproduced here should prove this not to be the case. That Epstein's sculpture lacked intimacy, that 'not one of his portraits suggests that it was born of a feeling of deep sympathy with some other human being' and that 'Epstein tended to read virtues, charms or failings with his sitters and relied on a broad delineation of character to assist him in obtaining a spectacular effect' are other charges which a study of these three busts made in 1951 should alone be sufficient to refute.

541

540. 541. 542
T. S. ELIOT

542

543

The sculptor had worked on the thirteen-foot-high group of the CAVENDISH SQUARE MADONNA AND CHILD for six months. 'Then', wrote Epstein, 'the day arrived for the Mother Superior to come and view it. She came with another sister and they immediately showed the warmest interest in the work and asked to be allowed to contemplate it quietly and alone for some time. After that they returned several times bringing different nuns on each occasion and eventually the work was cast. .. .' It was cast in lead.

[350]

543. 544. 545
CAVENDISH SQUARE MADONNA AND CHILD

546

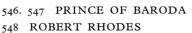
546. 547 PRINCE OF BARODA
548 ROBERT RHODES   547

As in the seated 'Madonna and Child' of 1927, the Mother looks thoughtfully down; but in the first group the Son — Enver — was a more human little boy, while this Christ, whose arms outstretched to embrace the world form a cross, has the shining face of a god. The group has a Byzantine simplicity and grandeur. There is justification for considering it Epstein's finest monumental work.

During the winter of 1952 the sculptor made one of his most perfect portraits of children. PRINCE OF BARODA, whose father the Maharajah had been modelled in 1950 (see Plate 531), was anyway a beautiful boy with serene classical features. The big musing eyes, the little nose and the clearly delineated lips are set in a face whose golden curves contrast with the horizontal lines of the hair brushed rightwards across the forehead.

Another boy's portrait of this time was that of the perky ROBERT RHODES.

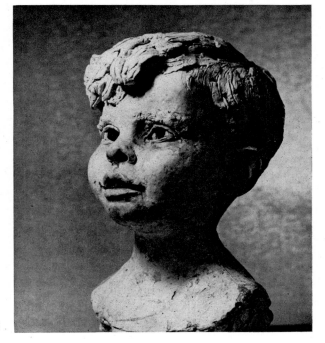

z   548

549
SOMERSET MAUGHAM

550
UNFINISHED CLAY
OF SOMERSET MAUGHAM

549

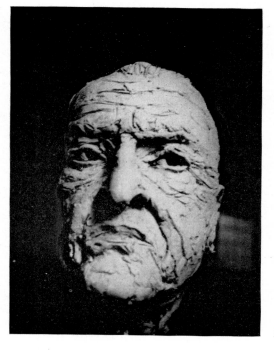

Of SOMERSET MAUGHAM, the playwright and novelist, whom Epstein sculpted in 1951, he wrote that 'he reminded me strongly of some old Roman patrician. In spite of his fastidious and aloof expression he proved a model sitter, was most genial whilst posing and discoursed on contemporary letters most entertainingly. We would leave the studio door open while a friend [Beth Lipkin] played Mozart on the piano much to his delight.' Both the unfinished clay and the plaster cast of this extraordinarily pungent portrait are here reproduced.

LOUIS CLARKE, Director of the Fitzwilliam Museum from 1937 to 1946, was portrayed with an air of cavalier elegance which cannot but have been pleasing to the genial host and fastidious collector. Between 1937 and his death in 1960 he was to give the Museum 2,700 works of art, and in his will would bequeath many

550

more, including his bust by Epstein. His whole face flickers with life and humour.

Another commissioned portrait of 1951 was that of MINDA BRONFMAN, heiress of a Canadian whisky fortune, who later became Baroness Ginsberg.

1952 was to be a year of triumph for Epstein, during which he would see the final placing of his 'Madonna and Child' and his 'Lazarus'; and enjoy a small premature apotheosis in his Retrospective Exhibition at the Tate. While modelling the huge group for Philadelphia he would nevertheless find time to execute several commissioned portraits. These were: PORTLAND MASON, daughter of the film actor James Mason; GINA LOLLO-BRIGIDA, the Italian film actress; DAME HILDA LLOYD of the Faculty of Medicine, Birmingham University; MARK JOFFE, writer and publisher; and LORD SIMON OF WYTHENSHAWE, the world-famous authority on Birth Control.

551 LOUIS CLARKE
552 MINDA BRONFMAN
553 PORTLAND MASON
554 GINA LOLLOBRIGIDA
555 DAME HILDA LLOYD
556 MARK JOFFE
557 LORD SIMON OF WYTHENSHAWE

551

552

553

554

555

556

557

558

Another cause of joy for Epstein was the purchase by New College of 'Lazarus'. Following the suggestion of Warden Smith, whom he had modelled in the previous year, he visited Oxford to consider the site. 'Beautiful and ideal as the green lawn in the centre of the cloisters is,' wrote the sculptor, 'in consultation with the Warden we decided that in view of the action of the English climate on stone, it would be better to place the carving in New College Chapel . . . the carving was bought and placed at the west end of New College Chapel. This was one of the happiest issues of my working life.'

In the autumn of 1952 the Arts Council staged a retrospective exhibition of Epstein's work at the Tate.

That the exhibition, his biggest yet, was attended by 70,000 people, gave Epstein further cause for satisfaction. The show, he wrote, 'resulted in a purchase for the

558 LAZARUS THE CHAPEL OF
NEW COLLEGE, OXFORD

559 CAVENDISH SQUARE
MADONNA AND CHILD

559

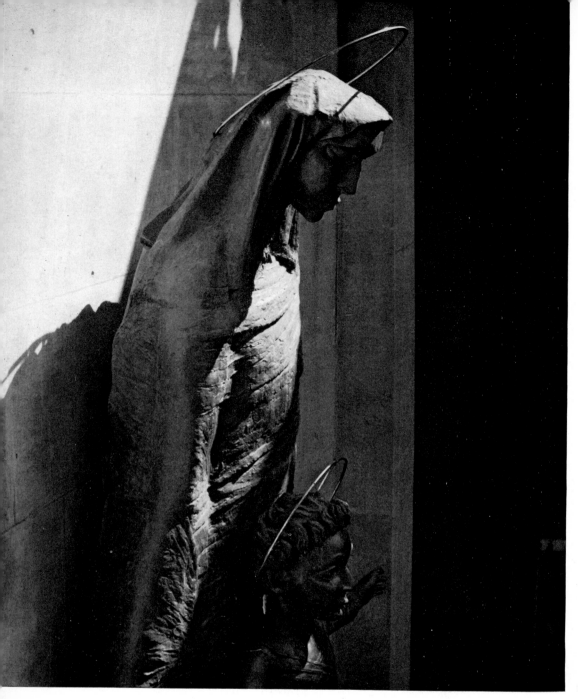

560

Gallery by the Chantrey Bequest of a small bust made over forty years ago' ('Mrs. McEvoy').

On Ascension Day 1953 the great 'Madonna and Child' was raised up and bolted to the side of Louis Osman's fine bridge between the two convent buildings in Cavendish Square. The day of its unveiling arrived. 'It was a May day,' wrote Epstein, 'and fortunately there were brief spells of sunshine for a considerable crowd had gathered and the street had to be cordoned off for the opening ceremony performed by Mr. R. A. Butler, the Chancellor of the Exchequer. This ceremony seemed to reach back to the days of the Renaissance when the appearance of a new religious work was the occasion for public rejoicing.

'No work of mine has brought so many tributes from so many diverse quarters. One which particularly pleased me by reason of its spontaneity was from a bus driver. Halting his bus as he passed the statue he suddenly saw me standing by and called out across the road, "Hi Governor, you've made a good job of it." '

[358]

561

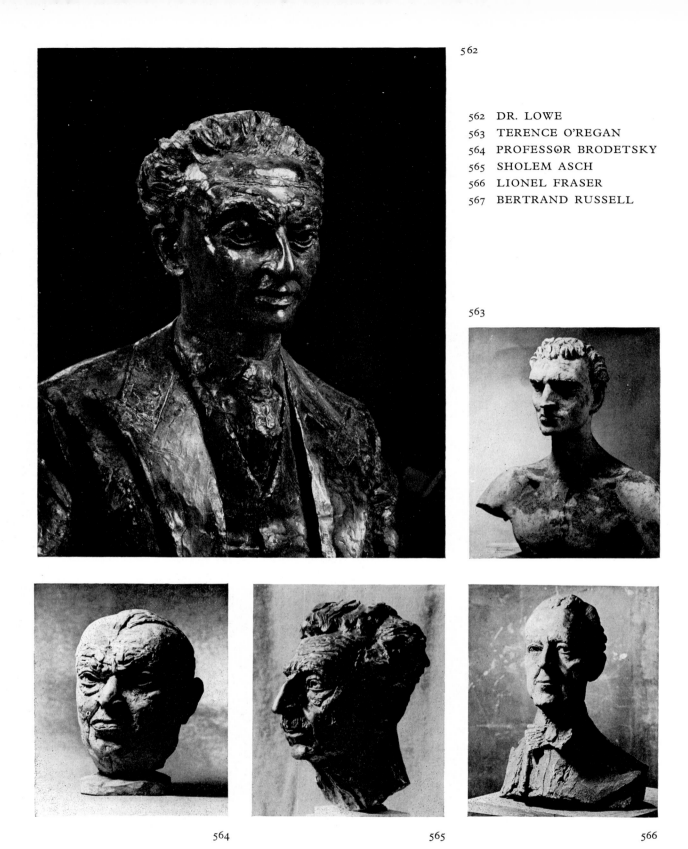

562

562 DR. LOWE
563 TERENCE O'REGAN
564 PROFESSOR BRODETSKY
565 SHOLEM ASCH
566 LIONEL FRASER
567 BERTRAND RUSSELL

563

564   565   566

DR. ELIAS LOWE was a friend from Epstein's youth. His over life-size bust was commissioned by Princeton University, and the sculptor made his sitter a gift of the plaster. Other portraits of 1953 were: TERENCE O'REGAN, a young actor; PROFESSOR BRODETSKY, who went from Leeds to the Hebrew University in Jerusalem; SHOLEM ASCH; LIONEL FRASER, Chairman of Tillings; and LORD RUSSELL, philosopher, and worker for peace.

[360]

567

Epstein had long wanted to model BERTRAND RUSSELL and the commission was realised when Russell married the American Miss Finch, who had ordered the bust of 'Professor Donelly' twenty years before. 'Lord Russell, far from being the ponderous philosopher of tradition, was gay and witty as, pipe in hand, he

[361]

568

568 FIRST PORTRAIT OF
ANNABEL FREUD
WITH BONNET

569 SECOND PORTRAIT OF
ANNABEL FREUD

570 MAI ZETTERLING

571 MACE HEAD

572 FRISKY

569

570

carried on a most sprightly conversation.'

It went without saying that Epstein's descendants became his models. In 1953 he sculpted the younger daughter of Kitty and Lucian Freud. There are two versions of the charming FIRST PORTRAIT OF ANNABEL FREUD (WITH BONNET), in one of which she has a bow under the left side of her chin. He also modelled her again later in the year. In the SECOND PORTRAIT OF ANNABEL FREUD, the curly-headed girl is looking down.

Epstein's bust of the Swedish actress MAI ZETTERLING, who had latterly made a name for herself on the London stage, was one of his late smooth portraits, which are still so far removed from the merely academic.

In a moment of relaxation Epstein amused himself by modelling his Shetland sheepdog FRISKY. This little bronze, which conveys well the gentle affectionate character of the animal, was Epstein's only animal sculpture apart from a less finished 'Cat' of 1920.

Another experiment of 1953 was a MACE HEAD with three figures back to back, designed for Singapore, but never realised.

571

572

573 MAQUETTE FOR
CHRIST IN MAJESTY

574 SERAPH

573

574

Meanwhile Epstein had received another commission from Llandaff Cathedral, one of the oldest foundations in the country, which had been bombed in 1941. He travelled to Wales with George Pace the architect and Stanley Spencer, who was to do a mural (never realised). His MAQUETTE FOR CHRIST IN MAJESTY was approved, and he decided to use as a basis for his face of Christ the 1923 'Seraph', a portrait of Marie Collins.

In 1954 Epstein undertook to make a posthumous bust of the Socialist statesman, SIR STAFFORD CRIPPS, for the Crypt of St. Paul's Cathedral. Of the boy CHARLES LANE, a nephew of Lord Rothschild, the sculptor made a delightful bust with bare shoulders. Two other commissioned portraits were those of DR. FREDERICK MALLON, the retiring Irish Governor of Toynbee Hall, whose face was full of comedy and character, and LORD BRAINTREE, the Managing Director of the Crittall Manufacturing Company, makers of metal windows, whose bust was wanted for the factory at Braintree in Essex.

In July 1954 Epstein was knighted. He went to Buckingham Palace to receive the accolade and the insignia of a Knight of the Order of the British Empire from Queen Elizabeth, the Queen Mother. (The Queen was abroad.)

575 SIR STAFFORD CRIPPS
576 CHARLES LANE
577 DR. FREDERICK MALLON
578 LORD BRAINTREE

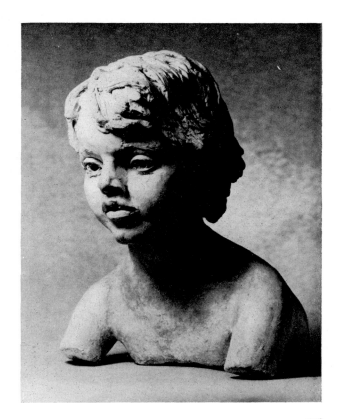

576

575

577

578

580

579 HEAD OF LIVERPOOL GIANT
580 MAQUETTE FOR THE PROW
OF A SHIP
581 HEAD AND SHOULDERS OF
LIVERPOOL GIANT

579

Throughout this year he was working on the Llandaff 'Christ' and another big statue. Because the studio in Hyde Park Gate was too low for these works to be made other than in sections, the Royal College of Art, whose sculpture school was only a few hundred yards away in Exhibition Road, put at his disposal a loftier workroom.

Shortly before this time, Epstein had been visited by Lord Woolton and the directors of Lewis's, the big Liverpool store. They asked him to make a statue to adorn the façade of their shop which would put new heart into Liverpool: the city, they said, had never really recovered from the bombing.

The sculptor decided to model a gigantic male nude striding forward on the prow of a ship, a kind of figurehead. He made a little MAQUETTE FOR THE PROW OF A SHIP, but it was decided to have a plainer base to the figure. Like the Llandaff 'Christ', the nude was modelled in sections in the Hyde Park Gate studio, then put together, finished and cast in plaster at the Royal College.

[366]

582

582 HEAD OF SEATED MOTHER. DETAIL OF SOCIAL CONSCIOUSNESS
583 THE GOOD SAMARITAN. DETAIL OF SOCIAL CONSCIOUSNESS

Throughout 1951 and 1952 Epstein had been working on the big group of five figures for Philadelphia, for which he was to be paid £4,000. In 1953 he finished the modelling, it was cast in plaster, and the plaster cast was taken to Fulham to recast in bronze.

It might be said that SOCIAL CONSCIOUSNESS was Epstein's answer to the Statue of Liberty. No one could claim that vast landmark as a work of art, yet it was dear to millions of American citizens and it was a symbol of American democracy welcoming disillusioned fugitives from the old world to the Land of the Free. 'Give me your tired, your poor, Your huddled masses yearning to breathe, free. . . .' Epstein's parents had been among those who had found a welcome in the United States. The group as a whole stood for the American ideal of Good Samaritanship which

[368]

[369]

2 A

585

had taken on a new meaning in the present century.

The central figure of the group, a seated, long-waisted figure in draperies, though she carries no torch, seems particularly to extend the welcome of the bountiful continent; raising her arms as if to say, 'Come unto me all ye that travail and are heavy laden.' Her features are Sunita's, and the sculptor said of her, 'I had in mind that line [from Whitman's "America"] about "A grand, sane, towering, seated Mother, Chair'd in the adamant of time".'

On her right, or to the left of the group as you look at it, a thirteen-foot high Christ-like Good Samaritan begins to raise from the ground the lifeless figure of another man: 'the Healer succouring the downfallen', wrote Epstein. This is the grandest unit of the group, a kind of

Deposition, the energetic limbs of the standing figure making with the limp arms and legs of the collapsed one an elaborate composition of diagonal lines.

On the right of the group another draped female figure, gliding on the surface of the ground, supports an almost naked youth who hangs from her shoulders by the crook of his elbows like a thief on the cross. This woman's face is that of Marcella Barzetti — indeed her head was evidently cast from the plaster of the 'Cavendish Square Madonna'. Epstein said of her 'I was thinking of Whitman again,' and quoted passages from the poem on Abraham Lincoln 'When Lilacs last in the dooryard bloom'd': 'Come, lovely and soothing death . . . Dark Mother always gliding near, with soft feet . . . Approach, strong Deliveress. . . .'

[371]

584 DETAIL OF SOCIAL CONSCIOUSNESS
585 BACK VIEW OF SOCIAL CONSCIOUSNESS

586

In June 1953 Epstein exhibited eighteen bronzes, including portraits of Warden Smith, Professor Blackett, Eliot, Bertrand Russell, Lady Anne Tree, Lady Melchett and his grand-children at the Leicester Galleries.

In July he received the honorary degree of Doctor of Letters at Oxford from Sir Maurice Bowra, the Vice-Chancellor, and was warmly applauded by the under-graduates as he walked in procession.

For a time the plaster cast of this triumphant pagan and that of the serene omniscient 'Llandaff Christ' shared Epstein's studio at the Royal College of Art.

[372]

586 SOCIAL CONSCIOUSNESS IN THE FOUNDRY
587 LIVERPOOL GIANT AND LLANDAFF CHRIST AT THE ROYAL COLLEGE

588

588 FIELD MARSHAL SMUTS
IN THE STUDIO

589 HEAD OF FIELD MARSHAL
SMUTS

When the Office of Works invited the sculptor to make a slightly over-life-size statue of FIELD-MARSHAL SMUTS for Parliament Square he decided, as a change from the usual static official effigy, gesticulating meaninglessly, to represent him in motion. Epstein had never met the great South African, but he was shown a number of photographs and a film, and decided that a pose with hands clasped behind the back was typical. So he decided to model Smuts in uniform striding along, head in air and hands clasped behind him. In spite of its vivacity — or perhaps because of it — the statue was to look rather odd when placed in position. Epstein always maintained that modern dress was as good as any to sculpt, but there is something about a well-fitting uniform with Sam Browne belt, breeches and laced leather leggings which does not lend itself to sculpture.

The head of Smuts, on the other hand, which was later cast separately, makes a powerful impression.

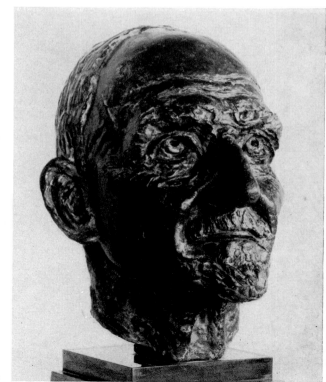

589

590

590. 591
SOCIAL CONSCIOUSNESS
IN PHILADELPHIA

By the time Epstein sailed off to America (on what was to be his last visit) to see his 'Social Consciousness' group unveiled at Philadelphia, he already had the prospect of more grandiose commissions to fulfil.

591

592

593

Some time after the unveiling of the 'Madonna' Louis Osman designed some door-handles which he suggested that Epstein should adorn with cherubs' heads as a present for the Convent in Cavendish Square. The FOUR DOOR-HANDLES took the form of oval knobs, each bearing the face of a different baby angel enclosed in wings. They were based on four child portraits (reproduced beneath them for comparison), namely 'Peter laughing', 'Ian', 'Annabel' and 'Isobel Hughes'. The first and third incorporated praying hands. Unique among Epstein's work, the little bronzes have a marvellous vivacity. A few years later the sculptor had another

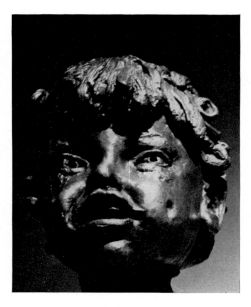

596 PETER

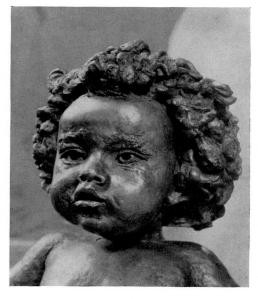

597 IAN

594

595

set cast for Coventry Cathedral.

The huge male nude is rather what one imagines the Colossus of Rhodes to have been like: in style it is a mixture of Archaic formalisation, as in the torso and pelvis, and Hellenistic naturalism, as in the striding legs. The arms are almost naturalistic in treatment too, but the stiff ritualistic gestures they are executing give them a stylised air: the right being raised in a semi-fascist, semi-communist salute, the left extended sideways with clenched fist. As with 'Youth Advancing', so with the

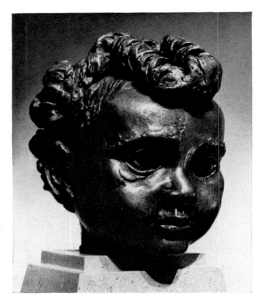

598 ANNABEL

599 ISOBEL

600

601

602

600 LIVERPOOL GIANT
     IN FOUNDRY
601 FRANKLIN MEDAL
     (OBVERSE)
602 FRANKLIN MEDAL
     (REVERSE)

LIVERPOOL GIANT we feel that Epstein in trying to express the ineffable — some *ne plus ultra* of inspiration and heroic uplift — has gone too far. Yet the giant's head, with its ideal and outlined features is resplendent: a Khmer angel with Tony Curtis hair.

The 'Liverpool Giant' was cast and ready to travel north to its final destination.

Epstein had been commissioned to make the silver FRANKLIN MEDAL for presentation to Sir Winston Churchill. On the obverse was a profile of Franklin, on the reverse the shining face of Prometheus peering through the rays of his stolen sun. The medal was presented to Churchill at Craven Street on January 1956, in the sculptor's presence.

[379]

603

603 THE WAVE
604 YOUNG BACCHUS
605 MUSE

604

605

Though busier and more in demand than ever before for large-scale works, Epstein was not too preoccupied, when he relaxed in the evenings, to engender new projects; and his restless fingers would readily transfer his thoughts to plasticine. At least three small sketches survived from 1956 to be cast in bronze after his death by his widow.

THE WAVE was an essay in the arresting of violent movement — that challenge he took up with the fearless daredevilry of old age. How mad to model a wave at the moment of its highest caracole, and a man riding it, his arm raised in triumph! Let another sculptor take over and carry through the thrilling project.

YOUNG BACCHUS, done on a suggestion of Kathleen Epstein, was modelled on the back of the sketch for the Seated Mother in the Philadelphia group, presumably because this was near him when the idea was proposed; and her upraised hands can be seen emerging at the sides. The plumpy god crowns himself with a garland, and inside the triangle formed by his upraised arms his sideways-projecting Infanta coiffure of grapes forms another.

Like 'Young Bacchus' the MUSE, presumably Terpsichore, is in high relief. With her chin tilted to heaven, her swinging arm and rippling transparent draperies she reminds us of Bourdelle's studies of Isadora.

Epstein had made his MAQUETTE FOR THE T.U.C. WAR MEMORIAL, a standing mother holding a dead son in her arms; and the great block of stone, the last he was to carve, was raised on its base in the courtyard off Great Russell Street.

Knowing as we do now how precarious was the state of Epstein's heart at this time, we are intimidated at the thought of this seventy-six year old man tackling the job of carving such a stone. He had never employed assistants in modelling or carving, and he did not do so now: but he was persuaded to allow stonemasons to cut away the rough of this last carving. We may reflect that there is no way of making the practise of sculpture easier for an artist just because he is old and famous: he still has to attack the hard stone with mallet and chisel, balanced precariously on scaffolding in all weathers.

606 MAQUETTE FOR THE
    T.U.C. WAR MEMORIAL

607 EPSTEIN WITH STONE ON SITE
    OF T.U.C. WAR MEMORIAL

606

607

608 WYNNE GODLEY

609   ROSALYN TURECK

Kitty had parted from Lucian Freud and in 1956, she married WYNNE GODLEY, the younger brother of Lord Kilbracken, a musician, who worked in the Treasury. Godley was strikingly handsome, and Epstein lost no time in enlisting him to pose. The result was one of the most carefully observed, subtlest and noblest of the late portraits; and a stylised version of it would supply the head for the Coventry 'St. Michael'.

Throughout his life music was a great solace to Epstein; in his 'seventies he had not abandoned the habit of concert-going formed when a boy in New York. He often heard ROSALYN TURECK play Bach in public and at her home; and when he modelled her head he gave her the look of a seraphic messenger.

[383]

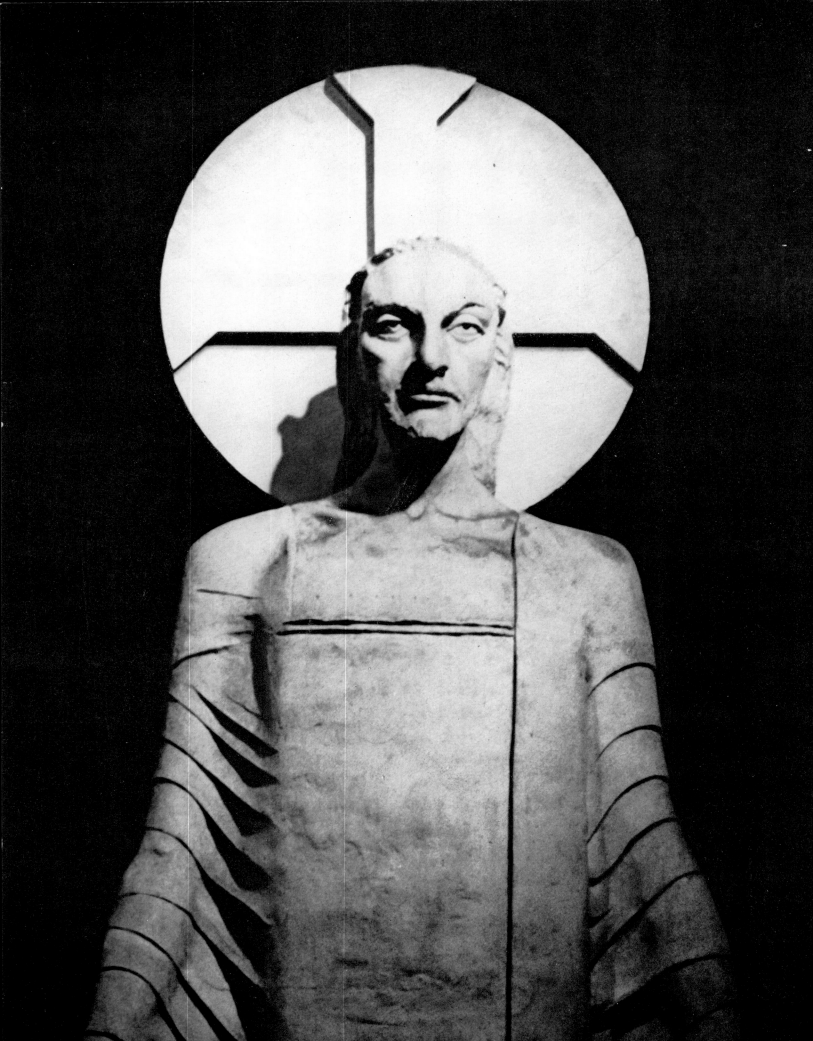

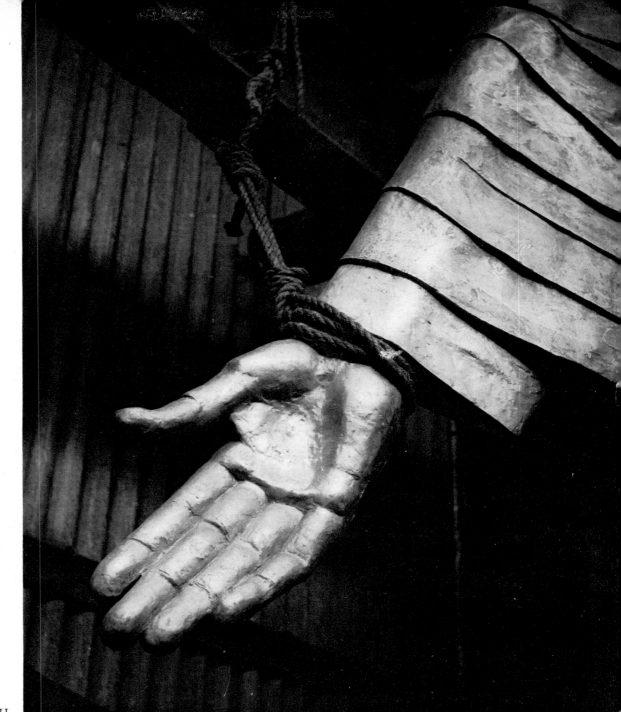

610
HEAD OF
CHRIST IN
MAJESTY
(PLASTER)

611
HAND OF
CHRIST IN
MAJESTY

611

The fee agreed for the CHRIST IN MAJESTY was £2,000 and it had been intended to cast it merely in plaster, then gild it. Epstein, however, quite understandably, was hungry for permanence; and he volunteered to sacrifice £500 of his money so that the statue should be cast in aluminium.

The 'Christ' was conceived as a Pantocrator in the spirit of Byzantine mosaics. The immensely long body and legs are concealed by a garment so simply rendered that it appears little more than a pilaster. Only over the arms which stand out at an angle of fifteen degrees from the body are there any folds. The garment's neck line is cut low and square, and from the bottom left-hand corner of the rectangular opening a seam runs straight down to the hem, dividing the flat pilaster into two un-equal parts. The open, giving hands and the hanging feet which touch no floor protrude, and are modelled with a large and simplified realism. But the most astonishing part of the statue is Christ's haloed head, which rises above the towering simplicity of his garment like the sun

2B

[385]

610

over a cliff. The long hair, the beard, the fine features and the intense eyes are traditional, but they transcend Byzantine, Renaissance, eighteenth- and nineteenth-century traditions. Only consider how the greatest painters have been unable to produce an acceptable image of Christ — not Michelangelo, not Titian; and how even Tintoretto, perhaps the foremost of Christian painters, was always weakest in portraying the founder

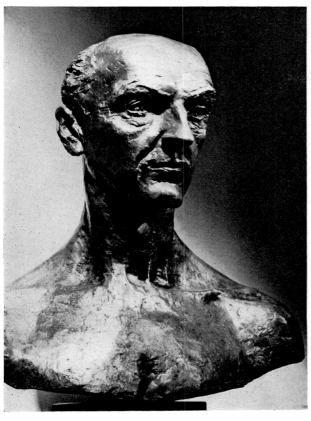

613

614

612 CHRIST IN MAJESTY IN FOUNDRY
613 MARQUESS OF NORMANBY
614 PROFESSOR SIR JAMES GRAY
615 DEAN LOWE

of his faith. Only Rembrandt and El Greco have rivalled Epstein in making heads of Jesus in which virile beauty is balanced by intellectual power.

The Llandaff Christ was cast in aluminium by the firm of Morris Singer in Clapham, who specialised in large-scale works and who were later to cast the Liverpool Giant, the Philadelphia group, St. Michael and the Bowater House group. At the time it was the largest casting in aluminium ever made in this country. The mystery of bronze-moulding was kept within a small group of inter-related firms. Parlanti, Benabo, Fiorini, Carney and Gaskin had cast for Epstein.

In 1956 Epstein executed the following portrait commissions: THE MARQUESS OF NORMANBY, a bust which stands in his house at Mulgrave Castle near Whitby, Yorkshire; PROFESSOR SIR JAMES GRAY for the Department of Zoology, Cambridge; DEAN LOWE of Christ Church, Oxford, for Christ Church Library; and Robert Hesketh for his mother Lady Hesketh to stand in the Hawksmoor house of Easton Neston.

615

616 FIRST SKETCH FOR ROBERT HESKETH
617 ROBERT HESKETH
618 FIELD MARSHAL SMUTS IN
      PARLIAMENT SQUARE

Epstein was dissatisfied with his FIRST SKETCH FOR
THE PORTRAIT OF ROBERT HESKETH and scrapped it.
The plaster is reproduced here for the sake of interest.
He again modelled the sturdy, individual little boy of
five in his sailor suit, and the second ROBERT HESKETH,
looking up, was more successful.

The statue of Smuts was to have been unveiled on
November 7, 1956, by Sir Winston Churchill, but it was
the time of Suez and the ceremony was performed by the
Speaker instead.

616

617

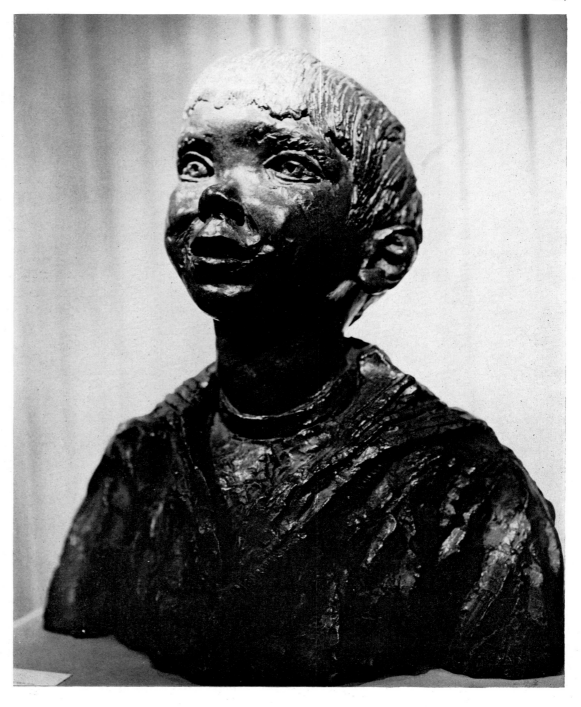

61

620

The 'Liverpool Giant' was unveiled by Lord Woolton in the presence of Sir Jacob and Lady Epstein on November 20, 1956; and buglers of the Royal Lancashire Fusiliers sounded a fanfare as the hanging parted and the colossus was revealed.

There were three spaces above the entrance of Lewis's shop, below the 'Giant'; and rather than have these filled by a lesser artist, Epstein, with a typical gesture of generosity, undertook to throw in three bas reliefs with his statue. He modelled the panels in his studio at the Royal College, and they were cast in concrete. The left hand relief represents CHILDREN FIGHTING and is a scrimmage of eleven boys. The centre relief, the simplest, shows ANNABEL AND FRISKY. Epstein's youngest grand-daughter is seated in a handleless pram with outspread arms, facing the spectator, while the Shetland sheepdog looks up at her, begging. The right-hand relief of CHILDREN PLAYING has a girl in a swing, a boy standing

621   621   ANNABEL & FRISKY

622   CHILDREN FIGHTING   RELIEFS FROM LEWIS BUILDING, LIVERPOOL   623   CHILDREN PLAYING

622   623

on his hands, two girls playing 'Tig' and another who is perhaps skipping, but it is dominated by two boys in the middle, one of whom is leapfrogging over the other towards the spectator.

The MAQUETTE FOR ST. MICHAEL AND THE DEVIL may conveniently be placed here, for it was some time in 1956 that Sir Basil Spence, the architect of the new Coventry Cathedral, set eyes on it for the first time: but the story of Sir Basil, St. Michael and Epstein goes back to the autumn of 1954 when the architect took Bishop Gorton to see the Cavendish Square Madonna. Spence tells in the record of his grand achievement *Phoenix at Coventry*, how the Bishop, bareheaded and 'oblivious of the traffic, stood looking up at this masterpiece. . . . The Bishop said simply "Epstein is the man for us".'

There had been opposition to overcome. 'When I mentioned Epstein to the Reconstruction Committee,' wrote Sir Basil, 'there was a shocked silence, at length broken by the remark, "But he is a Jew"; to which I replied quietly, "So was Jesus Christ." '

During 1955 Spence had gone to see Epstein while he was working on the Llandaff Christ in the Royal College of Art. 'When I asked him if he would accept the commission to do the great figure of St. Michael, he answered, "All my life I have wanted to do Michael. This is a great task." I asked what his fee would be,

624

626

625

624 MAQUETTE FOR
ST. MICHAEL AND THE DEVIL

625 SKETCH FOR ST. MICHAEL TORSO

626 ST. MICHAEL UNFINISHED IN
THE STUDIO

627 CHRIST IN MAJESTY IN LLANDAFF CATHEDRAL 628
628 MAQUETTE FOR BOWATER HOUSE GROUP

saying that funds were low, and he quoted a ridiculously small figure adding, "If the committee can't pay that, I shall reduce it." But his first figure was agreed.'

Then the Committee decided that Epstein was 'such a controversial figure that they must have the backing of the Cathedral Council for his appointment. I presented the case and the meeting was a stormy one. . . . At last by a majority decision it was decided that he should be commissioned to do a "maquette" about eighteen inches high to be submitted to the two committees before going any further.' Spence brought the Provost to lunch with the Epsteins. Asked what his religious beliefs were, the sculptor replied 'My beliefs can be clearly seen through my work (he pronounced it "woik").' Dr. Gorton died and was succeeded by Cuthbert Bardsley, who also proved a warm supporter.

One day Spence read in a paper that Epstein had said his St. Michael for Coventry would be his masterpiece, and hurried round to see what was going on. The sculptor, without waiting to submit the maquette, had begun the upper part of the huge statue, and Wynne Godley's features had already emerged on the face of the

saint. 'Am I going too fast?' Epstein asked. Then added 'Look, I'm not working for the Committee any more, I am working for myself.' Luckily the new Bishop and the Provost, being hastily summoned next day, were quick to appreciate the sculpture's merits. Photographs were taken, which both Committee and Council approved.

On April 10, 1957 the Epsteins travelled up to Cardiff for the dedication of the restored cathedral of Llandaff. The Archbishop of Wales rose from his deathbed to conduct the service, which was attended by three hundred clergy. The great aluminium 'Christ in Majesty' or 'Majestas' as it is also called, was seen in position at last.

About this time Epstein was approached by the directors of Bowaters, the paper manufacturers to design a group to stand before their new building which was to go up next to the Hyde Park Hotel, and which would be pierced by a new entrance to the Park. The sculptor decided to make a kind of Bacchic rout, a group of figures driven by Pan from the city into the woods. He prepared a small MAQUETTE FOR THE BOWATER HOUSE GROUP, and this was approved.

[395]

629

630

629 MARCHIONESS
OF BATH

630 SIR WILFRED
LE GROS CLARKE

631 MARIA DONSKA

631

632. 633
DR. OTTO KLEMPERER

632

633

In 1957, while carving the T.U.C. Memorial, the sculptor made several portraits. THE MARCHIONESS OF BATH, formerly Virginia Parsons, was daughter of Viola Tree and Dennis Parsons, grand-daughter of Sir Herbert Beerbohm Tree. Her aunt Iris Tree and her cousin Marie Beerbohm had posed for Epstein in 1916.

SIR WILFRED LE GROS CLARKE was commissioned for the School of Human Anatomy at Oxford, of which he was head. The bust of MARIA DONSKA was made as a present for the sitter. She had been a friend of the painter Mark Gertler in Vortex days, taught now at the Royal College of Music, and often played the piano for Epstein, who said she was like the young Mozart.

Epstein, always a keen concertgoer, was impressed by the first Beethoven cycle of DR. OTTO KLEMPERER. Hearing this, Mr. T. A. Bean, Manager of the Royal Festival Hall, arranged for the conductor to sit. While the grand, tragic head was being made, a conversation was carried on in German and English; and Klemperer

634

would exclaim 'Heroic!' or 'Wunderbar!' at other works in the studio.

By the summer of 1957 Epstein's heart was in a bad condition, though he never felt conscious of age or weakness when he was working, scorned to call in a doctor and was convinced the practice of sculpture was a panacea against all ills. Kathleen had to look after him tactfully without letting him suspect he was in a precarious state; and she persuaded him against his will to take a holiday in Scotland. Accompanied by young Roland Joffé, they went by Edinburgh to Atholl Palace Hotel, Pitlochry in Perthshire. Epstein soon accustomed himself to being away from the studio and took a fancy to the grim pass of Glencoe. But he could not do without working and daily made pastels of the Perthshire landscape, regardless of bad weather, while Kathleen and Roland prepared a picnic lunch. One day he had an attack and was struck motionless. Kathleen had to leave him with Roland by the roadside while she went to Perth in search of a car to fetch him back.

On his return to London Epstein modelled the THIRD PORTRAIT OF KITTY, his last. Kitty is shown with bare shoulders, the right higher than the left, and with short hair which radiates in neat flames from a point above the

[398]

635

634. 635
  3RD PORTRAIT OF KITTY

636
  SKETCH OF KITTY

637
  1ST PORTRAIT OF KITTY

638
  2ND PORTRAIT OF KITTY

636

637

638

639

forehead. Her face, tense and thin, with its chiselled lips
and scooped out eyes, suggests a tragic mask.

Epstein had been working on an imaginary portrait of
WILLIAM BLAKE, commissioned by the Blake Society for
Poets' Corner in Westminster Abbey. 'It wasn't a
portrait,' he later told Sir Russell Brain. 'It was what I
imagined him to be.' Nevertheless, before making the
over life-size bust he had studied what likenesses of the
painter-poet he could find. The National Portrait Gallery
would not lend him their life mask, but sent him three
photographs of it. He got together all the portraits he
could, including sketches by Stothard. The result was a
powerful image. Its base in black Jerusalem stone was
given by Epstein: it was cut from a block brought back
as a present for him from the Holy Land before the war
by Sir Patrick Geddes, the town planner.

641
LADY LEPEL
PHIPPS

642
TABITHA

641

642

The bust was dedicated by Dean Don in November 1957. Epstein told Brain that not many of the 'Blake people' turned up. He thought they disapproved of him.

That winter of 1957–58 the sculptor made a bust of LADY LEPEL PHIPPS, eldest daughter of Lord Normanby, which, with its long hair and party frock, would remind one of Alice in Wonderland if it were not for the girl's intense and brooding expression.

A little head of TABITHA with curls forms a carefree contrast.

North Staffordshire University had commissioned a bust of their Chancellor, Princess Margaret, and in

2C

February 1958 Her Royal Highness came to the Hyde Park Gate studio for sittings.

The portrait of H.R.H. PRINCESS MARGARET was more than a bust; it continued to below the waist. The Princess, in evening dress and wearing the sash of the Royal Victorian Order over her right shoulder, has short hair combed with feigned negligence over the forehead. She looks down, smiling slightly, and extends her bare arms as if to rest them on the full skirt of her dress.

Epstein was seriously ill, but he worked away as if unconscious of the fact. To make him visit a specialist Kathleen resorted to a trick. She asked a friend to tea, explaining the situation, and at the same time ordered a car to take her husband to the doctor. The car came while they were at tea, and Epstein, as Kathleen had guessed, was unable to make a scene in front of a friend, and went

[403]

643 H.R.H. PRINCESS MARGARET

644 T.U.C. WAR MEMORIAL

645. 646
T.U.C. WAR MEMORIAL

645

quietly. He was suffering from pleurisy and thrombosis. Wallace Brigden could not understand how he was still alive, and feared he might drop dead at any moment. There was no question even of returning to Hyde Park Gate to pack a suitcase: Epstein was driven straight to the London Hospital in Whitechapel, where he was lodged in the nurses' wing. So the sittings of Princess Margaret were interrupted.

While he was in hospital the TRADES UNION COUNCIL WAR MEMORIAL was unveiled. Epstein had worked on the carving throughout most of 1957, balancing on a narrow plank on the face of the building, accompanied by the sound of electric drills. Stopping work in the evening he had found taxis reluctant to take him home because he was covered in marble dust. Kathleen had

hired a car, but even then the chauffeur hurt Epstein's feelings by starting to brush out the back before his illustrious client was out of sight.

Even more than the 'Risen Christ' of 1919, the T.U.C. Memorial is a fearful indictment of the horror of war. Clasping her dead son in her arms this maddened, disbelieving mother glares accusingly at a world which has bereaved her. In this work Epstein returned to the 'primitive' style of 'Night', 'Day' and the titanic images of the 'thirties; and comparing the T.U.C. Mother with the earlier Pietà, 'Night', we feel almost as if the calm Goddess who had sat lulling her son to sleep was now suddenly aroused by a bullet which had left him dead in her arms. This is a terrifying work.

The Memorial to the T.U.C.'s dead in two wars was

[404]

646

unveiled by Sir Thomas Yates, the current chairman, on 27 March, 1958.

Epstein submitted with fortitude to his illness, but Kathleen had to visit him twice a day for fear he walked out of hospital. He recovered, and because he did not really understand what illness was, and had no interest in it, he put it completely out of his mind.

With Kathleen and Beth Lipkin, he set off for a holiday in Italy. May was spent happily in Venice at the Pensione Seguso, on the Zattere. The sculptor had never set eyes on Verrocchio's equestrian statue of Colleoni before: he went to see it four times, and spent hours entranced before it. Then the party spent a few days at Padua, and Epstein discovered Donatello's Gattamellata with equal joy.

In April, 1958 the plaster cast of the huge group of ST. MICHAEL AND THE DEVIL went to Morris Singer's foundry in Clapham to be cast in bronze.

St. Michael's head, we have seen, was based on that of Epstein's son-in-law Wynne Godley; and it is interesting to compare the portrait with the monumental head, observing how the subtle planes were simplified and dramatised to register at a distance, how the human was made divine. The saint's bare torso, to which his tensed and rigid arms are fixed in a strange, individual way, is formalised like a Roman cuirass. His legs — the right one covered with unrealistic drapery, and both twined about with celestial garters — are parted wide and seem to be standing at ease on the ether. With the outspread wings they form an X; just as the arms and wings form another squatter and more three-dimensional one. Michael clasps a spear in his right hand, and his left foot dominates the horned head of the recumbent Devil.

There was no model for the angelic torso, but Epstein required one for the musclebound fiend, who presented a problem. It was not before Jack Solomons' gymnasium and several agencies had been combed that a suitable model was found in the person of Gordon Bagnall-Godfrey, a chartered surveyor living in Kensington. The Devil, with arms transfixed behind his back, and chained feet, stares brutishly upwards and seems not to comprehend the harm he has done.

The group clearly stands for the victory of the spiritual over the animal instincts of man.

648

649

647 ST. MICHAEL AND
    THE DEVIL (PLASTER)
    IN FOUNDRY

648 HEAD OF ST. MICHAEL

649 WYNNE GODLEY

647

650 BISHOP WOODS, PLASTER

651 BISHOP WOODS IN LICHFIELD CATHEDRAL

In 1953 Mr. Cannon Brookes, solicitor and executor to the late Bishop Woods of Lichfield, rang up to enquire if Epstein could recommend a young sculptor who might make a memorial to the Bishop for a moderate fee. Kathleen Epstein had associations with Lichfield — as a girl she used to ride on weekly visits to the Deanery with her father — and she arranged for Epstein to undertake the work. The sculptor travelled to Lichfield and the clergy turned out to meet him with black cloaks against the snow. Working from photographs, Epstein managed to get what was considered a remarkable likeness. In his over-life-size image of a priest with bowed head and praying hands he rethought an ancient formula; and the saintly character of BISHOP WOODS transcends the formality of his pose and the grandeur of his vestments.

After the monument was cast and despatched to Lichfield, Epstein was upset to hear it was not to be placed in the spot selected by him, but too high up, in a bad light and in a different part of the church. If he had meant it to be seen from below he would have planned it differently. He was disappointed and declined to attend its dedication.

at Basle, and Epstein saw the drawings of the monuments of the Duke and Duchess of Berri whom he had recognised in Bourges. But the great event of the return journey was the sculptor's first sight of Grünewald's Isenheim altarpiece at Colmar, and he studied with rapture and at length the masterpiece which has held so direct a message for many artists of our day.

We noted as early as the time of Epstein's first visit to Florence in student days how he was not cut out for sight-seeing; nor was he a habitual holiday-taker or -maker. Yet Kathleen remembers how from the very beginning of this tour, motoring through Kent, it was as if he had suddenly discovered what fun travel and sight-seeing were, and how he wanted to stop and look at everything. When, nearing home, he espied Laon cathedral on its hill and wanted to go there, the Cowies revealed that his sight-seeing had worn them out by exclaiming 'Not *another* cathedral!'

The first sitter in 1959 was PROFESSOR MCINNES of Bristol University. The historian was the kind of many-sided man who might be expected to appeal to Epstein: although blind, he used to ride daily, and translated poetry from the French. Epstein made an extraordinarily successful portrait of him.

652 SIR WILLIAM HALEY   652
653 PROFESSOR MCINNES

653

He had to be back to make a portrait of SIR WILLIAM HALEY, Director-General of the B.B.C. (now Editor of *The Times*) in June, so he returned to London to execute this commission. Haley told the sculptor about his voyage, as a boy, on a cholera ship; and how he had once been office-boy to Scott of the 'Manchester Guardian', whom Epstein had modelled in 1926. He told Kathleen that he had never been so happy as when posing for Epstein; and his portrait had all the subtlety of the sculptor's most careful work.

During the summer the Epsteins went with their friends Drs. John and Valerie Cowie on a sight-seeing tour of French cathedrals. They drove to Beauvais, Senlis, Chartres and Bourges, where the sculptor saw the kneeling figures of the duc de Berri and his duchess, and remarked 'Holbein drew this couple.' They continued to Nîmes and Arles, where Epstein saw the Romanesque St. Trophime and went to bathe in the sea at Les Saintes-Maries. By the Côte d'azur and Portofino, still bathing daily, they came to Milan, Como and Parma, where Kathleen wanted Epstein to see the twelfth-century reliefs of Antelami. Arrived in the church of S. Antonio, Epstein suddenly said, 'Everything's gone dark. I can't see anything.' After a while he recovered from this attack and looked at the carvings.

On the way back they struck an exhibition of Holbein

[410]

654 EARL LLOYD GEORGE

Back in London, the Epsteins attended a garden party at the Deanery, Westminster. Dr. Fisher, Archbishop of Canterbury, said to Kathleen, 'Do you think the great man would do me?' The sculptor was pleased at the idea of having a bust in the grand setting of Lambeth Palace near the Holbein of Bishop Warham, and a plan was made. During the autumn Princess Margaret resumed her sittings.

Besides continuing work on the big Bowater House Group, Epstein began a statue of DAVID LLOYD GEORGE commissioned by the Office of Works for the House of Commons. Only the head of this over life-size posthumous portrait was completed: the figure in a morning coat got no further than a rough, doll-like maquette, and after Epstein's death the money advanced on the statue had to be refunded. The Prime Minister's children, Lady Megan Lloyd George and Lord Lloyd George came more than once to the studio and approved the likeness.

655 PLASTER CAST OF
DR. FISHER
WITH EPSTEIN

656 DR. FISHER
ARCHBISHOP OF
CANTERBURY

655

656

Next came DR. FISHER, ARCHBISHOP OF CANTERBURY, to the studio. On seeing the big horned figure of Pan which had been cast in plaster to form part of the Bowater House Group he exclaimed 'That's my enemy!' Epstein protested that Pan and the Devil were far from being the same person.

The Royal College of Physicians had ordered a bust of their president, SIR RUSSELL BRAIN (now Lord Brain); and Epstein modelled him in his presidential gown with folded hands. The neurologist, whose memory qualifies him for a Boswell, wrote down a detailed record of his conversations with the sculptor which is published in his book *Some Reflections on Genius*. They spoke of poetry, sculpture and past sitters, of Shakespeare, Michelangelo, Monet's waterlilies and Cleopatra's nose. 'At the end of one sitting, Epstein looked rather wistfully at his work and said: "There comes a time when you don't know if you're making any progress! I'm still learning. I'm like a beginner!" ' During these sittings Brain tells us that Epstein and Kathleen spent a day at Oxford visiting Warden Smith, and enjoyed Uccello's 'Night hunt' in the Ashmolean. Oxford had adopted him and made him part of its university. He had portrayed three Heads of Colleges, besides a Professor of Human Anatomy; there were bronzes by him in the Ashmolean and his 'Lazarus' was in New College Chapel.

At the beginning of April the Epsteins travelled with Kitty and Beth Lipkin to Bristol for the presentation of Professor McInnes's head to the Gallery of Art. A few days later they set off for a holiday in Paris with Epstein's brother, Dr. Irving Epstein and his wife.

After a week of intensive sightseeing in the Louvre and elsewhere the sculptor saw his brother and sister-in-law off to America; then travelled with Kathleen and Beth to Venice. He revisited Verrocchio's equestrian statue and crossed the lagoon to see the mosaics at Torcello.

On the way home through Paris Epstein bought two pieces of African sculpture to add to his collection which was now perhaps the most distinguished in the world. Charles Ratton, who sold him these carvings, was later to help in disposing of the collection.

During May, June and July the sculptor's last sitters came to Hyde Park Gate. IVAN SANDERSON was the head of the wallpaper and textile firm, for whose lately rebuilt premises in Berners Street the bust was ordered. Epstein's last adult portrait was of SIR BASIL SPENCE, the architect of Coventry Cathedral, who had commissioned 'St. Michael' and who was now President of the Royal Institute of British Architects. The money offered for the commission was only for a head, but the sculptor said the head needed the support of shoulders and made a bust. We have seen how Epstein had

657

658

659

[413]

657 SIR RUSSELL BRAIN

658 IVAN SANDERSON

659 SIR BASIL SPENCE

660

660 LADY SOPHIA CAVENDISH
661 LADY EVELYN ROSE PHIPPS

throughout his life worked in several different styles concurrently. While the portrait of Sanderson was essentially in his late psycho-analytical manner, that of Spence is more architectural, with a touch of classical stylisation, and could almost have been made in 1916.

Before modelling Sir Basil, Epstein had made a little bust with bare arms of LADY SOPHIA CAVENDISH, the Duke of Devonshire's four-year-old youngest daughter, whose aunt Lady Anne Tree had posed in 1951. This girl was one of the best behaved sitters Epstein ever had; and her Nanny made up such fascinating stories that the sculptor and his plaster-moulders would break off work to listen.

Another small girl, LADY EVELYN ROSE PHIPPS, was Epstein's last portrait. She was the youngest daughter of Lord Normanby, who had sat for Epstein in 1956; and her elder sister Lepel had sat in 1957. Several of the characteristics most peculiar to Epstein's work can be observed in this bust: the irregularities of surface —

despite the mainly smooth finish, the dissymetry of the eye-pupils to give expression, the feeling for the growth of hair, the dramatic vitality.

On Wednesday, August 17th the sculptor's old friend Sir Matthew Smith, who was himself a dying man, telephoned to invite the Epsteins to visit him. On the way up in the lift at Chelsea Cloisters Epstein was seized with dizziness and chewed his emergency heart pills, but still insisted on going in. The painter was immaculately dressed but too weak to lift the bottle of champagne which he had provided; and the sculptor looked robust in comparison. Both men were in high spirits and spent nearly two hours discussing painting, sculpture and the old days in Paris. Smith could not believe Epstein was ill. He himself was to die six weeks later.

On August 19th, after working all day on the almost completed Bowater House group, and giving instructions to Parrott, his bronze moulder, for its elaborate casting, Epstein went with Kathleen and Beth to dine at Ciccio's Restaurant on Campden Hill. It was unusual for him to walk if he could get a taxi, but this evening he suggested walking home through Kensington Gardens. Kathleen, however, would not allow this. It was a warm night, so Epstein took a chair out on the porch, saying 'Let's watch the stars come out.' He began to sing Schubert songs, then fell asleep. When he woke up he said, 'I don't know when I've slept so deeply. I'm going into the studio to look at my group.' Kathleen begged him to go to bed, but he was firm about covering up his clay. 'You've done everything for me in life, Kitty, but that's one thing you can't do'; and he went into the studio.

Epstein was fearless, but he had once said he was afraid Kathleen might not be with him when he died. In this, as in may other ways, he was lucky.

When he came out of the studio he said 'All's well. The group is finished'; and he went up to his room. Kathleen felt something was wrong, and told Beth to telephone for the doctor. She followed her husband upstairs. Epstein's eyes were open, so that he saw Kathleen when she came in to find him lying on the floor by the bed. He died a few seconds later.

[414]

662 KATHLEEN EPSTEIN UNVEILING ST. MICHAEL AND THE DEVIL AT COVENTRY

[417]

2D

to have been his portraits (particularly his portraits of men, whom he saw with a greater objectivity than that which a man of his direct and personal vision could turn upon women) and also such pieces of sculpture as his "Madonna and Child", one of his best and last works, that is now in Cavendish Square. Of the sculptor's media, his was surely clay. . . . In his old age he even came to resemble Rembrandt physically. His warmth and his vitality and his courage will not be quickly forgotten. We have lost a great sculptor.'

The Editorial of the November issue of the scholarly *Burlington Magazine* turned the tables on Bloomsbury. After establishing that the reason why the Philistines attacked Epstein was that 'he turned to barbaric arts as models, realistic or otherwise, for the expression of ideas which were too dear to the hearts of Englishmen to be bearable in any visual language but English', the writer went on: 'The highbrows attacked Epstein from the opposite flank. Their weapons may have been sharper because they knew how to write, but they also missed the point. They had learnt these "outrageous" languages and were no longer perplexed by their re-emergence in contemporary art. But they resented the re-use of these languages for the purpose for which the languages had been evolved. They believed that the only permissible re-use of barbaric forms was the transformation of them into formal harmonies and suspected, correctly, that Epstein was using them, as they were originally devised, for expressionist purposes. And such vulgarity was inexcusable. Even his portrait busts (never particularly objectionable to the general public) were cleverly ridiculed by the highbrows for concentrating too obsessively on the personalities of the sitters at the expense of sculptural qualities. . . . The best criticism of this kind is that of Roger Fry who says: "It may be, of course, that I am so carried away, so disturbed if you like, by all these other qualities of drama and actuality, which Mr. Epstein's work [i.e. his bronze busts] displays that I cannot feel the purely formal stimulus to the imagination which is what I seek for in sculpture. . . . If these are sculpture, then I want another word for what M. Maillol and Mr. Dobson practise, let alone Luca della Robbia and the Sumerians." What word would we have wanted for the sculptors at Moissac, for Andrea Pisano, Donatello, Michelangelo and Rodin?'

Epstein was buried in Putney Vale Cemetery, on August 24, Dr. Hewlett Johnson, Dean of Canterbury, taking the funeral service. Matthew Smith was there.

On November 10 a Memorial Service was held in St. Paul's Cathedral. Canon C. B. Mortlock preached a fine sermon; and from a temporary wall blocking off the north transept where repairs were taking place shone forth the countenance of the Llandaff 'Christ', the plaster cast of which had been hung there for the occasion. Canon

663 ST. MICHAEL AND THE DEVIL
      WITH THE SPIRE OF OLD
      COVENTRY CATHEDRAL

Mortlock concluded with the words 'If we ask how it was that a boy born and bred in the Jewish Faith and never embracing any other, should become the interpreter of the sublime mysteries of our religion there can be no clear answer. Such things belong to the inscrutable wisdom of God. . . . His work on earth being finished, let us pray that he may come at last to the enjoyment of Him, the Supreme Artist, at the sight of whose creative work "the morning stars sang together and all the sons of God shouted for joy".'

In March 1960 the Arts Council held an exhibition of the Epstein collection of Tribal and Exotic Art at their premises in St. James's Square. This wonderful show contained no less than 347 exhibits, African, Mexican, Oceanic, Greek, Roman, Egyptian and from the Far East. In his introduction to the catalogue, William Fagg of the British Museum wrote: 'Epstein collected boldly and with remarkable insight in a number of fields . . . in which expert scholars have learnt to be chary of giving firm opinions. . . . In general it must be said that a great sculptor's appreciation of artistic sincerity in the work of others has in this case proved an almost unerring guide for the collector, and there can have been few collectors anywhere in the world who have been so well equipped to recognise mastery in sculptural form and craftsmanship. This is without doubt the finest such private collection in Great Britain, and is equalled by few in the world.'

On June 10, 1960, an exhibition of 'Fifty Years of Bronzes and Drawings by Sir Jacob Epstein' opened at the Leicester Galleries. This included the 'Risen Christ' of 1919, which no one had seen for years.

On June 24, 1960, 'St. Michael and the Devil' was

unveiled by Lady Epstein on the east wall of Sir Basil
Spence's still unfinished cathedral at Coventry.

Meanwhile, Lady Epstein had invited the present
writer to make a book on Epstein's sculpture; and he had
in turn suggested to Lord Harewood a comprehensive
memorial exhibition of the sculptor's work for the
Edinburgh Festival of 1961. It was while collecting
material for this that the writer learned the four carvings
at Blackpool might be for sale. Lord Harewood and Mr.
I. Jack Lyons bought these on February 6, 1961.

During April, 1961, the BOWATER HOUSE GROUP was
erected inside the new Duke of Edinburgh Gate to Hyde
Park, and the public were at last able to study the
sculptor's final huge and unpredictable creation.

Epstein's first London lodgings had been at 219
Stanhope Street, St. Pancras, within a few minutes' walk
of Regent's Park; and the London Parks had always
meant a lot to the sculptor, who, like many artists, would
probably have settled in the country if it were not more
difficult to earn a living there. 'Rima' was made for Hyde
Park; and Epstein's home from 1928 until his death had
been at 18 Hyde Park Gate, near the Albert Hall. The
subject of the Bowater House group certainly had a

665

666

special meaning for him: namely, the flight from civilisation into a golden, uncomplicated, natural world — a return to Eden. It seems strange, however, to find the creator of such static immutable creatures as 'Genesis' or 'Night', or even of the 'Byzantine' Madonnas and Christ, making so violent and baroque a group — strange, that is, until one finds (in Haskell's *The Sculptor Speaks*) how much he admired the 'Marseillaise' of Rude on the Arc de Triomphe, in Paris.

The surge of figures, man, woman, child and dog, driven by the music of Pan's pipes, is a daring, elaborate composition, which seems to open fanlike from Pan's hindmost hoof and which is dominated by the uninhibited diagonal of the diving woman. What an extraordinary salute to youth, to life and to joy in life was this wild vision of the dying master! He saw another spring and another summer come to London and knew that children and lovers would impatiently seek the green places to play, to lie in the sun, to forget care, to sleep and to make love.

On June 8, 1961 Mr. Billy Rose, the American impresario, who owned the 'Third Marble Doves', entertained Lady Epstein and the present writer to luncheon in his suite at the Savoy. Mr. Rose had been for some years devoted to the promotion of art galleries for Israel; he said that if Lady Epstein would give Epstein's plaster casts to Jerusalem he would see that a special museum was built to house them. She consented at once; and later added the early carving of 'Maternity' to her benefaction.

On August 19, 1961, the second anniversary of Epstein's death, the great Memorial Exhibition opened in the Waverley Market, Edinburgh. The two hundred and thirty exhibits included a selection of bronzes, drawings, photographs of monumental works which could not be transported, and most of the other large carvings and bronzes. For the first time the 'Garden Figure', 'Maternity', 'The Rock Drill', the 'Risen Christ', 'The Visitation', 'Genesis', the Epping Forest carvings, 'Ecce Homo', 'Consummatum est', 'Jacob and the Angel', 'Adam', 'Lucifer', 'Lazarus', and the plaster casts of the head and torso of the Liverpool Giant, of 'Bishop Woods' and 'Christ in Majesty' were to be seen under one roof. The plaster of 'St. Michael and the Devil' was displayed *on top of* the roof, and for a month became one of the sights of Princes Street. The Edinburgh exhibition attracted 125,000 visitors, more than twice as many as had paid to see the works of any artist in the previous fourteen festivals.

Later in the year the Arts Council mounted a smaller — but still large — show at the Tate Gallery, for which Sir John Rothenstein selected the exhibits. In 1961 and 1962 exhibitions of Epstein's work were held throughout the British Isles.

667 BOWATER HOUSE GROUP

CATALOGUE RAISONNÉ

Works are placed under years when they are believed to have been begun.

All works are in bronze unless listed otherwise.

All portraits are lifesize unless otherwise stated. As most of them were cast several times no owners' names are given.

Measurements of carvings and monumental bronzes are given, where discoverable, height first; as are the museums, institutions or collectors to whom they belong.

Works believed to have been destroyed are printed in italics.

N.R. means 'not reproduced'.

1902–04

Baby Awake
Sleeping Baby
Temple of Love (marble)   N.R.
Temple of the Sun (marble)   N.R.

1905

Epstein, Mrs., 1st portrait (leaning on one hand)
Relief of Mother and Child, 14″ × 14″

1907–08

John, Romilly (Rom)
Old Italian Woman
Strand Statues (Portland stone), $1\frac{1}{2}$ times life size

1909

Chadburn, Mrs. (marble), Schinman Coll., U.S.A.
English Girl
Hamblay, Hilda
McEvoy, Mrs. Ambrose (bronze)
McEvoy, Mrs. Ambrose (marble), Johannesburg Art Gallery
Maternity (marble) 82″, Lady Epstein Coll.
Nan, bust of

1910

Garden Figure (Euphemia), (marble), 53″, Mrs. Arthur Clifton Coll.

Narcissus
Sunflower, 24″, Schinman Coll., U.S.A.
Sungod (Hoptonwood stone), Sally Ryan Coll., U.S.A.

1911

Clifton, Mrs. Arthur
Dodd, Mrs. Francis
Euphemia (Lamb), 1st portrait of (bust)
Euphemia (Lamb), 2nd portrait of (bust)
Gertrude, Half length figure of
Gregory, Lady
Nan (The Dreamer), 11″
Nan, seated, 19″
Rankin, Marie (Irish Girl)
Standing Mother & Child (Marie Rankin), 71″ × 26″

1912

Self Portrait in a cap
Wilde, Oscar, Tomb of (Hoptonwood stone)

1913

Cursed be the day whereon I was born
Female figure in Flenite
Figure in Flenite, 18″
Flenite Relief, 12″ × 11″
Granite Mother & Child
Marble Mother & Child, $16\frac{1}{4}$″, Museum of Modern Art

Rockdrill, $27\frac{3}{4}''$
Venus, 1st, 47″, Baltimore
Venus, 2nd, 96″, Yale University

1914–15

Beerbohm, Marie
Bird Pluming itself   N.R.
Drogheda, Countess of
Fisher, Admiral Lord
Gordon, Billie
Hamilton, Duchess of
Hulme, T. E.
Marble Doves (1st Group), 29″ × 26″, Private Coll.,
    London
Marble Doves (2nd Group of)   N.R.
Marble Doves (3rd Group of), $19\frac{1}{4}''$ × 29″, Billy
    Rose Collection
Marcelle
Tree, Iris

1916

Bone, Muirhead
Davies, W. H.
Epstein, Mrs., 2nd portrait of (Mask with ear-
    rings)
John, Augustus
Meum, 1st portrait of (bust)
Shelley, Lilian, 1st portrait of (head)
Tin Hat, The
Van Dieren, Bernard, 1st portrait of (head)

1917

American Soldier
Andrews, Mrs.   N.R.
Deacon, Gladys (later Duchess of Marlborough)
Holbrooke, Josef
Keane, Doris
Matthews, Harley   N.R.
Meum, 2nd portrait of (head)
Newbolt, Francis   N.R.
Nielke, Marguerite
Scott-Ellis, Hon. Elizabeth
Sheridan, Clare

1918

Casati, Marchesa
Epstein, Mrs., 3rd portrait of (with a ribbon)
Epstein, Mrs., 4th portrait of (with a scarf)
Epstein, Mrs., 5th portrait of (in a Mantilla)
Gray, Cecil   N.R.
Hunter, Sgt. David Ferguson, V.C.

Meum, 3rd portrait of (mask)
Meum, 4th portrait of (with a fan)
Peggy Jean, 1st portrait of, age 3 months   N.R.
Shelley, Lillian, 2nd portrait of (bust)

1919

Dervich, Eve
Head of a Girl
Helène
May, Betty, 1st portrait of (bust)
May, Betty, 2nd portrait of (head)
Noreen   N.R.
Peggy Jean, 2nd portrait of (smiling)
Peggy Jean, 3rd portrait of (aged 1 year)
Risen Christ (Bernard van Dieren), 86″
Soene, Gabrielle
Van Dieren, Bernard, 2nd portrait of (head)

1920

Peggy Jean, 4th portrait of, aged 18 months
Peggy Jean, 7th portrait of, with arms out
Putti, 5th and 6th portraits of Peggy Jean
Self Portrait with a beard

1921

Kathleen, 1st portrait of (bust)
Kramer, Jacob
Peggy Jean, 8th portrait of, with very curly hair N.R.
Peggy Jean, 9th portrait of, laughing
Peggy Jean, 10th portrait of, sad   N.R.
Plichte, Miriam, 1st portrait of (bust)
Plichte, Miriam, 2nd portrait of (bust with arms)
Senegalese Girl

1922

Dolores, 1st portrait of (La Bohémienne) (bust)
Dolores, 2nd portrait of (head)
Kathleen, 2nd portrait of (small bust)
Old Smith
Roselli, Fedora
Selina
Weeping Woman, The, 23″

1923

Angel of the Annunciation (Ferosa Rastoumji)
    (Torso, $62\frac{1}{2}''$)
Dolores, 3rd portrait of (bust with arms)
Dolores, 4th portrait of (head)
Dolores, reclining study of, $27\frac{1}{2}''$ × 10″
Graham, R. B. Cunninghame
Marble arms, 37″ long, Mrs. Clare Crossley Coll.

Marlborough, Duchess of (sketch head of)
Marlborough, Duke of (head)
Oko, Dr. Adolph S.
Old Pinager
Proudfoot, Eileen
Rastoumji, Ferosa

1924

Conrad, Joseph
Epstein, Jacob, of Baltimore   N.R.
Erskine, David   N.R.
Lanchester, Elsa
Seraph, The (Marie Collins), 11″
Sheila

1925

Alexander, Prof. Samuel O. M.
Enver, 1st portrait of (head)
Hudson, W. H., relief of, 13″ × 17½″
Marlborough, Duke of (bust), 36″ × 38″
Rima (Hudson Memorial)
Ross, Oriel, 1st portrait of (bust)
Sunita, 1st portrait of (bust)
Sunita, 2nd portrait of
Thorndyke, Sybil

1926

Anita
Feibleman, James K.
Good, Edward (Mosheh Oved)
MacDonald, Ramsay, 1st portrait of (small bust)
Mijinska   N.R.
Peggy Jean, 11th portrait of (age 7½ with long hair)
Ross, Oriel, 2nd portrait of (head)
Scott, C. P.
Sunita, 3rd portrait of (bust with a necklace)
Tagore, Rabindranath
Tennant, Hon. Stephen
Visitation, The, 65″, Tate Gallery

1927

Boas, Prof. Franz
Dewey, Prof. John
Dunn, Daisy
Good, Mrs. Edward (Mrs. Mosheh Oved)   N.R.
Jay, Virginia   N.R.
Madonna and Child, Riverside Church, New York
Oko, Pearl
Zeda

1928

Cohn, David, N.R.
Peggy Jean, 12th portrait of (sick child)
Phillips, Mrs. Godfrey (a portrait)
Robeson, Paul
Rothermere, Viscount

1929

Day
Night
Night (maquette for), 14½″

1930

Betty (Esther)
Genesis, 31″ × 48″, Coll. Sidney Bernstein
Germaine (Miss Bras)
Goldie, May
Greenwood, Joan (as a child)
Kindler, Hans
Little Eileen
Lydia, 1st portrait of (bust)
Powys, Isobel
Rebecca
Tirrenia (Mrs. Gerrard)

1931

Beatty, Mrs. Chester
Bendon, Malcolm
Blandford, May
Cotts, Sir William M.   N.R.
Cramer, Dr.
Donnelly, Prof. Lucy
Heath, Mrs. Sonia
Israfel (Sunita)
Jansen, Ellen
Joel, Mrs. Betty (La Belle Juive)
Kathleen, 3rd portrait of (bust)
Lydia, 2nd portrait of (bust with short hair)
Sunita reclining, 35″ × 22½″
Young Paul Robeson

1932

Ahmed
Chimera, 10″ × 26″, Schinman Coll., U.S.A.
Elemental, 31″, Schinman Coll., U.S.A.
Hochter, Harriet
Isobel, 1st portrait of (bust)
Louise, 1st portrait of
Nicolle, Arthur
Oved, Mrs.

[426]

Peggy Jean, 13th portrait of (Jeunesse)
Phyllis
Roma of Barbados, 1st portrait of (head)
Rose
Ross, Oriel, 3rd portrait of
Woman possessed, 17″ × 40″, Schinman Coll., U.S.A.

1933

Aran, Man of ('Tiger' King)
Beaverbrook, Lord
Burton, Basil
Cramer, Mrs. Belle
Einstein, Prof. Albert
Flaherty, Robert
Gielgud, John
Isobel, 2nd portrait of (bust)
Kathleen, 4th portrait of (bust)
Neander
Ostrer, Isidore
Primeval Gods (Hoptonwood stone), Coll. Sally Ryan
Roma of Barbados, 2nd portrait of (bust)
Sungod (finished), Coll. Sally Ryan
Weizmann, Chaim

1934

Balcon, Michael
Ecce Homo (subiaco marble), Epstein Estate, 132″
Hallé, Hiram
Lydia, 3rd portrait of (bust, laughing)
MacDonald, Ramsay, 2nd portrait of (bust)
Myers, M. S.
Olive
Rani Rama
Shaw, Bernard
Walpole, Hugh
Williams, Emlyn

1935

Collins, W. H.
Deborah
Jackie, 1st portrait of (a baby)
Kathleen, 5th portrait of (bust with arms)
Levy, Benn
Martin, Sir Alec   N.R.
Peggy Jean, 14th portrait of
Shulamite Woman   N.R.

1936

Abyssinia, Haile Selassie, Emperor of

Consummatum Est (alabaster), 24″ × 88″ × 32″, Schinman Coll., U.S.A.
Elsa
Fletcher, Sir Frank
Goldston, E.   N.R.
Morna
Oko, Mrs. Adolph S.
Priestley, J. B.
Rosemary
Van Dieren, Bernard, 3rd portrait of (bust)
Walker, Sir Alec

1937

Castle Stewart, Countess of
Givenchy, Pola
Jackie, 2nd portrait of (with long hair)
Leona
Louise, 2nd portrait of (Berenice)
Morris, David
Nerenska, Pola
Norman (Hornstein), 1st portrait of
Rita
Ryan, Sally
Tanya

1938

Adam (alabaster), 86″, Base 26″ × 32″, Coll. Earl of Harewood
Adam & Eve, 4¾″
Ballon, Ellen
Burial of Abel, 9¾″
Cecil, Betty
Dave
Maisky, Ivan
Tracy, Marie

1939

African Mother & Child
Leda, 1st portrait of (aged 2 months)
Leda, 2nd portrait of (aged 4 months)
Leda, 3rd portrait of (aged 6 months)
Norman (Hornstein), 2nd portrait of
Pearson, Mrs. Melinda
Peters, Betty
Sainsbury, Mrs. Robert (Lisa)   N.R.
Wise, Rabbi Stephen

1940

Jacob and the Angel, 84″, Base 43″ × 46″, Coll. Sidney Bernstein
Leda, 4th portrait of (with cockscomb)

Piccaninny
Ragamuffin (Jackie), 3rd portrait of

1941

Deirdre, 1st portrait of (with arms)
Deirdre, 2nd portrait of (with a slip)
Girl with Gardenias (Kathleen)
Grace   N.R.
Kathleen, 6th portrait of (bust with arms)
Resurrection Study
Slave hold

1942

Berkeley, Countess of
Black, George
Chia-Pi
Deirdre, 3rd portrait of (leaning forward)
Ian (Ossian)
Juanita (Forbes) (bust)
Lewis, Lalage
Margulies, Alexander
Patton, Helen   N.R.
Pritt, D. N.   N.R.
Pritt, Mrs. D. N.   N.R.
Sainsbury, Robert
St. Francis, 12″

1943

Bevin, Ernest
Cunningham, General Sir Alan
Menuhin, Yehudi
Mexican Girl (nude study)
Nude Studies (A–J)
Portal, Air-Marshal Viscount
Wavell, Field-Marshal Earl

1944

Braganza, Princesse de
Esther, 1st portrait of (with long hair)
Girl from Baku
Kitty, 1st portrait (with curls)
Leda, 5th portrait of (pouting)
Lucifer, Height 124″, Width of wings 76″, Base
    24″ × 24″
Lucifer, Relief (the Fall of Lucifer), 24″ × 25″
Mexican girl (bust)   N.R.
Satan, Beelzebub & Belial

1945

Juanita (nude study), 22½″ × 9″

Little Girl with Bow
Waverley, Viscount

1946

Churchill, Winston
Duncan, Ronald
Frankel, Anna
Guardians of Paradise, 10″
Hess, Myra (Dame)
L'Homme aux serpents, 6½″ × 5½″
Narcissus (Maquette for unrealised project)
    7¼″ × 4¾″
Neptune
Lovers on an eagle's back (Bird in Flight), 9″ × 7″
Nehru, Pandit, sketch of
Oved, Ymiel
Silberman, F. H.   N.R.
Whittaker, Dr. William

1947

Anthony
Anthony in a Balaclava Helmet
Freud, Lucian
Lazarus (marble), 100″
Lindsay of Birker, Lord
Myers, Isaac

1948

Balcon, Jill
Christian, Linda
Dyall, Franklin
Esther, 2nd portrait of
Esterman, Helen
Greenwood, Joan
Jackson, Mrs. Robert (Muriel)   N.R.
Kathleen, 7th portrait of (bust with arms)
Peter, laughing

1949

Baby with arms (Michael Stewart's daughter)
Bloch, Ernst
Chinese Boy
Desta, Princess
Elizabeth   N.R.
Esther, 3rd portrait of
Janner, Sir Barnett   N.R.
Kitty, 2nd portrait of
Lytton, Lady Madeleine
Margulies, Judith
Menan, Princess
Neagle, Anna   N.R.
Nehru, Pandit, bust of

Prinz, George   N.R.
Siobhan
Tindall-Lister, Elizabeth
Victor
Youth Advancing (marble), 82″, Manchester City
    Art Gallery
Zefira, Bracha

1950

Baroda, Gaekwar of
Barzetti, Marcella
Blackett, Prof.
Canterbury, The Dean of   N.R.
Cavendish Square Madonna & Child, 160″
Cavendish Square Madonna & Child, Maquette,
    $13\frac{3}{4}$″
Dorne, Sandra   N.R.
Freud, Ann
Hill, Diana Coppinger
Hughes, Christine
Hughes, Christopher
Hughes, Isobel
Hughes, Penelope
Joffé, Roland
Melchett, Gwen, Lady
Samuel, Lord
Solomons, Dr. Bethel
Williams, Ralph Vaughan

1951

Bronfman, Minda
Clarke, Louis C. G.
Eliot, T. S.
Lade, Judith
Little Prince, The
Maugham, Somerset
Rhodes, Robert
Smith, A. H.
Social Consciousness, Fairmount Park Association,
    Philadelphia
Social Consciousness, 3 maquettes for
Tree, Lady Anne

1952

Joffé, Mark
Lloyd, Dame Hilda
Lollobrigida, Gina
MacLeod, Prof. J. W.   N.R.
Mason, Portland
Simon of Wythenshaw, Lord

1953

Annabel
Annabel (Freud) with bonnet
Asch, Sholem
Brodetsky, Prof.
Cat, A
Fraser, Lionel
Frisky, 12″
Lowe, Dr. Elias
Mace-Head, 16″
O'Regan, Terence
Russell, Earl
Zetterling, Mai

1954

Annabel & Frisky (concrete) (Liverpool Reliefs),
    Lewis's Store, Liverpool
Braintree, Lord
Children Fighting (concrete) (Liverpool Reliefs),
    Lewis's Store, Liverpool
Children Playing (concrete) (Liverpool Reliefs),
    Lewis's Store, Liverpool
Christ in Majesty, Maquette, $26″ \times 9\frac{1}{4}″$
Cripps, Sir Stafford
Lane, Charles
Liverpool Giant (torso), 84″, Lewis's Store,
    Liverpool
Mallon, Dr. Frederick

1955

American Girl   N.R.
Christ in Majesty (Llandaff), 175″
Rogers, Nancy   N.R.
Smuts, Field-Marshal

1956

Blake, William
Bowater House Group, Maquette, $13\frac{1}{4}″ \times 4\frac{1}{4}″ \times 11″$
Door Handles, Four, $5″ \times 4″$
Franklin Medal, $3\frac{1}{2}″$ diam.
Godley, Hon. Wynne
Gray, Sir James
Hesketh, Hon. Robert (1st sketch)
Hesketh, Hon. Robert
Lowe, Dean
Muse, The, $10\frac{1}{2}″ \times 7\frac{1}{2}″$
Normanby, Marquess of
St. Michael and The Devil — maquette, $20″ \times 9″$
Streen, Dr.
T.U.C. War Memorial, maquette, 22″

Tureck, Rosalyn
Wave, The, $11\frac{1}{2}'' \times 7\frac{1}{2}''$
Young Bacchus, 10″

1957

Bath, Marchioness of
Clarke, Sir Wilfred Le Gros
Donska, Maria
Kitty, 3rd portrait of
Klemperer, Dr. Otto
Phipps, Lady Lepel
Tabitha
T.U.C. War Memorial (marble)

1958

Haley, Sir William

Lloyd George, Earl (maquette), 49″
McInnes, Professor
Margaret, H.R.H. Princess
St. Michael and The Devil, tip of wing to base of
    Devil, 420″; St. Michael, 234″; wingspan,
    276″
Woods, Bishop

1959

Bowater House Group
Brain, Sir Russell
Cavendish, Lady Sophia
Fisher, Dr., Archbishop of Canterbury
Phipps, Lady Evelyn Rose
Sanderson, Ivan
Spence, Sir Basil

LIST OF ILLUSTRATIONS

Plate No.

Abyssinia, Haile Selassie, Emperor of   346, 347, 348
Adam   378, 379
Adam (before polishing)   376, 377
Adam & Eve   369
African Mother & Child   385
Ahmed   300
Alexander, Prof. Samuel O. M.   217
American Soldier   138
Angel of the Annunciation (Ferosa Rastoumji)   201
Anita   228
Annabel   569, 598
Annabel (Freud) with bonnet   568
Annabel & Frisky   621
Anthony   477
Anthony in a balaclava helmet   476
Aran, Man of ('Tiger' King)   309
Asch, Sholem   565

Baby Awake   11, 12
Baby with Arms (Michael Stewart's daughter)   501, 502
Baku, Girl from   439
Balcon, Jill   486
Balcon, Michael   325
Ballon, Ellen   374
Baroda, Gaekwar of   561
Baroda, Prince of   546, 547
Barzetti, Marcella   533
Bath, Marchioness of   629
Beatty, Mrs. Chester   277
Beaverbrook, Lord   313
Beerbohm, Marie   111
Bendon, Malcolm   282
Berenice (2nd portrait of Louise)   367
Berkeley, Countess of   416
Betty (Esther)   266
Bevin, Ernest   425
Bird in Flight (Lovers on an Eagle's back)   466
Black, George   417, 418, 419
Blackett, Prof.   532
Blake, William   639, 640
Blandford, Mary   284

Plate No.

Bloch, Ernest   504
Boas, Prof. Franz   241
Bohémienne, La (1st portrait of Dolores)   180, 185
Bone, Muirhead   126
Bowater House Group   664, 665, 666, 667
Bowater House Group, maquette   628
Braganza, Princesse de   441
Brain, Sir Russell   657
Braintree, Lord   578
Brodetsky, Prof.   564
Bronfman, Minda   552
Burial of Abel   370
Burton, Basil   314

Casati, Marchesa   147
Castle Stewart, Countess of   363
Cavendish, Lady Sophia   660
Cavendish Square Madonna & Child   543–545, 559–561
Cavendish Square Madonna & Child, maquette   534
Cecil, Betty   420
Chadburn, Mrs. (marble bust)   54
Chia-Pi   420
Children Fighting   622
Children Playing   623
Chimera   290
Chinese Boy   516, 517
Christ in Majesty (Llandaff)   610, 611, 612, 627
Christ in Majesty Maquette   573
Christ in Majesty with Liverpool Giant in Royal College of Art   587
Christ, Risen (Bernard van Dieren)   153, 154, 155
Christian, Linda   484
Churchill, Winston   463, 464
Clarke, Louis C. G.   551
Clarke, Sir Wilfred Le Gros   630
Clifton, Mrs. Arthur   79
Collins, W. H.   343
Conrad, Joseph   202, 203
Consummatum Est   355
Cramer, Mrs. Belle   318
Cramer, Dr.   280

[431]

Plate No.

Cripps, Sir Stafford 575
Cunningham, General Sir Alan 424
Cursed Be The Day Whereon I Was Born 1c8

Dave 373
Davies, W. H. 124
Day 254, 256
Deacon, Gladys (later Duchess of Marlborough) 134
Deirdre, 1st portrait of (with arms) 401, 402
Deirdre, 2nd portrait of (with a slip) 403
Deirdre, 3rd portrait of (leaning forward) 423
Dervich, Eve 158
Desta, Princess 512
Dewey, Prof. John 242
Dodd, Mrs. Francis 80
Dolores, 1st portrait of (La Bohémienne) (bust) 180, 185
Dolores, 2nd portrait of (head) 181, 186
Dolores, 3rd portrait of (bust with arms) 183, 184, 187
Dolores, 4th portrait of (head) 188, 189, 190
Dolores, Reclining Study of 182
Donnelly, Prof. Lucy 283
Donska, Maria 631
Door Handles, Four 592, 593, 594, 595
Doves, marble (1st group of) 119, 120
Doves, marble (3rd group of) 121, 122
Dreamer, The (Nan) 83, 86
Drogheda, Countess of 112
Duncan, Ronald 469
Dunn, Daisy 235
Dyall, Franklin 487

Ecce Homo 333, 334, 335, 336
Eileen, Little 263
Eileen (Proudfoot) 198
Einstein, Prof. Albert 320
Elemental 287, 288
Eliot, T. S. 540, 541, 542
Elsa 352
English Girl 53
Enver, 1st portrait of (head) 214
Epstein, Mrs. 1st portrait of (leaning on one hand) 13
Epstein, Mrs. 2nd portrait of (mask with earrings) 128
Epstein, Mrs. 3rd portrait of (with a ribbon) 140
Epstein, Mrs. 4th portrait of (with a scarf) 141
Epstein, Mrs. 5th portrait of (in a mantilla) 142, 143, 144
Esther, 1st portrait of (with long hair) 449–455
Esther, 2nd portrait of 482
Esther, 3rd portrait of 509, 510, 511
Esterman, Helen 483
Euphemia (Lamb), 1st portrait of (bust) 74
Euphemia (Lamb), 2nd portrait of (bust) 75

Plate No.

Euphemia (garden figure) 72, 73

Feibleman, James K. 229
Female Figure in Flenite 99
Figure in Flenite 100, 101
Fisher, Admiral Lord 116, 117
Fisher, Dr., Archbishop of Canterbury 655, 656
Flaherty, Robert 307, 308
Flenite Relief 97, 98
Fletcher, Sir Frank 353
Forbes, Juanita (bust) 413
Frankel, Anna 468
Franklin Medal 601, 602
Fraser, Lionel 566
Freud, Annabel 569
Freud, Annabel (with bonnet) 568
Freud, Ann 521, 522
Freud, Lucian 475
Frisky 572

Garden Figure (Euphemia) 72, 73
Genesis 269, 270, 271, 272
Germaine (Miss Bras) 264
Gerrard, Mrs. (Tirrenia) 261, 262
Gertrude, Half length figure of 76
Gielgud, John 315
Girl from Baku 439
Girl with Gardenias (Kathleen) 407, 408, 409
Girl, Head of a 159
Givenchy, Pola 364
Godley, Hon. Wynne 608, 649
Goldie, May 267
Good, Edward (Mosheh Oved) 230
Gordon, Billie 110, 113
Graham, R. B. Cunninghame 195, 196
Granite Mother & Child 106
Gray, Sir James 614
Greenwood, Joan 485
Greenwood, Joan (as a child) 260
Gregory, Lady 81
Guardians of Paradise 465

Haley, Sir William 652
Hallé, Hiram 332
Hamblay, Hilda 52
Hamilton, Duchess of 118
Head of a Girl 159
Heath, Mrs. Sonia 278
Helène 157
Hesketh, Robert (1st sketch) 616
Hesketh, Robert 617
Hess, Myra (Dame) 467
Hill, Diana Coppinger 523
Hochter, Harriet 301
Holbrooke, Josef 135

	Plate No.			Plate No.
Hornstein, Norman (1st portrait of)	356, 357, 381		Leda, 3rd portrait of (aged 6 months)	388
Hornstein, Norman (2nd portrait of)	380		Leda, 4th portrait of (with cockscomb)	389
Hudson Memorial (Rima)	209, 210		Leda, 5th portrait of (pouting)	440
Hudson, W. H., Relief of	207		Leona	359
Hughes, Christine	527		Levy, Benn	342
Hughes, Christopher	528		Lewis, Lalage	412
Hughes, Isobel	525, 599		Lindsay of Birker, Lord	473
Hughes, Penelope	526		Little Eileen	263
Hulme, T. E.	115		Little Girl with Bow	459
Hunter, Sgt. David Ferguson, V.C.	139		Little Prince, The	546, 547
			Liverpool Giant	579, 581, 600, 619, 620
Ian (Ossian)	422, 597		'Liverpool Giant' with 'Christ in Majesty' in	
Irish Girl (Marie Rankin)	78		Royal College of Art	589
Isobel, 1st portrait of (bust)	294		Liverpool Reliefs	621, 622, 623
Isobel, 2nd portrait of (bust)	321, 322		Llandaff Christ, maquette	5
Israfel (Sunita)	273		Llandaff Christ (Christ in Majesty)	610–612, 627
			Lloyd, Dame Hilda	555
Jackie, 1st portrait of (a baby)	338		Lloyd George, Earl	654
Jackie, 2nd portrait of (with long hair)	362		Lollobrigida, Gina	554
Jackie, 3rd portrait of (Ragamuffin)	391		Louise, 1st portrait of	299
Jacob & the Angel	394–400		Louise, 2nd portrait of (Berenice)	367
Jansen, Ellen	281		Lovers on an Eagle's Back (Bird in Flight)	466
Jeunesse (14th portrait of Peggy Jean)	303		Lowe, Dean	615
Joel, Mrs. Betty (La Belle Juive)	279		Lowe, Dr. Elias	562
Joffé, Mark	556		Lucifer	446, 447, 448
Joffé, Roland	524		Lucifer Relief (The Fall of Lucifer)	445
John, Augustus	127		Lydia, 1st portrait of (bust)	268
John, Romilly (Rom)	16, 17		Lydia, 2nd portrait of (bust with short hair)	276
Juanita (Forbes) (bust)	413		Lydia, 3rd portrait of (bust laughing)	328
Juanita (nude study)	461, 462		Lytton, Lady Madeleine	505
Juive, La Belle (Mrs. Betty Joel)	279			
Kathleen, 1st portrait of (bust)	171, 493		MacDonald, Ramsay, 1st portrait of (small	
Kathleen, 2nd portrait of (small bust)	176, 494		bust)	226
Kathleen, 3rd portrait of (bust)	285, 495		MacDonald, Ramsay, 2nd portrait of (bust)	324
Kathleen, 4th portrait of (bust)	316, 496		Mace-Head	571
Kathleen, 5th portrait of (bust with arms)	339, 340, 341, 497		McEvoy, Mrs. Ambrose (bronze)	55, 56
Kathleen, 6th portrait of (bust with arms)	406, 498		McEvoy, Mrs. Ambrose (marble)	57
Kathleen, 7th portrait of (bust with arms)	490, 491, 492, 499		McInnes, Professor	653
			Madonna and Child	239, 240
Kathleen (Girl with Gardenias)	407, 408, 409		Madonna and Child (details)	237, 238
Keane, Doris	132		Madonna and Child (Cavendish Square)	559–561
Kindler, Hans	258		Madonna and Child (Cavendish Square)	
King, 'Tiger'	309		(details)	543–545
Kitty, 1st portrait (with curls)	456, 457, 458, 637		Madonna and Child (Cavendish Square),	
Kitty, 2nd portrait of	508, 638		maquette	534
Kitty, 3rd portrait of	634, 635		Maisky, Ivan	375
Klemperer, Dr. Otto	632, 633		Majestas	573
Kramer, Jacob	173, 174		Mallon, Dr. Frederick	577
			Man of Aran ('Tiger' King)	309
Lanchester, Elsa	204		Marble Arms	191
Lane, Charles	578		Marble Doves (1st group)	119, 120
Lazarus	478–481, 556		Marble Doves (3rd group of)	121, 122
Leda, 1st portrait of (aged 2 months)	383		Marble Mother and Child	107
Leda, 2nd portrait of (aged 4 months)	387		Marcelle	114
			Margaret, H.R.H. Princess	643

2 E

Plate No.

Margulies, Alexander — 421
Margulies, Judith — 507
Marlborough, Duchess of (Sketch head of) — 192, 193
Marlborough, Duke of (bust) — 211
Marlborough, Duke of (head) — 194
Mason, Portland — 553
Maternity — 64–68
Maternity (with Epstein) — 63
Maugham, Somerset — 549, 550
May, Betty, 1st portrait of (bust) — 149
May, Betty, 2nd portrait of (head) — 150
Melchett, Gwen, Lady — 518
Menan, Princess — 513
Menuhin, Yehudi — 438
Meum, 1st portrait of (bust) — 130
Meum, 2nd portrait of (head) — 131
Meum, 3rd portrait of (mask) — 145
Meum, 4th portrait of (bust with arms and fan) — 146
Morna (Stewart) — 345
Morris, David — 366
Mother & Child (granite) — 106
Mother & Child (marble) — 107
Mother & Child Relief — 14
Mother & Child, Standing (Marie Rankin) — 77
Mourner — 537
Muse, The — 605
Myers, Isaac — 474
Myers, M. S. — 331
Nan, bust of — 59, 60
Nan (the dreamer) — 83, 86
Nan seated — 84, 85
Narcissus (destroyed statue) — 71
Neander — 317
Nehru, Pandit (Sketch of) — 471
Nehru, Pandit (Bust of) — 503
Nerenska, Pola — 365
Nicolle, Arthur — 305
Nielke, Marguerite — 133
Night — 255, 257
Night, Maquette for — 252
Night (with Epstein on site) — 253
Norman (Hornstein), (1st portrait of) — 356, 357, 381
Norman (Hornstein), (2nd portrait of) — 380
Normanby, Marquess of — 613
Nude Studies A–J — 428–37

Oko, Dr. Adolph S. — 199
Oko, Mrs. Adolph S. — 350
Oko, Pearl — 234
Old Italian Woman — 18
Old Pinager — 197
Old Smith — 179
Olive — 329
O'Regan, Terence — 563
Ossian (Ian) — 422, 593

Plate No.

Ostrer, Isidore — 312
Oved, Mosheh (Edward Good) — 230
Oved, Ymiel — 470
Old Italian Woman (with shawl) — 37

Pearson, Mrs. Melinda — 384
Peggy Jean — 160–163
Peggy Jean (age 7½ with long hair) — 227
Peggy Jean (Jeunesse) — 303
Peggy Jean (last portrait) — 337
Peggy Jean, Laughing — 170
Peggy Jean (Sick child) — 244–6
Peter Laughing — 488–9, 596
Peters, Betty — 382
Phillips, Mrs. Godfrey (a portrait) — 248
Phipps, Lady Evelyn Rose — 661
Phipps, Lady Lepel — 641
Piccaninny — 390
Plichte, Miriam, 1st portrait of (bust) — 168
Plichte, Miriam, 2nd portrait of (bust with arms) — 169
Portal, Air-Marshal Viscount — 427
Portrait, A (Mrs. Godfrey Phillips) — 248
Powys, Isobel — 259
Priestley, J. B. — 354
Primeval Gods — 310
Proudfoot, Eileen — 198
Prow of a ship, Maquette for — 580
Putti — 161

Ragamuffin (Jackie, 3rd portrait of) — 391
Rani Rama — 330
Rankin, Marie (Irish Girl) — 78
Rastoumji, Ferosa — 200
Rebecca — 265
Reclining Goddess (Sunita reclining) — 275
Relief of Mother and Child — 14
Resurrection Study — 410, 411
Rhodes, Robert — 548
Rima (Hudson Memorial) — 209, 210
Risen Christ (Bernard van Dieren) — 153–55
Rita — 361
Robeson, Paul — 243
Rock drill — 94, 95, 96
Roma of Barbados, 1st portrait of (head) — 302
Roma of Barbados, 2nd portrait of (bust) — 306
Romilly John (Rom) — 16, 17
Rose — 304
Roselli, Fedora — 177
Rosemary — 349
Ross, Oriel, 1st portrait of (bust) — 212, 296
Ross, Oriel, 2nd portrait of (head) — 231, 297
Ross, Oriel, 3rd portrait of — 295, 298
Rothermere, Viscount — 247
Russell, Earl (Bertrand Russell) — 567
Ryan, Sally — 358

	Plate No.
Sainsbury, Robert	414
St. Francis	415
St. Michael (head)	648
St. Michael and the Devil	662, 663
St. Michael and the Devil — in foundry	647
St. Michael and the Devil — maquette	624
St. Michael and the Devil — in studio	626
Samuel, Lord	529
Sanderson, Ivan	658
Satan, Beelzebub & Belial	444
Scott, C. P.	218
Scott-Ellis, Hon. Elizabeth	136
Seated Mother, Maquette for Social Conscious- ness	538
Selassie, Haile, Emperor of Abyssinia	346, 347, 348
Self Portrait with a Beard	164, 165, 166, 167
Self Portrait in a Cap	91
Selina	178
Senegalese Girl (Madeleine Béchet)	172
Seraph, The (Marie Collins)	206, 574
Shaw, Bernard	323
Sheila	205
Shelley, Lillian, 1st portrait of (head)	123
Shelley, Lillian, 2nd portrait of (bust)	148
Sheridan, Clare	137
Sick Child (Peggy Jean)	244, 245, 246
Simon of Wythenshaw, Lord	557
Siobhan	506
Slave Hold	404
Sleeping Baby	10
Smith, A. H.	535
Smuts, Field-Marshal	588, 589, 618
Social Consciousness	582, 586, 590, 591
Social Consciousness, 3 maquettes for	537, 538
Soene, Gabrielle	156
Solomons, Dr. Bethel	530
Spence, Sir Basil	659
Standing Mother and Child (Marie Rankin)	77
Strand Statues	20, 50
Study, A (The Visitation)	220, 221, 222
Sunflower	69
Sungod	70
Sunita, 1st portrait of (bust)	213
Sunita, 3rd portrait of (bust with a necklace)	223
Sunita (Israfel)	273
Sunita reclining	275
Tabitha	642
Tagore, Rabindranath	224, 225

	Plate No.
Tanya	360
Tennant, Hon. Stephen	219
Thorndyke, Sybil	216
Tin Hat, The	129
Tindall-Lister, Elizabeth	515
Tirrenia (Mrs. Gerrard)	261, 262
Ti-yi	372
Tracy, Marie	368
Tree, Lady Anne	539
Tree, Iris	109
T.U.C. War Memorial	644, 645, 646
T.U.C. War Memorial, maquette	606
T.U.C. War Memorial (site of, with Epstein)	607
Tureck, Rosalyn	609
Van Dieren, Bernard, 1st portrait of (head)	125
Van Dieren, Bernard, 2nd portrait of (head)	152
Van Dieren, Bernard, 3rd portrait of (bust)	351
Vaughan Williams, Ralph	519, 520
Venus, 1st	102, 104
Venus, 2nd	103, 105
Victor	500
Visitation, The	220, 221, 222
Walker, Sir Alec	344
Walpole, Hugh	326
Warrior with Sword	537
Wave, The	603
Wavell, Field-Marshal Earl	426
Waverley, Viscount	460
Weeping Woman, The	175
Weizmann, Chaim	319
Whittaker, Dr. William	472
Wilde, Oscar, Tomb of	88, 89, 90
Williams, Emlyn	327
Williams, Ralph Vaughan	519, 520
Wise, Rabbi Stephen	386
Woman Possessed	291, 292, 293
Woods, Bishop	650, 651
Young Bacchus	604
Young Communist (Norman Hornstein)	356, 357
Young Paul Robeson	286
Youth Advancing	536
Zeda	233
Zefira, Bracha	514
Zetterling, Mai	570

INDEX

Abbey Theatre (Dublin), 57
Abyssinia, Empress of, 331
Abyssinia, Haile Selassie, Emperor of, 125, 170, 224, 226, 276
Adam, 170, 181, 240, 244–5, 416, 422
Adam & Eve, 240–1
African Carvings, 63
African Mother & Child, 251
Agar Street, 26, 27, 34
Ahmed, 197
Akhnaton, 15
Albany Street, 20
Albert Hall, Royal, 42, 44, 421
Albert, Prince, 136
Alexander, Prof. Samuel, O.M., 143
Allied Artists' Exhibition, 42
Alma-Tadema, 22
'America' (Walt Whitman), 371
American Soldier, 85, 91
Amina — see *Sunita*
Anderson, Sir John (Viscount Waverley), 300
Angel of the Annunciation (Ferosa Rastoumji), 128, 145
Anita, 150, 170
Annabel, 363, 376–7
Annabel (Freud) with bonnet, 363
Annabel & Frisky, 391, 393
Antelami, 410
Ashmolean Museum (Oxford), 412
Anthony, 310
Anthony, In a Balaclava Helmet, 310
'Apres-midi d'un Faune, L' ', 293
Aran, Man of ('Tiger' King), 200
Arc de Triomphe, 422
Arles, 410
Armstrong, Miss, 37
Artist's Rifles, 80, 88
Arts Council of Great Britain, 332, 345, 356, 416, 420, 422
Arts Student League, 10, 160
Asch, Sholem, 360

Ashe, Oscar, 113
Assisi, 272
'Atalanta in Calydon', 187
Aumonier, E., 104

Baby Awake, 19
Baby with Arms (Michael Stewart's Daughter), 323
Bagnall-Godfrey, Gordon, 407
Bagrit, Sir Leon, 299
Bakst, Leon, 63
Ballad of Reading Gaol, The, 63
Baku, Girl from, 285
Bakunin, Michael, 18
Balcon, Jill, 212, 316
Balcon, Michael, 212
Baldwin, Stanley, 136
Balliol College (Oxford), 309
Ballon, Ellen, 242
Bardsley, Dr. Cuthbert, 395
Barnard, George Gray, 10, 145
Barnes, Dr., 161
Baroda, Gaekwar of, 340, 353
Baroda, Prince of, 332, 353
Bartok, Bela, 22
Barzetti, Marcella, 343, 371
Basle, 410
Bath, Marchioness of, 397
Battersea Park, 315, 349
Baudelaire, Charles, 170, 281
Bax, Clifford, 87
Bazell, Mrs. Anna, 23
Bazile, Georges, 63
Bean, T. A., 397
Beatty, Mrs. Chester, 184
Beauvais, 410
Beaux-Arts, Ecole des, 14, 15, 16, 18
Beaverbrook, Lord, 80, 204
Béchet, Madeleine (Senegalese Girl), 109
Beerbohm, Marie, 74, 397
Belloc, Hilaire, 136
Belloni, Rue, 14, 16

[436]

Benabo, Count, 387
Bendon, Malcolm, 184
Bennett, Arnold, 136
Berenice (2nd portrait of Louise), 238
Berg, Alban, 22
Belcher, George, 22
Berkeley, Countess of, 272
Bernstein, S., 181
Berri, Duc & Duchesse de, 410
Betty (Esther), 174
Bevin, Ernest, 276
Billy's Gallery, 14
Binyon, Laurence, 34, 88
Bird in Flight (Lovers on an Eagle's back), 305
Bird Pluming Itself, A, 78
Birmingham City Art Gallery, 288
Birmingham, Lord Mayor of, 288
Black, George, 275
'Blackbirds', 153, 174
Blackett, Prof., 340, 372
Blackpool, 416, 421
Blake Society, 400
Blake, William, 332, 400
Blandford, Mary, 187
'Blast', 65, 68
Bloch, Ernest, 325
Bloomsbury, 23, 65, 68, 160, 170, 311, 416, 418
Boas, Prof. Franz, 158, 160
Bobinet Music Hall, 16
Bohémienne, La (1st portrait of Dolores), 115
Bone, Muirhead, 22, 23, 36, 60, 82, 130, 136
Bonnard, Pierre, 14
'Book of Affinity', 151
Borodine, Alexander, 22
Bossom, Sir Alfred, 181
Boston, 11
Bouguereau, William Adolphe, 16
Bourdelle, Antoine, 380
Bourges, 410
Bowater House Group, 241, 332, 387, 411, 412, 414, 421
Bowater House Group, maquette, 395
Bowery, The, 11, 160
Bowra, Sir Maurice, 372
Braganza, Princesse de, 287
Brain, Sir Russell, 400, 412
Braintree, Lord, 365
Brancusi, Constantin, 13, 49, 63, 73, 161
Brangwyn, Frank, 65
Braque, Georges, 14, 65
Brzska, Henri Gaudier, 13, 59, 60, 65, 68, 78
Brzska, Sophie, 59
Brigden, Wallace, 404
Bridges, Robert, 22
Brodie's, Steve (Saloon), 11

Bristol Art Gallery, 413
Bristol University, 410
British Medical Association, 24, 32, 35, 38, 163
British Medical Journal
British Museum, 18, 23, 42, 91, 310, 420
Brookes, Canon, 409
Brodetsky, Prof., 360
Brodzky, Isaac, 60
Bronfman, Minda, 355
Brooklyn Bridge, 11
'Brothers' (Dostoevsky), 171
Brown, Henry Kirk, 9
Browne, Maurice, 184
Bruges, 14, 100
Bryn Mawr (Philadelphia), 187
Beethoven, Ludwig van, 240
Burial of Abel, 240-1
Burlington Magazine, 418
Burton, Basil, 204
Busoni, Ferruccio, 104, 343
Butler, R. A., 358

Café Royal, 20, 91, 96, 118, 184
'Calamus' (Whitman), 22
Camden Town Group, 65
Cameo Corner, 151
Campden Hill, 414
Canadian Pacific Railway, 235
Canova, Antonio, 9
Canterbury, Dean of (Dr. Hewlett Johnson), 418
Caprice Restaurant, 316
Caravaggio, 68
Carlton Club, 332
Carney (Foundry), 387
Carpeaux, Jean Baptiste, 57
Carrara, 104
Casati, Marchesa, 91, 96
Castle Stewart, Countess of, 237
Catskill Mountains, 11
'Cave of the Golden Calf', 80
'Cave of Harmony', 132
Cavendish, Lady Sophia, 414
Cavendish Square Madonna & Child, 332, 341, 343, 349, 350, 353, 355, 358, 371, 376, 393, 418
Cavendish Square Madonna & Child Maquette, 343
'Cauldron of Anwyn, The' (Holbrooke), 91
Cecil, Betty, 242
Central Park, 10, 11
Century Magazine, 13
Cerracchi, Giuseppe, 9
Cézanne, Paul, 14, 15, 16, 20, 161
Chadburn, Mrs. (Marble Bust), 39, 40
Chandos, Duke of, 341

Chantrey Bequest, 356
Charterhouse School, 230
Chartres, 410
Chartwell, 302
Chelsea Cloisters, 414
Cheyne Walk, Studio in, 24, 42, 50, 57, 60
Chia-Pi, 275
Children Fighting, 391, 393
Children Playing, 391, 393
Chimera, 191
Chinese Boy, 331, 345
Chirk Castle, 90
Christchurch College, Oxford, 387
Christ in Majesty (Llandaff), 332, 366, 373, 385, 387, 395, 418, 422
Christ in Majesty, Maquette, 365
Christ, Risen (Bernard van Dieren),
Christian, Linda, 316
'Chu Chin Chow', 113
Churchill, Winston, 91, 252, 302, 311, 337, 379, 388
Ciccio's Restaurant, 414
Cladel, 15
Clark, Sir Kenneth, 35
Clarke, Louis C. G., 354
Clarke, Sir Wilfred Le Gros, 397
Clifton, Arthur, 50, 57
Clifton, Mrs. Arthur, 57
Cloisters Museum, New York, 10
Coburg Hotel, 88
Coghlan School (Bulawayo), 37
Cohn, David, 151
Cole, Horace, 99
Collins, José, 132
Collins, Marie, 132, 365
Collins, W. H., 224
Colmar, 410
Colossus of Rhodes, 379
Columbia University, 158
Comédie Française, 16
Commonwealth Conference (1946), 308
Como, 410
Conder, Charles, 14
Condron, Nan (see under *Nan*)
Conrad, Joseph, 22, 82, 125, 130, 416
Constable, W. G., 35
Consummatum Est, 170, 181, 232, 233, 235, 416, 422
Convent of the Holy Child Jesus (Cavendish Square), 339, 341
Cooper, Douglas, 349
'Corn is Green, The' (Emlyn Williams), 212
Côte d'Azur, 410
Council for the Care of Churches, 221
Cournos, John, 88
Courtauld, Samuel, 136

Coventry Cathedral, 339, 376-7, 393, 414
Coventry, Provost of, 395
Cowie, Drs. John & Valerie, 410
Cox, Trenchard, 288
Cramer, Mrs. Belle, 204
Cramer, Dr., 184
Craven Street, 379
Craxton, John, 308
Cripps, Sir Stafford, 365
Crittall Glass Co., 365
Cromer, 206
Crowley, Aleister, 98
Cubism, 65, 68
Cumberland Market, 20
Cunningham, General Sir Alan, 276
Curle, Richard, 130
Cursed be the day whereon I was born, 73, 88

'Daily Express', 181
'Daily Mail', 136, 181
'Daily Telegraph', 35, 181
Dalou, Jules, 57
Dave, 242
Dave, Victor, 18
'David' (Michelangelo), 17
Davies, W. H., 39, 80, 88
Davison, Jo, 211
Day, 82, 163-7, 191, 218, 251, 332, 404
Day-Lewis, Cecil, 316
Deacon, Gladys (later Duchess of Marlborough), 88, 122
Debussy, Claude, 14, 293
'Deerhurst', 189, 191
Deirdre, 1st portrait of (with arms), 11, 264, 271, 297
Deirdre, 2nd portrait of (with a slip), 267
Deirdre, 3rd portrait of (leaning forward), 275-6
Degas, Edgar, 14, 20, 59
Delacroix, Eugène, 283
Delmer, Sefton, 209
Delys, Gaby, 65
Deposition, The, 110, 145
Derain, André, 14
Derby, Earl of, 80
Derbyshire, 38
Dervich, Eve, 102
Desta, Princess, 331
Devonshire, Duke of, 414
Dewey, Prof. John, 158, 160
Diaghilev, Serge, 22, 170
Dicksee, Sir Frank, P.R.A., 136
Dobson, Frank, 418
'Doctor's Commons' (Paul Vaughan), 24
Dodd, Francis, R.A., 22, 23, 24, 60, 77, 82, 136
Dodd, Mrs. Francis, 23, 57, 59

Dolores, 1st portrait of (*La Bohémienne*) (Bust), 80, 96, 106, 194, 209, 285
Dolores, 2nd portrait of (*head*), 115
Dolores, 3rd portrait of (*bust with arms*), 116
Dolores, 4th portrait of (*head*), 118
Dolores, Reclining Study of, 59, 115
Don, Dean, 401
Donatello, 11, 17, 32, 113, 315, 393, 404, 416
Donnelly, Prof. Lucy, 170, 187, 361
Donska, Maria, 397
Door Handles, Four, 376–7
Dordogne Caves, 65
Dorking, 334
Doves, Marble (1st group of), 65, 78
Doves, Marble (2nd group of), 65, 78
Doves, Marble (3rd group of), 65, 78
Doyle, Sir A. Conan, 136
Dreamer, The (*Nan*), 57
Dreyfus, 14
Drinkwater, John, 145
Driver, Dr. S. R., 256
Drogheda, Countess of, 74, 75, 88
Dublin, 57
Dukes, Ashley, 77, 349
Duncan, Isadora, 16, 380
Duncan, Ronald, 306
Dunlop, Margaret (see under Mrs. Epstein), 92
Dunn, Daisy, 153
Durand-Ruel, 11, 13
Duveen, Lord, 158
Dyall, Franklin, 316
'Dying Centaur', 10

Eakins, Thomas, 11
Earp, T. W., 36
East River (New York), 73
Ecce Homo, 170, 216, 221, 416
Edinburgh, 398
Edinburgh Festival, 37, 421
Edinburgh Gate (Hyde Park), 421
'Egoist, The', 78
Eiffel Tower Restaurant, 118
Eileen (*Proudfoot*), 127, 173
Einstein, Prof. Albert, 125, 170, 206, 337, 416
Elemental, 189
Elgar, Sir Edward, 22
Elgin Marbles, 18
El Greco, 387
Eliot, George, 39
Eliot, T. S., 22, 237, 252, 321, 332, 349, 372
Elizabeth, H.M. Queen (The Queen Mother), 365
Ellis, T. E., 90
Elsa, 228
Emerald Street, 42, 203

Emerson, 10
English Girl, 39, 54
Enver, 1st portrait of (*head*), 141, 142, 182, 353
Epping Forest, 125, 134, 145, 153, 170, 174, 189
Epstein Memorial Exhibition, Edinburgh, 37, 252, 315
Epstein, Jacob: born, 9; travels to Europe, 13; student at Ecole des Beaux Arts, moves to Julian Academy, 16; leaves school, 16; first visit to Italy, 17; meets Margaret Dunlop (later his first wife), 18; comes to London, takes studio in St. Pancras, 20; travels to New York for a fortnight, 22; takes studio in Fulham Road, 22; moves to Cheyne Walk and starts Strand Statues, 24; becomes British Citizen, 39; to Paris for erection of Oscar Wilde Tomb, 65; takes bungalow at Pett Level, 65; called up and demobilized, 80; returns to London and takes house in Guildford Street, 80; first one man show, 85; Peggy Jean born, 103; meets Kathleen Garman (later his second wife), 109; carves Hudson Memorial, 134; works in shed in Epping Forest and models 'The Visitation', 145; models the first 'Madonna and Child'; lease of Guildford Street given up and he goes to New York, 158; exhibition in New York, 158; returns to London, 161; takes 18 Hyde Park Gate, 163; commissioned to do Underground Headquarters groups, 163; completes 'Genesis', 174; rents 'Deerhurst' in Epping Forest, 189; works on 'Ecce Homo', 216; works on 'Adam', 244; works on 'Jacob and the Angel', 256; works on 'Lucifer', 289; carves 'Lazarus', 311; Mrs. Epstein dies, 332; Cavendish Square 'Madonna and Child' commissioned, 341; travels to U.S.A. and agrees to model 'Social Consciousness' group, 346; 'Lazarus' placed in New College, Oxford Chapel, 356; is knighted, 'Christ in Majesty' commissioned for Llandaff Cathedral, 365; is lent studio in Royal College of Art, 366; commissioned to make 'Liverpool Giant', 366; receives Degree at Oxford, 372; sails to America for unveiling of 'Social Consciousness', 375; starts on T.U.C. War Memorial, 381; 'St. Michael and the Devil' commissioned for Coventry Cathedral, 395; re-dedication of Llandaff Cathedral, 395; commissioned to execute Bowater House group, 395; holiday in Scotland, 398; taken to Hospital, 404; sight-seeing tour of French Cathedrals and into Italy, 410; holiday in Paris, 413; dies, 414
Epstein, Mrs., 1st portrait of (*leaning on one hand*), 20, 23, 54, 158, 332
Epstein, Mrs., 2nd portrait of (*mask with ear-rings*), 85, 88

Epstein, Mrs., 3rd portrait of (with a ribbon), 92
Epstein, Mrs., 4th portrait of (with a scarf), 92
Epstein, Mrs., 5th portrait of (in a Mantilla), 80, 93
   252
Esther, 1st portrait of (with long hair), 252, 293–7, 337
Esther, 2nd portrait of, 315
Esther, 3rd portrait of, 326, 328
Esterman, Helen, 315
Etchells, Frederick, 65
Eumorfopoulos Collection, 136
Euphemia (Lamb), 1st portrait of (bust), 52
Euphemia (Lamb), 2nd portrait of (bust), 52, 88
Euphemia (garden figure), 50, 52
Euston Road Group, 20
'Evening Standard', 34, 167

Fairmount Park, Philadelphia, 11
Fairmount Park Trust (Philadelphia), 346
Fagg, William, 420
'Falling Gladiator' (William Rimmer), 10
Fauves, Les, 14, 65
Feibleman, James K., 151
Fels (A Chemist), 38
Female Figure in Flenite, 59, 73
Fénelon, Bertrand de, 14
Festival of Britain, 331, 338, 345
'Fidelio' (Beethoven), 267
'Fighting Lions' (William Rimmer), 10
Figure in Flenite, 69, 153
Finch, Miss Edith, 187, 361
Fine Arts Gallery, New York, 245
Fiorini (Foundry), 387
Fish, Mrs. Styyvesant, 10
Fisher, Admiral Lord, 77, 85
Fisher, Dr., Archbishop of Canterbury, 411, 412
Fitzwilliam Museum (Cambridge), 288, 354
Flaherty, Robert, 170, 200
Flenite Relief, 69, 73
Fletcher, Sir Frank, 230, 235
'Fleurs Du Mal' (Baudelaire), 170
Florence, 11, 17, 410
Forain, Jean Louis, 13
Forbes, Juanita (bust), 272
Ford, Ford Maddox (Hueffer), 77
Forster, E. M., 22
Fothergill, John, 22
Foundlings' Hospital, 80
France, 9, 39
France, Anatole, 15
Frankel, Anna, 306
Frankel, Benjamin, 306
Franklin Medal, 379
Fraser, 256
Fraser, Lionel, 360

Frazee, John, 9
Freud, Annabel, 363, 376–7
Freud, Annabel (with bonnet), 363, 372
Freud, Ann, 337, 372
Freud, Lucian, 326, 383
Freud, Lucian, 308, 337
Freud, Sigmund, 308
Frisky, 363
Fry, Roger, 170
Fulham Road, 22

Gainsborough, Thomas, 347
Gallati, Mario, 316
Galsworthy, John, 65, 134
Gandhi, Mahatma, 325
Garden Figure (Euphemia), 50, 52, 283, 422
Gardner, Albert, 10
Gardner, Isabella, 11
Garman, Kathleen — see under Kathleen, 80, 109,
   122
Gaskin (Foundry), 387
Gauguin, Paul, 14, 20, 22, 42, 65
Geddes, Sir Patrick, 400
'Gems for Life', 151
Genesis, 49, 69, 153, 170, 174–81, 240, 356, 416, 422
Germaine (Miss Bras), 173
German Expressionists, 13
'George' (Emlyn Williams), 212
Georgian Poets, 80
Gerrard, A. H., 164
Gerrard, Mrs. (Tirrenia), 173
Gertler, Mark, 397
Gertrude, Half length figure of, 54
Ghetto, The New York, 10, 11
Ghiberti, 17
Gill, Eric, 164
Gilman, Harold, 65
Gielgud, John, 204
Ginsberg, Baroness, 355
Girl from Baku, 285
Girl with a dove, 49
Girl with Gardenias (Kathleen), 252, 268–71, 332
Girl, Head of a, 102
'Gitanjali', 147
Givenchy, Pola, 238, 272
Giverny, 14
Glencoe, 398
Glenconner, Lord, 143
Godley, Hon. Wynne, 332, 383
Godley, Hon. Wynne (as model for St. Michael), 395,
   407
Goldie, May, 174
Goldston, E., 235
Gollancz, Victor, 242

'Good Companions, The' (J. B. Priestley), 230
Good, Edward (Mosheh Oved), 151
Goodhart — Rendel, H. A., 36
Gordon, Billie, 75
Gorton, Bishop, 393, 395
Grafton Galleries, 42
Graham, R. B. Cunninghame, 125, 136
Granite Mother & Child, 72, 88
Grant, Mrs. Blanche, 210
Gray, Cecil, 82, 104, 171
Gray, Sir James, 387
Great Exhibition, The, 10
'Greek Slave' (Hiram Powers), 10
'Green Mansions' (Hudson's), 134
Greenough, Horatio, 10
Greenwich, 57
Greenwood, Joan, 316
Greenwood, Joan (as a child), 172
Greenwood Lake, 11
Greffuhle, Comtesse, 14
Gregory, Lady, 22, 50, 57, 77
Griller Quartet, 306
Grünewald, 410
Guardians of Paradise, 305
Guggenheim, S. R., 237
Guilbert, Yvette, 16
Guildford Street, 42, 80, 85, 91, 98, 99, 118, 158, 203
Guino, 32
Gussow, Bernard, 9, 11, 14, 16, 346

Haley, Sir William, 410
Hallé, Hiram, 216
Halliday, Johnny, 331
Hamblay, Hilda, 39
Hamilton, Duchess of, 77
Hamnett, Nina, 78
Hampstead Road, 20
Hapgood, Hutchins, 11, 12, 13, 170
Hardy, Thomas, 22
Harewood, The Earl of, 181, 421
Harewood House (Yorkshire), 245
Harlem, 160
Harlequin Club, 98, 132, 171
Harris, Frank, 60
Haskell, Arnold, 16, 54, 109, 170, 199, 422
Hastings, 65
Head of a girl, 102
Heath, Mrs. Sonia, 184
Hebrew Union College Library, 127
Hebrew University of Jerusalem, 360
Heidelberg, 160
Helène, 102
Helleu, Paul-Cesar, 14
Hesketh, Robert (1st sketch), 388

Hesketh, Robert, 388
Hess, Myra, 306
Hester Street, 9, 12
Hill, Diana Coppinger-, 337
Hill, G. F., 36
Hochter, Harriet, 197
Holbein, Hans, 410, 411
Holbrooke, Josef, 90
Holden, Charles, 24, 26, 36, 50, 163, 251
Holmes, Sir Charles, 34
Homer, Winslow, 11
Hopkins, G. M., 22
Hornstein, Norman, 250, 275, 346
Hornstein, Norman (1st portrait of), 170, 235, 337, 346
Hornstein, Norman (2nd portrait of), 248
Houdon, Jean Antoine, 9, 346
House of Commons, 411
Howard de Walden, Lord, 90, 136
Hudson Memorial (Rima), 82, 106, 125, 134, 136, 153, 212, 218, 416
Hudson River, 11
Hudson, W. H., Relief of, 134
Hughes, Christine, 339–40
Hughes, Christopher, 339–40
Hughes, Isobel, 339–40, 376–7
Hughes, Penelope, 339–40
Hughes, Mr. & Mrs. Peter, 339
Hugo, Victor, 9, 240
Hulme, T. E., 63, 69, 75, 77, 78–88, 349
Hunter, Sgt. David Ferguson, V.C., 85, 91
Hyde Park, 23, 82, 125, 134, 421
Hyde Park Gate (No. 18), 163, 170, 203, 323, 332, 366, 403, 404, 413, 421
Hyde Park Hotel, 395

Ian (Ossian), 275, 337, 376–7
Ibsen, Henrik, 20
'Importance of Being Earnest, The', 20
Impressionists, The, 161, 184, 349
Ingres, Jean Domenique, 14
Irish Girl (Marie Rankin), 54
Ishmael (2nd portrait of Norman Hornstein), 248
Isobel (1st portrait of (bust), 11, 194, 252, 285, 416
Isobel (2nd portrait of (bust), 209
Isola Bella Restaurant, 98
Israel, 422
Israfel (Sunita), 181
Italian Woman, Old — (see *Old Italian Woman*)
Italy, 65, 104
Ivy Restaurant, 249

Jaberwu, Namtanda, 251
Jackie, 1st portrait of (a baby), 170, 249, 281, 337
Jackie, 2nd portrait of (with long hair), 237

Jackie, 3rd portrait of (*Ragamuffin*), 254
Jackson, Holbrook, 136
Jackson, Robert, 20
Jacob & the Angel, 181, 240, 252, 256–64, 416, 422
Jacob, Max, 14
James, Henry, 22
Jansen, Ellen, 184
Jardin des Plantes, 16
Jefferson, Thomas, 9
Jerome, Celia, 16, 18
Jerusalem, 422
Jeunesse (14th portrait of Peggy Jean), 199
'Joan of Arc' (Bernard Shaw), 321
Joel, Mrs. Betty (*La Belle Juive*), 184
Joffé, Mark, 337, 355
Joffé, Roland, 337, 398
Johannesburg Art Gallery, 41
John, Augustus, 22, 23, 40, 50, 60, 82, 83, 88, 136, 145, 170
John, Admiral of the Fleet Sir Caspar, 23
John, Romilly (*Rom*), 23, 82, 88, 249, 328
Johnson, John G., 11
Johnson, Samuel, 77
Joseph, Michael, 170
Joyce, James, 22
Juanita (*Forbes*) (bust), 272
Juanita (nude study), 272, 300
Juive, La Belle (Mrs. Betty Joel), 184
Julian Academy, 16
Jupiter and Semele, 305

Kandinsky, Wassily, 65
Kathleen (Garman), 109, 170–1, 182, 189, 249, 285, 318, 326, 332, 341, 343, 380, 398, 403–4, 409, 412–14
Kathleen, 1st portrait of (bust), 109, 170
Kathleen, 2nd portrait of (small bust), 113
Kathleen, 3rd portrait of (bust), 187
Kathleen, 4th portrait of (bust), 204–14
Kathleen, 5th portrait of (bust with arms), 222
Kathleen, 6th portrait of (bust with arms), 268–71, 315
Kathleen, 7th portrait of (bust with arms), 318–22, 252
Kathleen (Girl with the Gardenias), 252, 268–71, 332
Keane, Doris, 88
Kensington Palace Gardens, 184, 414
Kilbracken, Lord, 383
Kindler, Hans, 171
King, 'Tiger' (Man of Aran), 200
Kitty, 308
Kitty, 1st portrait (head, with curls), 297–9, 337, 383, 413
Kitty, 2nd portrait of (head), 326
Kitty, 3rd portrait of (bust), 398
Klemperer, Dr. Otto, 397

Kopf, A. F., 91
Kramer, Jacob, 110

'Lady of Elche', 15
La Gandara, Antonio de, 14
Lamb (Euphemia) — see under *Euphemia*
Lambert, Constant, 209
Lambeth Palace, 411
Lanchester, Elsa, 132
Lane, Charles, 365
Lane, Sir Hugh, 57
Lang, Dr. (Bishop of Stepney), 34
Laughton, Charles, 132
Laurel Hill Cemetery (Philadelphia), 10
Laurens, Jean-Paul, 16
Lautrec, Toulouse-, Henri de, 14, 75
Lavery, John, 63, 136
Lawrence, D. H., 22
Lawrence, Professor, 288
Lazarus, 252, 311–15, 341, 345, 349, 355, 356, 412, 422
League of Nations, 170
Le Cannet, 14
Leda, 1st portrait of (aged 2 months), 250, 275, 337
Leda, 2nd portrait of (aged 4 months), 250
Leda, 3rd portrait of (aged 6 months), 251
Leda, 4th portrait of (with cockscomb), 252, 416
Leda, 5th portrait of (pouting), 285
Léger, Fernand, 14, 203
Lehmbruck, Wilhelm, 59
Leicester Galleries, 85, 88, 100, 145, 170, 177, 191–2, 203, 221, 244, 281, 288, 305, 306, 311, 315, 341, 372
Leona, 237
Levy, Benn, 224
Lewis, Lalage, 272
Lewis, Wyndham, 65, 77
Lincoln College, Oxford, 143
Lewis's Store (Liverpool), 366
Lichfield, 409
Lincoln, Abraham, 371
Lindsay of Birker, Lord, 309
Lipkin, Beth, 354, 404, 413, 414
Little Eileen, 173
Little Girl with Bow, 299
Little Prince, The, 332, 353
Littler, Emile, 352
Liverpool Giant, 332, 379, 387, 391, 393, 422
Liverpool Reliefs, 391, 393
Livorno, 104
Llandaff Cathedral, 365
Llandaff Christ, Maquette (Majestas), 365
Llandaff Christ (Christ in Majesty), 132, 332, 366, 372, 385–7, 395, 418
Llewellyn, Sir William, P.R.A., 36

Lloyd, Dame Hilda, 355
Lloyd George, Earl, 332, 411
Lloyd George, Lady Megan, 411
Locker-Lampson, Commander, 206, 224
Lollobrigida, Gina, 355
London Group, 65, 68
London Hospital (Whitechapel), 404
London Transport Headquarters, 164
London University, 37
Long Island, 11
Louise, 1st portrait of, 197
Louise, 2nd portrait of (Berenice), 238
Louvre, The, 11, 15, 18, 413
Lovers on an Eagle's Back (Bird in Flight), 305
Lowe, Dean, 387
Lowe, Dr. Elias, 360
Lucifer, 181, 252, 283, 287-8, 332, 356, 416, 422
Lucifer, Relief (The Fall of Lucifer), 288
'Ludovisi Throne', 134
Luxembourg Museum, 63
Lydia, 1st portrait of (bust), 11, 174
Lydia, 2nd portrait of (bust with short hair), 183
Lydia, 3rd portrait of (bust laughing), 214
Lyons, I. J., 181, 421
Lytton, Lady Madeleine, 326

MacDonald, Ramsay, 1st portrait of (small bust), 136, 149
MacDonald, Ramsay, 2nd portrait of (bust), 21F, 235
Mace-head, 363
Maclagan, Eric, 36
McEvoy, Ambrose, 22, 52, 136
McEvoy, Mrs. Ambrose (bronze), 23, 39, 40, 356
McEvoy, Mrs. Ambrose (marble), 41
McInnes, Professor, 332, 410, 413
'Madame Chrysantheme' (Ashton — Rawsthorne — Isobel Lambert), 209
Madonna and Child (First), 141, 142, 154, 158, 235, 242
Madonna and Child (Cavendish Square), 332, 341, 343, 349, 350, 353, 355, 358, 371, 376, 393, 418
Madonna and Child (Cavendish Square) Maquette, 343
Maeterlinck, Maurice, 14
Maillol, M., 418
Maisky, Ivan, 242
Majestas, 365, 395
Mallarmé, Stéphane, 14
Mallon, Dr. Frederick, 365
Man of Aran ('Tiger' King), 200
Manchester City Art Gallery, 345
'Manchester Guardian', 143
Manet, Edouard, 11, 14, 281
Manhattan, 9

Manson, J. D., 36
Marble Arms, 122
Marble Clock, 88
Marble Doves (1st Group), 78
Marble Doves (2nd Group), 65, 78
Marble Doves (3rd Group of), 78, 422
Marble Mother and Child, 65, 73, 88
Marcella, 75
Margaret, H.R.H. Princess, 103-5, 411
Margulies, Alexander, 275, 326
Margulies, Judith, 275, 326
Marinetti, Filippo, 65
Marlborough, Duchess of (sketch head of), 125, 139
Marlborough, Duke of (bust), 88, 139
Marlborough, Duke of (head), 123, 125
Martin, Sir Alec, 235
Mason, James, 355
Mason, Portland, 355
Maternity (Marble), 42, 44, 49, 69, 153, 422
Matisse, Henri, 14, 22
Maugham, Somerset, 354
May, Betty, 1st portrait of (bust), 96, 98, 99
May, Betty, 2nd portrait of (head), 99
Maxim's Restaurant, 14
Maxwell, Henry, 332
Medici Chapel,
Medrano, Cirque, 16
Melchett, Gwen, Lady, 332, 372
Melchett, Lord, 332
Menan, Princess, 331
Menuhin, Yehudi, 285
Mercury Theatre, 349
Meredith, George, 22
Metropolitan Museum, 91, 161
Metsu, Gabriel, 163
Metropolitan Opera House (New York), 285
Meudon, 14
Meum, 1st portrait of (bust), 87, 88
Meum, 2nd portrait of (head), 87, 88
Meum, 3rd portrait of (mask), 94
Meum, 4th portrait of (with a fan), 94
Michelangelo, 11, 15, 16, 17, 32, 167, 177, 283, 386, 412, 416, 418
Middlesex Hospital, 224
Milan, 410
Millais, John Everett, 40
Ministry of Information, 276, 302
Minton, John, 308
Miriam Patel (see under Anita)
'Miserables, Les' (Hugo), 9
Modigliani, Amedeo, 13, 49, 63, 102, 177, 416
Moissac, 418
Monet, Claude, 14, 412
Monro, Harold, 80

Montesquiou, Comte Robert de, 14
Montparnasse, Cimetière de, 14
Moore, George, 136
Moore, Henry, 13, 60, 164, 191–2, 332, 416
Morgan, Hon. Evan, 88
Morna, 224, 235
'Morning Post', 136
Morrell, Lady Ottoline, 50, 57
Morris, David, 238
Mortlock, Canon C. B., 418, 420
Mother & Child (granite), 72–88
Mother & Child (marble), 65, 73, 88
Mother and Child Relief, 20
Mother and Child, Standing (Marie Rankin), 54
'Mother and Child' (Henry Moore), 192
Mount Auburn Cemetery (Boston), 10
Mount Vernon, 9
Mourner, 346
Mulberry Street, 11
Munich, 65
Munnings, Sir Alfred, 136
'Murder in the Cathedral' (T. S. Eliot), 349
Muse, The, 380
Museum of Modern Art, 73, 235
Mussolini, Benito, 170, 212
Mussorgsky, Modeste, 22
Myers, Isaac, 308
Myers, M. S., 216

Nabis, The, 14
Nan (bust of), 41, 42, 49, 57, 88
Nan (the dreamer), 57
Nan (seated), 57
Napoleon (Buonaparte), 9
Narcissus (destroyed statue), 50
National Gallery, 40
National Gallery of Canada, 75
National Gallery of Modern Art (The Tate), 163
National Portrait Gallery, 82, 130, 132, 400
National Vigilantes Society, 34
Neander, 204
Nehru, Pandit, Sketch of, 306–7
Nehru, Pandit, Bust of, 325
Nerenska, Pola, 238
Nevinson, Henry, 65, 136
'New Age', 77, 88
New Born Baby (sleeping baby), 88
New College, Oxford, 315, 345, 356, 412
New English Art Club, 23, 65, 82
'New English Weekly', 235
New Jersey, 11
'New Statesman', 88
New York, 9, 11, 22, 73, 158, 160, 161
New York 'Daily Mirror', 245

Newport Art Gallery, 88
Nicholson, William, 22
Nicolle, Arthur, 199
Nielke, Marguerite, 88
Night, 44, 82, 163–7, 191, 218–19, 251, 332–404, 422
Night, Maquette for, 164
Nijinsky, Vaslav, 49
Nîmes, 410
Noailles, Anna de, 14
'Noli me tangere' (Titian), 40
Norfolk, 170
Norman (Hornstein), 250, 275, 346
Norman (Hornstein), 1st portrait of, 170, 235, 252, 337
Norman (Hornstein), 2nd portrait of, 248
Normanby, Marquess of, 401, 414
North Staffordshire University, 403
Nude Studies A–J, 281–3

'Observer, The', 181
Office of Works, 134, 374, 411
Oko, Dr. Adolph S., 127, 153, 228
Oko, Mrs. Adolph S., 128, 228
Oko, Pearl, 128, 153, 228
Old Italian Woman, 23, 88
Old Italian Woman (with shawl), 23, 311
Old Pinager, 127, 278
Old Smith, 113, 278
'Old Testament Drawings', 189, 240, 281
Olive, 214
Orage, G. R., 77, 210, 349
Order of the British Empire, 365
O'Regan, Terence, 360
Oriel (see under Ross, Oriel)
Orpen, William, 22, 41, 136
Ossian (Ian), 275, 337, 376–7
Ostrer, Isidore, 204
Othello, 184, 189
'Other Men's Flowers' (Wavell), 278
Oxford University, 372, 387, 412
Oved, Mosheh (Edward Good), 151, 306
Oved, Ymiel, 306

Pace, George, 365
Paderewsky, Ignace, 16
Padua, 404
Palais Rose (Avenue du Bois), 96
Palazzo Venier (Venice), 96
Palisades, New Jersey, 11
'Paradise Lost' (Milton), 287
Paris, 14, 16, 60, 63, 65, 153, 413, 416
Parlanti (Foundry), 387
Parliament Square, 374
Parma, 410
Parrott (Foundry), 414

Parsons, Virginia, 397
Parthenon, The, 27
Partridge, Bernard, 136
Pasha, Zeda (see under *Zeda*)
Pasiphaë, 305
'Passage to India, A' (E. M. Forster), 170
Patel, Miriam (Anita), 141
Paulett, Earl, 139
Pearson, Lionel, 251
Pearson, Mrs. Melinda, 251
Peerbhoy, Amina (see under *Sunita*)
Peerbhoy, Enver, 141
Peggy Jean, 20, 103, 158, 160, 172, 235, 249, 250, 252,
    275, 337, 346
Peggy Jean (2nd portrait of), 103
Peggy Jean (4th portrait of), 103
Peggy Jean (Putti) (5th and 6th portraits of), 103
Peggy Jean (7th portrait of), 103
Peggy Jean (age 7½ with long hair), 149
Peggy Jean (Jeunesse), 199
Peggy Jean (14th portrait), 221
Peggy Jean, laughing, 106
Peggy Jean (the Sick Child), 106, 160
'Pelléas et Mélisande' (Debussy), 14, 16
Père Lachaise Cemetery, 63
Peter, laughing, 318, 376–7
'Peter Pan' (J. M. Barrie), 136
Peters, Betty, 59, 170, 249, 252, 281, 283
Pett Level, Sussex, 65, 70, 78, 80
Pevsner, Dr. Nikolaus, 164
Philadelphia, 11
Philadelphia Gallery of Art, 346
Phillips, Mrs. Godfrey ('A portrait'), 163
Phipps, Lady Evelyn Rose, 414
Phipps, Lady Lepel, 401, 414
'Phoenix at Coventry' (Sir Basil Spence), 393
Picasso, Pablo, 13, 14, 42, 49, 65, 177, 281, 349
Piccaninny, 254
Pisano, Andrea, 418
Pissarro, Camille, 11, 14
Pissarro, Lucien, 14
Plichte, Miriam, 1st portrait of (bust), 106
Plichte, Miriam, 2nd portrait of (bust with arms), 106
Plymouth, 80
Poetry Bookshop, 80
Poiret, 102
Poland, 9, 125
Portal, Air Marshal Viscount, 278
Porteous, H. G., 235
Portofino, 410
Portrait, A (Mrs. Godfrey Phillips), 163
Post Impressionist Exhibition, 22
Pound, Ezra, 60, 68, 77, 78
Power, Tyrone, 316

Powers, Hiram, 10
Powys, Isobel, 172
Powys, T. C., 172
Poynter, 22
Praxiteles, 283
Priestley, J. B., 230, 235
Primeval Gods, 170, 203, 237
Princes Street, Edinburgh, 422
Princeton University, 360
Pretoria, 63
Proudfoot, Eileen, 127, 173
Proust, Marcel, 14
Prow of a Ship, Maquette for, 366
'Punch', 22
Putney Vale Cemetery, 418
Putti, 103

Quinn, John, 70, 72, 73, 74, 75, 78, 88

Rabinovitch, F., 164
Ragamuffin (Jackie, 3rd portrait of), 254
'Railway Accident, The', 22, 24
Raleigh (State house at), 9
Rani Rama, 214
Rankin, Marie (Irish Girl), 54, 74, 82, 252, 328
Rastoumji, Ferosa, 128
Rattner, Joseph, 158
Ratton, Charles, 413
Rawsthorne, Alan, 209
Read, Herbert, 63
Rebecca, 174
Reclining Goddess (Sunita Reclining), 59, 170, 182–3
Redfern Gallery, 170, 189, 332
Reed, Miss, 37
Reform Club, 340
Regent's Park, 20, 421
Reid-Dick, William, 36
Relief of Mother & Child, 20
Rembrandt, 13, 161, 206, 278, 387, 416, 418
Renoir, Auguste, 11, 14, 32
Resurrection Study, 238, 272
Retrospective Exhibition (Tate Gallery 1952), 355,
    356
Rhodes, Robert, 353
'Richard of Bordeaux' (Gordon Daviot), 204
Ricketts, Charles, 34
Rima (Hudson Memorial), 82, 106, 125, 134, 136, 153,
    212, 218, 416, 421
Rimmer, William, 10
Risen Christ (Bernard van Dieren), 80, 99, 100, 106,
    145, 404, 420, 422
Rita, 237
Ritz Hotel, 38
Riverside Church (New York), 158, 235

Robbia, Luca della, 418
Robeson, Paul, 158, 160, 184, 187, 189
Rockdrill, The, 68, 88, 422
Rodin, Auguste, 11, 13, 14, 16, 40, 49, 57, 63, 77, 88,
    90, 122, 211, 235, 241, 416, 418
Roerich, Nicolas, 49
'Rogue Herries' (Hugh Walpole), 212
Roma of Barbados, 1st portrait of (head), 197
Roma of Barbados, 2nd portrait of (bust), 199
'Romance', 88
Rom (Romilly John), 23, 82, 88, 249
Roosevelt, Franklin D., 20
Rose, 199
Rose, Billy, 78, 422
Roselli, Fedora, 113
Rosemary, 228
Ross, Oriel, 1st portrait of (bust), 139–41
Ross, Oriel, 2nd portrait of (head), 151
Ross, Oriel, 3rd portrait of, 194, 197
Ross, Robert, 38, 63
Rothenstein, Sir John, 422
Rothenstein, William, 22, 41
Rothermere, Viscount, 163, 204
Rothschild, Lord, 365
Rotunda Hospital (Dublin), 340
Royal Academy, 36, 170
Royal College of Art, 136, 366, 372
Royal College of Music, 397
Royal College of Physicians, 412
Royal Festival Hall, 397
Royal Institute of British Architects, 414
Royal Lancashire Fusiliers, 391
Royal Society, The, 82
Royal Society of British Sculptors, 59
Royal Society for the Protection of Birds, 134
Russell, Earl (Bertrand Russell), 187, 360, 361, 372
Russia, 9
Ryan, Sally, 158, 203, 235, 237, 242
Ryan, Thomas Fortune, 235

'Sacre du Printemps, Le' (Stravinsky), 42, 192
'Sacred Service' (E. Bloch), 325
Sadler, Michael, 136
Sainsbury, Robert, 272
Sainsbury, Mrs. Robert (Lisa), 272
Saint-Gaudens, Augustus, 10
St. Francis, 272
'St. Francis receiving the stigmata' (Van Eyck), 11
'St. James's Gazette', 34
'St. John the Baptist' (Rodin), 14
St. Martin's Hotel, 331
St. Matthew Passion (J. S. Bach), 334
St. Michael and the Devil, 283, 383, 387, 395, 407, 414,
    420, 422

St. Michael and the Devil — maquette, 393
St. Paul's Cathedral, 365, 418
St. Trophime, Arles, 410
Saintes Maries, Les, 410
Samuel, Lord, 340
San Michele (Capri), 96
Sanderson, Ivan, 413–14
Sandy Hook, 158
Sargent, John Singer, 14, 22, 88
Sassoon Family, 80
Satan, Beelzebub & Belial, 287
Savoy Hotel, 422
Schönberg, Arnold, 22
School of Human Anatomy (Oxford), 397
Scott, C. P., 143, 410
Scott, Harold, 130
Scott-Ellis, Hon. Elizabeth, 90
'Sculptor Speaks, The' (Haskell), 422
Seated Mother, Maquette for Social Consciousness, 346,
    380
Selassie, Haile, Emperor of Abyssinia, 125, 170, 224,
    226, 276
Selby Abbey (Yorkshire), 221
Self Portrait with a beard, 104
Self Portrait in a cap, 63
Selina, 113
Senegalese Girl, 109
Senlis, 410
Seraph, The (Marie Collins), 132, 365
Serpotta, Giacomo, 328
Seurat, Georges, 14, 22
Seven Pillars of Wisdom Trust, 288, 356
'Seventy Five drawings by Jacob Epstein', 150, 153,
    170
Shakespeare, William, 68, 412
Shannon, Charles, 34
Shaw, Bernard, 20, 22, 63, 100, 136, 142, 210–11, 315
Sheila, 132
Shelley, Lillian, 1st portrait of (head), 57, 80
Shelley, Lillian, 2nd portrait of (bust), 96
Sheridan, Clare, 91, 96
'Sherman, General' (Saint-Gaudens), 10
Sick Child (12th portrait of Peggy Jean), 161, 163,
    199, 285
Sickert, Walter Richard, 20, 22, 35, 36, 170
Simon of Wythenshaw, Lord, 355
Singer, Morris (Foundry), 387, 407
Siobhan, 326
Sistine Chapel, 104
Slade School, 22, 40, 136
'Slaves' (Michelangelo), 15
Sleeping Beauty, 19
Smith, A. H., 332, 345, 349, 356, 372–412
Smith, Sir Matthew, 128, 170, 216, 332, 339, 414, 418